MW00946637

Vitalis and Justa

A STORY OF SLAVERY IN ANCIENT ROME

T. GRIFFITH

Copyright © 2023 by T. Griffith

All rights reserved.

No part of this book may be reproduced in any form or by any electronic or mechanical means, including information storage and retrieval systems, without written permission from the author, except for the use of brief quotations in a book review.

All images are public domain or created by the author. AI in Canva was used for the book cover.

✺ Created with Vellum

Dedicated to
Jeff who always encouraged

There is no greater love than to sacrifice yourself for another.

❧

Map of Herculaneum and the Pompeii Region

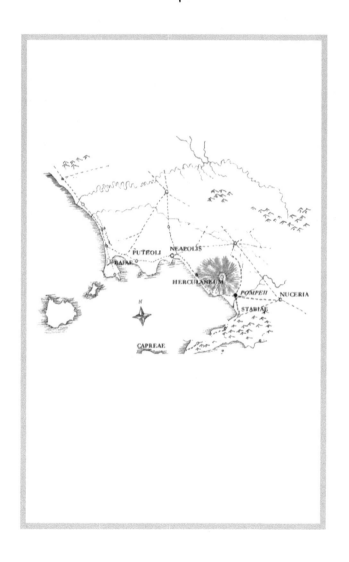

Prologue

T his was a story given to me very gradually, beginning with an experience at the age of sixteen. At that time, I visited Pompeii with my father. That personal experience has followed me throughout my life, coming back to me and reminding me of a vision until I finally began to write it down. At times the story would come as if someone was telling it to me. I was even surprised at the events as they unfolded.

I have researched many of the details and corresponding political influences but this is a work of fiction, and should be regarded as a jumping off point for other readers and historians to dig more deeply into the fascinating time of Pompeii and Herculaneum.

The story is based on real events involving Vitalis and Justa recorded on wax tablets found in the debris of Herculaneum.

What was daily life like in this coastal town?

What was slavery like in ancient Rome?

What opportunities were available to women?

What current events were happening that might influence this family?

What was it like to worship Roman gods, or be Jewish or Christian at that time?

Chapter One

Slave Market in Pompeii A.D. 59

VITA WAITED HER TURN, her child-body curled over her knees. She stopped breathing, then suddenly gasped for air. Sounds pounded the walls of the windowless shed. Her throat begged for water. A slit under the door rendered voices of auctioneers shouting numbers and praising the attributes of human property for sale. She watched her toes dig into the dirt. A spider examined her toe. She shook the creepy leggy thing off. *I know how to feel safe.*

She forced memories of her father, like the cool feel of his tunic when she wrapped her arm around his waist or the look in his blue eyes when he grinned at her with pride. She dug deep into her soul to concentrate on how much he loved her. These cherished thoughts whirled back to the last morbid moments before he died.

The door opened with a flash of light. Hands came and pulled her from her corner, shoved her up wooden stairs to a platform, dropped her tunic and displayed her for all to see. A wisp of a girl and filthy from her long sea journey, she appeared frail. Mourning the loss of her father, nauseated from the movement of the boat, repulsed by the offerings of putrid nourishment, and fear of the other captured slaves had produced this skeletal body. Maybe in death she could be with her father again, for she had no will to live without anyone to love her.

A stick pulled up her chin so bidders could see her features and naked body on the revolving pedestal. White chalk dust on her foot announced that she was being offered as a new slave. She closed her eyes to cloak her intelligence. A *tituli* hung around her neck which listed her native origin and age and would have listed her attributes and talents but Vita had refused to reveal any, so the rest of the sign was blank. She wore a round *pillei* cap relaying a message to the purchaser that the seller was free of any responsibilities or guarantees of health, intelligence, or skills. Her arms closed across her body. No bids were offered.

"Come on, gentlemen, this sweet girl just needs some training and a good meal." One voice bellowed, then, "Sold! to the only bidder." Two men captured her and dragged her down steps while dropping her soiled shift over her head.

"Where am I going?" she asked in Greek with no answer.

"Where am I going?" she tried in Latin.

The short auctioneer and banker, Jucundus, pulled out his wax tablet to document the sale. His ears sat low on his bald head, and the giant wart on his cheek forced a stare. He registered Vita as a slave belonging to Gaius Petronius Stephanus, a soldier and citizen of the Roman Empire, value—the same as sheep or pigs.

Gaius reached for her hand and led her away from the Pompeii auction to the West Marine Gate. Vita had seen plenty of soldiers in her life, but if she had to draw a perfect Roman soldier of the Empire, it would be a trite picture of Gaius: short dark hair, chiseled jaw, and a powerful stallion body. At first, he navigated from behind to shove her, pushing her into strangers, down Via del'Abbondanza, past the baths and temples to the sea, then steered in front to cut the crowd. They were caught in a current of chaotic human beings. Now she stumbled behind, clinging to his tunic, watching his massive bare legs confidently plod over cobbled pavement. Gaius pulled her close under his arm which should offend but made her feel safe. She paused when they passed a glorious Temple with columns leading to a massive statue of Venus. *So that is who Venus is.* She remembered how the white Temple beckoned her from the sea on her arrival to Pompeii, and how the sailors gave this statue praise for a safe voyage. Gaius reached back and took her hand this time with a look of encouragement and pulled her through the crowd.

They were caught up in a mass of people leaving the city, like a river running to the sea, confronted by another crowd entering the city to do business. An explosion of humanity going nowhere made Gaius twist left and right to keep them together as their steps became smaller and smaller. Once they passed through the western gate, Pompeii's dazzling marina opened up before them. The hectic city extended on to the sea with wild dancing vessels moving to unsynchronized rhythms, each precariously avoiding other boats, pretending to have some control and yet nothing was secure.

Vita watched large ships with imported goods being unloaded by burly laborers. The men lowered the weighty clay amphorae onto flat-bottomed boats where slaves and merchants stood waiting for the goods. A loud crack startled Vita sounding like timbers breaking, which they were, as a flat-bottom boat was caught between two large ships lurching together, smashing the delivery boat as they all rose up on a wave. Sailors and slaves shouted and swam out from shore to try to save the amphorae that stored something priceless, but all were lost as the containers fell to the floor of the bay.

Vita looked up from the chaotic retrieval to stare at the grandiose villas lining the cliff. Their plastered architecture glittered with large picture windows facing the sea. Probably the benefactor was watching his ships from his villa, hoping for a generous profit, but now calculated his loss as he watched his imports disappear beneath the water. They shuffled through the crowd along the dock to reach the same boat that Gaius had chartered that morning, tethered and ready to return to a less hectic city twelve miles up the coast called Herculaneum.

The captain of the small bobbing transport hurried passengers aboard. Gaius turned to face Vita and help her step over the side and settle on a plank bench. The frenzied port disappeared as they followed the coast west, then north against the wind to Herculaneum.

It had been a long day for Gaius. He'd left his small, refined town of vacationing aristocracy in the dark of dawn to carry out business in Pompeii, full of its sailors and struggling businessmen, because he heard that healthy slaves were to be auctioned off. Perhaps bulky farm workers would be presented to work his farm on the side of fertile Mount Vesuvius. Scheduled to serve his duty in the Roman army, finishing his commitment to the Empire as a Legionnaire, he feared the farm might suffer while he performed his assignment.

Unfortunately, the most coveted slaves were sold to wealthier citizens who outbid him. He returned empty-handed but for this one little female. A shy endearing child standing on the auction pedestal, he'd rationalized that she would be a cheap price being so young and small with no attributes or talents. He could use more household slaves. The child, exported from Ephesus, probably spoke both Greek and Latin bringing with her some status to the household. Gaius had watched her during the auction with compassion witnessing her pitiful countenance. If he did not buy the young girl, she might be purchased and ruined by the unsavory brothel proprietors of Pompeii. Detecting a hidden intelligence, he bid on her. Perhaps she would also be a companion to his new wife who seemed so restless and lonely, and still in her own late teens, not much older than this young girl.

"What were you thinking!" shouted Calitoria as she walked toward Vita and grasped her hair. "Not only do you come back to our villa without purchasing the needed slaves for the farm, but you bring me an impossible situation of an incompetent house slave who appears to be no more than a child, if you can see beneath the filth and grime on her. She is nothing!"

Calitoria jerked Vita's head to the side as she released her hair. "I will have to teach her everything. An embarrassment to our household! What did you think? That I needed a playmate! I am not a lonely, unhappy child missing my mother. You say I am sullen and unhappy. If I am sullen, it is because you disappoint me. I certainly do not need this added to all my responsibilities of running this place as your wife."

It was not hard for Gaius to hold his retort. He was trained as a soldier. No answer would come from his mouth. Of course, buying a new slave was the right decision to make for the family that he was creating. *A child will act like a child, I shouldn't expect more.* he thought.

"She is so small she can't even fetch water, although she must. The kitchen slaves will find her a nuisance, rather than a help. How much did you pay for her? Too much whatever it was. She is beneath us in every way. I am trying to be respected and have prestige in this community! Your career depends on it! Now, instead of supporting me you bring me an impossible task. I won't let her be seen. Send her up to one of the back rooms until I can decide what to do with her."

Vita avoided looking at Calitoria with her unusual blonde hair. She stopped listening, wondering if it hurt that woman's neck to hold her chin so high. Her voice pierced like needles to make up for small stature. *This one is going to be trouble,* she thought. Otherwise, Calitoria was beautiful.

Vita searched the atrium of this grand house realizing that Gaius Petronius Stephanus must be a wealthy man to have such a home. In fact, he was a hardworking middle-class Roman citizen trying to create a fortune. He was not a Patrician, one who could trace his lineage back to the founding one hundred families of Rome; he was part of the rising middle class in the Empire. The glorious home had been inherited from his father, who purchased it during an economic upturn and would be by tradition, passed down from generation to generation. The original owners had added more grandeur to the furnishings and wall decorations creating one of the grandest villas in Herculaneum. The atrium, with its high open ceiling and black and white mosaic floor, had few pieces of furniture, merely a table and a couch around the rectangle *impluvium* filled with water. Vita's mouth dropped with awe as she studied the dark vermillion walls of black and gold geometrics surrounding simulated columns and detailed architecture.

Her eyes traveled the room and settled on an old woman sitting in a corner. Arms folded across an ample abdomen, lips set in a pout, she stared at the tirade of Gaius's wife. This woman wore plain garments of fine fabric. *She must be part of the immediate family, a mother or aunt but her gnarled fingers show calluses from hard work,* thought Vita.

Additional doorways lined the *atrium.* One had a wooden lattice gate protecting something precious inside. Later she would learn this room was forbidden to her and the other slaves. There was no time to observe further, for a nameless slave entered and led Vita through the atrium past an interior garden called the *peristyle* with manicured greenery and ornate statues. Grand columns lined the garden fluted with spirals and carvings to their tops. She followed along the mosaic walkway and up a stairway to a small cubicle on the second floor that contained a couch with soft pillows. The kind slave left water and part of a loaf of bread to eat. No words were said, the slave retreated, and peace was finally upon her. Now she could finally hide from all her trauma of the day and past weeks. She rolled to her side on the couch and fell into a deep sleep.

ANGRY DREAMS ENCIRCLED Vita as they did every night. This time there was someone in white chasing her through the streets; hiding and dashing, she would barely escape only to be discovered and the chase would begin again. A new dream revealed that the one in white carried a knife and wanted to kill her. She fitfully awoke trying to wrestle away from arms that imprisoned her. She struggled, pushing away pillows and illusive demons that had enormous strength. No one could be trusted. She slept again only to experience her need to shout at strangers, argue with masters, hit and spit at unknown phantoms and generally rage at the world.

GAIUS COLLAPSED on the bed in the *cubiculum* with Calitoria beside him. Disappointed that farm slaves were too expensive for him, he pondered what his father would do.

"I can't afford the price for more slaves for the farm, but to have the farm make more money I need more slaves." He spoke aloud but was really talking to himself.

"Well, the one you bought today is worthless."

"The girl is probably Greek and will bring something of merit to our household." Now he spoke directly to his young wife. "Underneath the dirt is an intelligent servant that can be prepared to serve in our expected style according to our position. In fact, I believe that buying one that is so young, we can expect fewer troubles. She can become part of our family, help rear children, become a handmaid to you, or if that does not work out she can always help preparing meals with the other slaves in the kitchen. Greek slaves normally go for three to five times as much as I paid for her. You have no idea what she is capable of at this point because you have not given it a chance." Gaius turned his back to leave.

"AND my decisions are not to be questioned by you. In the future, control your emotions, especially in front of the servants. I need for you to run a house that is not open to gossip if my career is to be firm and prosperous. And finally, Calitoria, you will never receive prestige in this community if you continue to act like an emotional child."

Chapter Two

Vita woke in the middle of the night and realized no one stirred in the house. Slipping the latch of the upstairs room, she stepped out onto the walkway that surrounded the peristyle and garden. She stood for a moment remembering how she arrived using a stairway and peered over the edge of the wooden railing. Shapes of plants and fountains danced below in the moonlight. Creeping silently around the outside walls past other doors, she found the stairway and padded down to the main level. The cold floor of the atrium shocked her feet. She shivered. Ahead of her beckoned the door to the street. Her heart pounded violently. No one would stop her.

I just want to be free. I could leave and disappear into the city. Maybe I could find my way back to Ephesus, hide on a ship. Maybe I could walk out of the city into the mountainside and live by myself. Some kind family would take me in and love me.

Her shaking hand wrapped around the massive door lever.

But there might not be food or shelter like there is here. I could do it.

She pulled down on the lever.

Father always said to have a plan before you begin. Maybe if I wait, I could walk away another time when I know where to go. It might be really hard to take care of myself out there.

Her hand let go of the lever. Every plan and possibility crowded her head at once.

I'll wait.

She leaned up against the door mapping infinite escape scenarios.

There, that really was a noise. Holding her breath, she tried to hear it again...nothing. The whispered sound must have been her imagination, yet her feet made a straight line across the smooth floor, past the *impluvium*, to the stairs next to the *tablinum*. She reached the third step just as a hand grabbed her ankle and held her firmly.

"Oh, ho, who is this? Who are you little one?" he said.

"Vita," she whispered and gazed at him with steady blue eyes. He did not look like a Roman soldier. He was rather tall and lanky and even had the hint of a beard. It was hard to tell what this stranger was in the dim light but his voice was kind.

"Vita, Vita,...you won't be called Vita here. Here you will be called something like Vitalia, we will see. Everyone gets their name transformed into a Latin name no matter where they are from. I am Telesphor**os**, presently Telesphor**us**, translated from Greek to Latin." He emphasized the last syllable. "How did you get here?"

Vita had no answer. *How can I explain that once I had a family, a mother and father and now I have no one, once I was safe and loved and now this strange place traps me where nothing is mine. How did I get here? I am an orphan and orphans become slaves.* A tear gave her thoughts away.

Telesphorus remembered his own interrupted life and purchase as an educated slave to work as bookkeeper and lawyer. The law of the present held him hostage and he found contentment. The past was gone. *Don't look backward,* he thought. *There is no transformation to the life I wanted. It is fate.*

He removed his hand from her ankle.

"Never mind, sometimes it is too painful to tell. It is best to not think so much about it. Be strong, little one, this is the life offered to you, take it. Your name, Vitalia, means 'living'. You have made it to this place and you are still alive. It is not so bad. Now back to bed with you. Morning will be here soon."

∽

BRIGHT LIGHT SEEPED through the small window of her room. A slave knocked.

"Come downstairs to help."

Vita slipped on sandals and followed the young girl to the back of the villa where several slaves were already preparing food. It didn't take long to realize who was in charge. A tall middle-aged woman moved gracefully from counter to table carrying a heavy earthenware bowl filled with flour. She scooped the contents out onto the rough worn table and added water to the center. Glancing up with a broad smile and hands poised to dive into the dough, this woman would not allow Vita to be a stranger.

"Oh my!" Lavinia gasped. "What happened to you? Poor dear." She took Vita's face in her floured hands, studied her nose to nose and declared, "I can't tell what you are, you are such a mess. Aquilina, come over here and take this girl to the stream to clean her up, get a new tunic and cloths on the way. Bring her back ready to work."

Aquilina was the young slave who knocked on the door that morning. Her too large nose and heavy eyebrows extinguished her promise of being a beauty at birth, but she possessed a broad smile saved for display with Lavinia. About the same age and height, the two girls could be sisters with their dark hair and slim bodies. She reached for Vita's hand and they stepped out on to the broad street. Already carts rumbled past pushed by people heading toward the markets. Vita soon learned Aquilina knew every part of Herculaneum. Born into slavery in this city, she loved the life in the kitchen, and Lavinia mentored her, teaching the skills of cooking.

Most of what Lavinia knew was simply an art of knowing what to do and memorizing how much of each ingredient was preferred. She did have access to recipes written down in a book by an author named Apicius that reminded her of key ingredients, but the amounts were really up to the cook's discretion. All this Lavinia was teaching her talented pupil, Aquilina. Female, and a slave, normally would be a precarious existence, but for Aquilina, if she mastered the skills, she would be assured of safety and security. This town of aristocrats demanded skilled cooks to impress and entertain.

"I hope you know how to swim," said Aquilina.

"Of course I do."

"Well, not everybody does!"

Both girls jumped into the water squealing, splashing the freezing and refreshing water all over Vita who returned the splash right into Aquilina's face. She screamed with delight but dove away dodging the next assault. Vita relaxed enough to continue to splash Aquilina giggling at her mischief. *This might be the most fabulous bath I have ever experienced,* she thought. All of the grime of her capture and voyage was rubbed off with cloths and floated away. With the filth, the memories and emotions disappeared for a moment. Vita surprised herself when she heard herself laugh, so much tragedy forgotten.

When they returned, Lavinia shoved her bowl and sieve at them commanding the girls to finish making reduced grape juice, *defrutum*. It was a day for making sauces to be stored for the future. The girls took the red grapes out to the unroofed area to begin squeezing them to drain the juices. Their hands pressed and pushed until the sieve separated the solid parts.

"Where are you from?" asked Aquilina.

"Ephesus."

"I don't know Ephesus. Were you captured in a war?"

"No, my parents both died. First my mother from something that made her sick inside her stomach. Then my father was injured working at the shipyard and the wound made him sick and then he was gone."

The girls poured the juice into a lead pot and placed it on the brazier to simmer until reduced to half, creating a sugary crust and sweet aroma. The white crust would be scraped and stirred into the reduced juice and stored in a pitcher to be added to several dishes.

The girls moved to a table in the cooking area. They pitted and chopped about ten dates, chopped and roasted almonds, chopped small onions, then added pepper, celery seeds, caraway, and safflower. They stirred in a spoonful of *garum* (a salty fish sauce), a bit of mild mustard, and poured in some of their freshly made defrutum and a bit of olive oil. This was placed in another pitcher and stored on a shelf as a sauce for chicken.

Pine nut sauce for eggs was a favorite of Gaius and his mother. While the eggs were boiling, Aquilina and Vita placed pine nuts in a bowl of vinegar, added honey, pepper, and lovage then crushed with a mortar and pestle and poured it over the eggs before serving.

Lavinia studied Vita, the first to get started and first to finish. "You have used a mortar and pestle before, lovely job, seems like you know how to cook."

"My mother taught me to cook in Ephesus. Our home was not so grand as this and we had no servants, so she taught me everything."

GAIUS LEFT for the public baths to join the men of the city in exercise to stage mock combats as he did everyday. Later, he would sit in the hot and cold pools followed by full body scraping, massage, and perfume. Proud Roman, he caught up with events in the Empire from messengers arriving and reporting. Gaius overheard men discussing new revolts and trouble in Britannia. He moved closer and sat with his back to them pretending not to listen, alarmed to hear about these new revolts.

"The time of peace between the barbarians and the Romans is unraveling. Emperor Nero considered withdrawing his soldiers from the encampments but now has decided to press on and tame the various tribes with force. He doesn't want to look weak and tolerate them. Risky business if you ask me, start another war on another front," said one.

"Nero is determined to have Britannia. He wants to expand and collect the resources, yet no one has been able to make a profit there because of the unrest," said another. "Even Julius Caesar gave up on it. The Druids run those tribes and I have heard about their rituals and sacrifices. Nothing you want your children to hear. Even the soldiers fear them," said another.

"That's enough said," an aristocrat warned as he looked from side to side checking for those who might be listening. "There are spies every-where who report back to the authorities of disloyal talk about the Empire."

Gaius needed to hear more. He was assigned to Britannia with fellow engineers to finish construction of the Roman capital, Camulo-dunum, including a magnificent Temple deifying the former Emperor Claudius. Roman soldiers and their families were retiring in the desired colony taking advantage of the local people. *Could the soldiers be causing trouble with the tribes?* he wondered.

His impatience to find out caused him to invite a widely respected local politician and friend, Marcus Nonius Balbus, to dinner. Fierce warring tribes against Roman soldiers was not the peace he expected while erecting a Temple in a new city. He preferred pleasant living not dealing with subhuman barbarians. Didn't they already have victory over these tribes?

~

RETURNING to his villa near the Forum, Gaius announced to his mother and Calitoria that dinner guests would be arriving, sending everyone into a frenzy. Calitoria calculated exactly how she wanted the evening to be constructed, from food to entertainment to how she would dress. She entered the kitchen to bestow the menu on Lavinia. Calitoria had been a slave in a Herculaneum family for many years, so she knew the customs of the rich. Moderation would convey taste and class rather than mimicking the activities of the newly rich, who smothered their dishes with every expensive seasoning they could acquire resulting in laughable concoctions that only screamed ignorance. She directed Lavinia to prepare courses that were delicious and impressive in flavor.

The handmaid delivered a gown to the fuller for pressing. House slaves tidied the garden, polished the silver plates, and filled lamps with oil. Calitoria scheduled her time to visit the Baths where she bathed and perfumed. During the bath she relaxed and collected her thoughts. *This must go well tonight. Marcus and Lasennia are the ladder to social movement upward. If I can make this connection people will forget I am a former slave. Dinner must be perfect.* Power and prestige came through her husband, not her birthright, for she had none. She needed social approval. What was not allowed for women by Roman law could be achieved through marrying well.

Later, she entered the kitchen. Vita and Aquilina, who stood together, instantly turned their backs and acted busy chopping and stirring. Vita motioned toward the door to the outdoor yard and they started inching their way to the exit.

"Girls!" They both jumped. "Aquilina and you, take this list to the market. Now!" She shoved Vita and Aquilina out the door and left.

Lavinia dried her hands on her tunic, picked up the unbaked loaves, and caught the girls outside.

"Here, take these to the baker." She stacked the bread in their arms. "You can pick them up on the way back." When so much bread was needed, Lavinia used the town baker's larger ovens. The name Petronius was scratched in the top of each round loaf to be sure to get her own bread back.

Lavinia reminded, "Be quick, girls. I need you back to help me with everything. You will also need to be dressed and groomed for this evening because you will be serving the dinner."

"What? I've never done that."

"It is fine, don't worry about anything. I will tell you what to do. Just watch me serving and do the same," said Aquilina.

THE FORUM WAS close to the Petronius villa, in fact, just across the road. Brightly colored awnings hung over tables and barrels filled with fresh and preserved produce. Vendor shops and crowds of slaves and laborers working or shopping for goods filled the whole open area. Vita hung on to the side of Aquilina's tunic so she would not be lost while her head spun left and right to see everything. She noticed a boy staring at her. She turned away and looked again, and he was still staring at her.

"Who is that boy staring at us?"

"Oh, he is not staring at us, he is staring at you. You know you are quite pretty, and he is such a nosy boy. That is Quintus the gem cutter's boy apprentice. He is freeborn. He is too cute and he knows it." Quintus had dark, curly, too long hair, with dark eyes that still looked at Vita. "Just ignore him," ordered Aquilina.

With that, Vita turned straight on to him, put her hand on her hip, and stared straight back. She flipped her head to the side and turned away. After taking several steps, she couldn't help but look back at him again. Quintus gyrated in a goofy dance back at her. There was no doubt his show was for her. She bit her lips to stifle a laugh.

The girls worked their way through their list: fresh eggs, lamb for the roast, six dormice, a lobster tail, and goose liver. Aquilina made sure the goose breeders had force fed the birds with figs to enlarge the livers then killed them by feeding them honeyed wine, (*mulsum*) which gave the birds a special flavor. Lavinia would roast these, stuff them with pork, pine nuts, and pepper, roll them in honey and poppy seeds and serve them as *gustum*, (appetizers). They made sure that the lamb had been sacrificed earlier that morning at the Temple and headed back with their arms loaded.

Exhausted but obedient they were sent out again to fetch water at the cross street. The girls each picked up a side of the amphora and struggled along the street making several trips.

"Do we really need this much water?"

"We need lots. Some have pipes delivering water inside their homes. This isn't so bad. It's just down the street. So, do you always complain? Probably should stop that."

Luigi Bazzani, 1836

LAVINIA COMMANDED the kitchen like a ship captain overseeing every minute detail. Dinner had an order of courses to follow with certain dishes to delight guests. Vita and Aquilina would serve the courses on tables preset with the dishes. It would be important for the girls to be well groomed and dressed in finer garments than their usual tunic. How the slaves were dressed was a way of judging the class of the household. They were handed longer garments with tooled leather belts to wear. Vita examined the pattern on the belt and stroked the smooth fabric. She tried on flawless sandals and wrapped the thin ties around her slim ankles. The girls scurried upstairs to a metal reflection mirror to admire their appearance.

"We look so good," said Vita. "Now, for the hair."

Aquilina combed Vita's hair straight back and tied it with a leather strip. Vita sectioned Aquilina's long hair and encircled delicate braids around her head leaving curls at her forehead and along the nape of her neck.

"Where did you learn how to do that?" Aquilina moved the hand mirror from side to side.

"From my mother. I used to love to play with my mother's beautiful hair. She would ask me to comb it in the evenings. I loved just being with her. She was so kind. Later, she taught me how to braid and I watched how the Greek women would fix their hair. I would fix my mother's hair that way and she would comb and braid mine in all sorts of styles. She used to help brides prepare for their wedding day. Style their hair, make lovely perfumes to wash away evil. It is a fond memory. Something we used to do."

"You must miss her very much," said her new friend.

"I do. I need her. I never thought I would be without my family. Someday I want to have a family again, one that loves me. I will be free again."

"You best stop thinking that way. Unless you marry some rich man who will buy you and pay for your freedom, that is not happening."

THE GIRLS WENT BACK DOWN to the kitchen areas to help place the appetizers artfully on plates. Just wearing nice clothes and having their hair fixed so attractively made them feel more grown up.

Gaius's elderly mother, Thana, perched on a stool in the kitchen to supervise the final preparations. Vita recognized her as the old woman in the atrium on that first night.

"Those are the wrong dishes for serving the gustum. If we use those we won't have any for the puddings!" said Calitoria.

Gaius's mother went over quietly to a shelf and pulled out some additional serving dishes to use.

"Not those!" Calitoria shouted at her mother-in-law.

"These are the proper dishes to use. I know what I am talking about," said Thana. Then she spoke in another language using the same sharp tone. Vita looked around at the others in the room, her eyes wide with surprise. The language was similar to her mother's first language, the one that Vita grew up with at home, and she understood every word. Thana told everyone in the room that Calitoria was a lowborn girl who was putting on a show. That the whole town knew she had been nothing more than a slave and her son had made a huge mistake bringing her poor breeding into this home and some of the slaves in this room had better breeding than her.

Didn't anyone else hear that? Vita studied the faces around the room. No one, including Calitoria, reacted. Vita decided to pretend she did not understand, but wondered if Thana had seen her mouth drop open. Thana sat back on her stool, folded her arms across her large abdomen and waited without emotion, glaring at her daughter-in-law. The slaves were confused. No one moved. Thana was still the rightful matriarch of the house until Calitoria produced children. All were quiet. Time stopped. Finally, Calitoria submitted and left. Thana sat delighted in her small network of current power.

Vita raised her eyebrows and got back to work.

Chapter Three

A quilina stood ready to serve in the corner of Calitoria's bedchamber while another handmaiden styled the mistress's hair. Like an actress transforming into a role, she held her chin high and took on an air of aristocracy, perfecting her character for the evening. She admired her hands, turning them and spreading the slim fingers.

"Aquilina, thank you for all you have done today to help us prepare for this evening. Also, thank you for teaching our new slave how to accomplish so many tasks here in the household. I am pleased with all the preparations. Now I have one more task for this evening. The gem cutter has designed exquisite gold earrings with clusters of sea pearls especially for me. They are ready and I want to wear them tonight. You must run and fetch them for me." Aquilina reached out her hand to accept the coins for payment.

"May I take our new slave with me? Vitalia needs to learn where things are in the city."

"Vital...? Is that her name? Yes, go and hurry."

Unusual for the mistress to speak in such a respectful tone. To be treated as part of the family and respected diminished any previous insults.

Aquilina left Calitoria with her thoughts and concerns about the dinner to find Vita in the kitchen. They wrapped shawls around their heads and shoulders and skipped out the side door. It was quiet now with few people carrying out business. The cool evening welcomed a strong breeze as the sun started to drop below the horizon. The girls clutched their warm wraps shivering against the salty air carrying the scent of the sea. Vita listened to the tapping sounds of their steps on the stone pavement peeking in doorways left and right prying to see who lived there and wondering what secrets they hid from view.

As they approached the shop, Vita could see him. He stood alone behind a wooden table with his head bent, focusing on something lovely in his hands. The gravel crunched under their feet alerting him. He looked up. Was he really that handsome, or only handsome to her? Vita wasn't sure if it was his dark eyes, or the way he held himself, his dark softly curled hair, or his shockingly white smile that attracted her. His eyes smiled tenderly as if he knew she was coming and had waited for her. Aquilina asked for the pearl earrings for the mistress. Vita's tongue was broken. Her face flushed red. Her legs were stuck. Quintus said hello to her but all she could hear was the drumming in her ears, all she could feel were his eyes on her. He decided to speak to Aquilina hoping to get a response.

"Who is your new friend?" he asked.

"This is Vitalia, our new slave. She is kind of shy."

"I am not! Don't say that about me."

"Your eyes flash when you speak. Are you always without grace and civility?"

"No, I mean yes!"

"I like that about you. Come by to see me again, will you?"

He said it with such softness and lack of arrogance, truly as one child to another simply wanting a friend. It was all Vita could do to hold her breath and look back at him, a moment that she wanted to grip tightly as they both knew it was some sort of beginning. The earrings were exchanged for coins, and they returned to the villa. Vita began to breathe again but she knew she would revisit the cherished moment when he said he liked her.

While Aquilina walked to the cubiculum to deliver the beautiful earrings to Calitoria, Vita slipped toward the front of the villa to see the atrium after all had been prepared. A fine vase on a three-legged stool near the white marble impluvium held clipped blooms from the garden. Several bronze lamps created a flickering magic to the large room with its high ceiling. The red and black geometric frescoes were hardly visible in the subdued light but reflected a sheen from their waxed surfaces. The black mosaic floor glittered with white specks like stars at night and surrounded a ribbon of black and white outlining the impluvium with its regal braided design.

Such a beautiful room, she thought. *Black and white floor with crimson walls and a white border high near the ceiling rafters, delicate florals in geometric shapes, what artist brilliantly designed this room? His control of using only a few colors, black, white, red and gold, so elegant.*

～

Luigi Bazzanii, 1879, Beauties

THE HANDMAID CONTINUED to prepare Calitoria for the evening. She applied slight amounts of rouge made from oil and ground iron oxide to the cheeks and black charcoal near the eyelashes to enhance the eyes. Restrained elegance and refinement defined the aristocratic woman. Calitoria knew to keep her independent thoughts and intelligence suppressed when entertaining, only the expected admiration and compliments could elevate her to the level of the Balbus family. She felt no need to improve her inner self, only create an outer appearance.

Praying to the gods for their favors and benevolence completed her ritual of preparation.

"Oh great god, oh great goddess, I have no idea which one of you I should be asking for help so all of you please help Gaius and myself to rise in power and influence in this city. Ancient spirits of this house, use your influence to elevate us in prestige."

THE BRONZE DOOR knocker disturbed the tranquil scene with its loud echo. Vita watched servants respond to open the door with Calitoria and Gaius Petronius Stephanus close behind walking side by side with Gaius cupping her elbow, a soft gesture. Even though Gaius was middle class his massive presence rang with assuredness. He knew who he was and felt no inferiority to his important guest, only respect and trust for Balbus. He truly welcomed him and his wife, Lasennia.

Balbus, ever the politician, produced the hand shake and jovial smile. "Thank you for your invitation, so good to see you and your new wife."

"Peace and good fortune I ask from the god of all doors, Janus, and the goddess of doors and hinges, Cardea," said Lasennia. She touched the frame with a delicate hand and stepped purposely over the threshold with her right foot for luck entering behind her husband.

"It is my good fortune to have you in our home," said Gaius and led the group through the house towards the garden and peristyle.

"Such a lovely villa," stated Lasennia. "How long have you acquired it?" Lasennia had to know that the Petronia family was somewhat new to Herculaneum compared to the Balbus villa that held generations of family, all aristocrats who used their wealth to better Herculaneum.

"My father purchased this house when his farmlands began to produce profit many years ago, and it was his desire that the family would keep this home and pass it down for all the generations to come," Gaius explained.

"Ah, avoid the five percent inheritance tax. No taxes to pay for the widow or children to hold on to the property upon his death then," asserted Balbus. "A wise move."

"If the economy continues to prosper and grow, I will pass it on to my future child. It simply needs to be stated in my will that my heir will inherit the home."

They settled in the elaborately decorated *triclinium* which included a large window facing the peristyle. Balbus strolled over to the window admiring the placement of statues and flowering bushes and how meticulously they had been tended to, which were compliments and credit to Calitoria and Gaius's mother's command of the household.

"The goddess of the Earth, Fauna, and the goddess of flowers, Flora, must be showing you favor to have such a lovely garden," said Lasennia.

Calitoria motioned to three reclining couches arranged in a half circle. A hired musician played the lyre creating a pleasant atmosphere which also filled awkward moments of silence. Vita and Aquilina were summoned to remove the guests' sandals and brought water and towels to wash their hands.

Vita scurried back to the kitchen. Old Thana, with her gray hair pulled straight back on her head and in an everyday tunic, sat in her position on a three-legged stool to orchestrate the timing of the meal. She barked out orders in Latin with an occasional insult in Etruscan that only Vita understood.

"Hurry up! Simple headed girls!"

There were several courses served on small tables that Vita and Aquilina carried and placed in front of the guests as they reclined on the couches. The first tables included the *gustum,* which was a variety of appetizers including the roasted dormice accompanied by olive paste seasoned with coriander, fennel, and mint on toast, and artichokes with chopped eggs seasoned with a salty fish sauce called garum. Aquilina and Vita carried the tables in synchronized steps and set them in front of the diners. They were told to stand passively in the corners with soft napkins ready to wipe lips and fingers of the honored guests.

Conversation was light about the current events of the city. Gaius thought it would be best to discuss the unrest in Britannia when the men were alone. The conversation centered on upcoming festivals in the city celebrating agricultural planting and begging assistance from the gods for prolific growing seasons. The festival Robigalia would soon be upon them with the necessary sacrifice of an unweaned, rust-colored puppy to ask for good harvests and protection from grain disease and insect pests. Part of the celebration would include foot races, always something to look forward to with many of their friends and acquaintances participating.

"Would you be interested in helping me organize the games?" asked Balbus.

"Of course, friend. Whatever you need."

The couples discussed the fastest and most talented athletes who would pose a challenge. Those that did not run the races could cheer for their favorites then watch the award ceremony honoring their friends and family members. The theater would have some performances for the festival, and vendors would prepare snacks and sweets to sell in the streets at the festivities. As a member of the city counsil, Balbus financed the festival. He talked at length about the city's plans until Calitoria suppressed a yawn and examined her new bracelets.

The next table, or course, the *mensa prima*, included domesticated and wild animal meat. Small liver patties seasoned with garum and bay leaves, sliced chicken breasts smothered with onions in a date and wine sauce, and pork stew with apples served in small bowls were the meat dishes with sides of fried carrots seasoned with garum and white wine, boiled leek salad sliced in rounds, lentils with a chestnut puree, and vegetables. Rumors of Romans gorging themselves were popular, but in homes the fare was modest. Dining was a leisurely event. Each dish was highly flavorful and a small slice or piece was very satisfying. Fingers were used unless a spoon was needed for stews or soups. The girls removed these tables and went back to the kitchen.

"You do not know how to be a slave, Vitalia!" Aquilina burst out laughing. "You stood in the corner crossing your eyes at me and then winking! Don't make me laugh! This is serious." Aquilina pulled herself together. "You and I will be beaten if we move or make a noise. Just stand there, please. Don't try to make me laugh! This is not funny!"

New tables were presented, *mensa secunda* filled with sweets, fruit, cheeses and breads arranged attractively on circular trays. Of course, wine goblets were kept filled. The wine was diluted, not to stretch it but rather to reach a preferred taste, flavored with seeds and herbs such as fennel. Calitoria used the help of one of the local wine stewards, the *cellarius,* to help her with appropriate choices. *Passum*, a sweet raisin wine, was served with the desserts.

"Let's leave the men to speak privately," said Lasennia.

"I would like to show you our garden," Calitoria smiled.

Vita and Aquilina cleared the tables.

"Do you think we will get to eat anything?" asked Vita while she picked over the abandoned food on the plates.

"Yes, I saved some for breakfast for the master and all of us," answered Lavinia. "Now you are all finished and may go to your beds."

THE TWO WIVES strolled to the peristyle surrounded by its huge columns where Calitoria suggested sitting on one of the benches. The plants and damp earth mimicked the surrounding beauty of the mountainside and created a luxurious restful spot in the middle of the villa.

"I noticed the lovely hair design of one of your slaves, the one that was serving with braided hair. Your handmaiden must be very talented. I was wondering if I might hire her to style my hair sometime. In running a household, it is good to recognize individual talents and use them. It builds and binds the family. I think it is wonderful that you allow your slaves to look so fashionable, it is good for them. You must be very wise and kindhearted."

Calitoria had not even notice Aquilina's braided hair. Not knowing what Lasennia was talking about, and not knowing who styled Aquilina's hair, she covered by saying, "Of course, I would be pleased to share her talents with you. We are fortunate to have her with us. But your hair is lovely. I can't imagine how it could be more beautiful."

Calitoria's eyes dropped to Lasennia's very pregnant abdomen, her worth validated by being quite pregnant. Calitoria needed this validation, too. She could never take the primary role of administrator of this household until she produced a child. This would be Lasennia's second child.

"Are you familiar with the worship of Isis?" asked Lasennia as she adjusted the gold band on her crown that matched her beaded necklace and bracelet set with molded relief of Venus holding a myrtle branch. "At one time, Balbus and I were hoping to have children, but I was having some trouble. I love children and wanted my own. I turned to Isis. She is the goddess of fertility from Egypt. She is very popular here. I know some have criticized me for attending the worship with people from classes far beneath me, but I was desperate to have a baby. Within weeks of being inducted, I conceived my first son." She gently rubbed her stomach, closing her eyes, enjoying the thought of having another child very soon.

"During the rituals, we tap into the energy of the natural world. It brings us closer to the goddess and we combine our human energy with hers, which generates the natural fertility in us. I believe that without Isis I would not be having this child or any child. It is such a miracle. I am very careful to acknowledge Isis and all the gods in everything I do."

Calitoria wanted to say that she found it very confusing, she couldn't remember which god did what, there were so many, and new citizens from lands around the Empire were always bringing new religions and cults. Here was a woman who knew all about the gods and had studied them. Normally, it would be uncomfortable for Calitoria to feel that anyone had superior knowledge or was superior to her in any way, but she was drawn by the need and desire to have a baby. Each month she would dream that she was pregnant and build up hope and anticipation. Then when her menses flowed, she would be disheartened and irritable with everyone. There was some urgency with Gaius leaving for his duty to the Empire, and there would be no chance for pregnancy until he returned.

"I want to have a baby, too, but it has not happened for me yet. Perhaps you could help me know who Isis is and how to receive her miracles?"

" I will help you, I can take you to the Temple and show you," Lasennia replied. "We could go to the Temple here but the one in Pompeii is extraordinary."

GAIUS AND BALBUS moved to the tablinum. Gaius pulled the curtain giving them some privacy as they sat around the table.

"I am scheduled to serve in Britannia after my leave here in Herculaneum. I heard rumors today that there is unrest in that area of the Roman Empire," said Gaius. He leaned forward and lowered his voice. "I understood that there was peace. I thought Emperor Claudius achieved treaties with the barbarians and that the tribes welcomed the

Roman culture and economy. Now, I am unsure of my next assignment to oversee artisans and engineers finishing the Imperial Temple. How can I do this if the tribes are rebelling? Is there an invasion of these subhumans? What do you know of Britannia?"

"I have heard of the trouble," Balbus admitted. "Emperor Claudius did attain control by setting up treaties with client kings of several tribes in the south, mostly to exchange goods for grain, but I have heard that the expense of defending and protecting the outreach far outweighs the value of the grain imports. There are rich metal deposits that are being tapped but could be increased to help with the cost of the conquest, but those deposits of iron and silver sit in the midst of some of the most tenuous treaties.

"Those barbarians are uncivilized," Balbus added. "They value their independence over peace, even creating uprisings and wars between themselves. Some tribes have come over to our side enjoying the protection of the legions in the area, but that causes increased resentments and divisions with the other tribes. They are an undisciplined people, no structure to their fighting forces, no organization, so it has been easy to subdue their small factions of independent tribal attacks. But recently, they seem to be finding a way of joining forces against a common enemy, which would be us. They hate Roman occupation. It is partly due to our mistakes in judgment."

"Mistakes in judgment?" Gaius frowned. "I thought Veranius was in charge as Legate in that area. He has vast experience throughout the Empire."

"The Empire is strong, embracing all the Mediterranean, Egypt, Britannia, Europe and the Middle East. It may be stretched too far, as seen in Britannia where it is difficult to establish continued control. There are many fronts to be protected and supervised from our Rome. So many cultures, hundreds of languages, and various religions. Many struggle for power and control. There is concern that Rome cannot rule such a diverse and large expanse," Balbus reflected throwing his arms wide, then leaned close, confiding.

"My grandfather served Julius Caesar. He told me Caesar's appetite to expand the Empire is why he commanded his armies to secure Britannia after chasing the Gauls and Germanic tribes that far north. They gained an uneasy stability after bloody battles. He went on to serve as Tribune with Octavian Augustus in the civil wars, then Proconsul and he told me the Senate lost interest in Britannia since other regions could provide the same resources with less trouble."

Balbus stood and began to pace, one arm bent behind at his waist, his free hand gesturing to convey his thoughts.

"When Emperor Augustus came into power, he was distracted by Cleopatra's ambitions to take over Rome. After he triumphed, adding Egypt to the Empire, some Romans wanted peace. Emperor Caligula did not focus on establishing a strong Province in Britannia either. Later, Emperor Claudius's continued what Caesar had started. He was quite proud of securing the Province for Rome."

"But since then harsh liberties taken by the former Lagate have caused resentment from the barbarians. Taxes on the inhabitants were raised, laws against locals were harsh. Those found with weapons were severely tortured and punished. And worst of all the indigent landowners had their land confiscated and given to Roman veterans who have now settled in the area. It was unwise to mistreat the local residents no matter how subhuman they are. Those were the mistakes in judgment."

"After all that, if it's ungovernable and not worth the expense, why the sudden interest in Britannia again?" Gaius's initial concerns were blossoming into grave misgivings, though he had no way of getting out of his assignment.

"Nero. Those close to the young Emperor have invested in the area giving loans and are now calling them due. Seneca, one of Nero's closest advisors, is said to be heavily in debt to Britannia. If Rome decides to pull out of the Province because of the upheaval and expense, his loans will never be repaid. Which is a possibility, as many with political influence have criticized that Britannia is a waste to the Empire. The drain of soldiers, the cost of the navy and administration, and distraction from other more important areas are not worth the trouble. It costs more to run Britannia than any other Province, but because Seneca invested so heavily, it is rumored that he is convincing Nero to increase the Empire's control of the Province and expand the iron and silver mines so mineral deposits could be sold to the rest of the Empire, making it profitable, and Seneca would be repaid."

"Nero probably does not want to lose the Province during his reign as Emperor. That would diminish respect for him. He is barely out of his teens, and craves popularity from the people," Gaius remarked accepting the reality.

"At the moment it is quite a mess. Last year they sent Veranius up there to be the Governor."

"Veranius was Governor of Lycia and a great authority on military matters," said Gaius. "A strong, experienced leader could make all the difference."

"Except, he is dead of old age. What were they thinking, he was old when they sent him up there! He claimed he could conquer and expand the area in two years, but he was old, worn out. A new Governor has been sent to clean up the mess that he left and expand and secure the area. Shouldn't be too hard."

"You believe it will not be difficult to secure the Province?" said Gaius.

"Of course not. Barbarians are not soldiers, my opinion, but they are scary. They fight amongst themselves more than against us. They are animal-like, fractured tribes. And remember, they have no weapons. We took them away. What can they fight with?"

Balbus reseated himself, having resolved the situation in his own mind. He chuckled.

"A few tribes are still rebellious; the Silures have caused trouble and refuse to enjoy the peace and prosperity that Rome offers them. It should be easy to wipe them out along with the other rebelling tribes. Besides the Silures are in the far west and you will be in the east if you are working on the Temple deifying Claudius. The new Governor, Paulinus, is a great general and a mastermind in military strategy. He is seizing control and securing the area for Rome."

Gaius understood the minor conflict would be over before he got there.

Chapter Four

It was difficult for Vita to feel whole again. A young girl cut off from all connection to her past life. *Might as well be floating out at sea with no pier to grasp, no buoy, no anchor, no family, no home and no way to return,* she thought. Each day started with an uneasy sick feeling that made her want to hide.

She entered the kitchen early the next morning to hear Lavinia's motherly voice ask her, "Did you sleep well? Here, have something to eat before you start your day." Vita reached out and caught Lavinia, wrapping her arms around her broad waist, squeezing hard, holding her tightly. Lavinia grabbed a towel to dry her busy hands so she could embrace Vita. She held her snuggly until both spirits felt the human need satisfied. Vita's eyes were moist when she released her. "Now, come on, cat. We have lots to do today."

The oven fires were already started in the hearth, spreading joy throughout the kitchen equal to the warmth of Lavinia's heart. Hands were active stirring and chopping.

"We need the bread to be ready by lunchtime. Olives need to be crushed. Girls, you will have to shop for fresh fish. I heard that spices have arrived at the market, and I want to shop for those myself," directed Lavinia. "Telesphorus has asked to speak with you, Vitalia, about helping with a trip to the vineyards and olive groves tomorrow. You need to see him this afternoon."

Old Thana was up early as usual and perched on her territorial stool hoping for leftovers from the night before. Her favorite place to be in the household, she had no pretensions, most comfortable with Lavinia and the servants in the kitchen.

"Thana, how are your bones today?"

"Oh, not bad for an old lady," she replied. She mopped up egg yolk with a wedge of bread. Thana began to mutter in her native Etruscan, "It is this cold weather, it hurts the bones of the ancients."

Vita unconsciously answered her back in Etruscan. "Perhaps you should try warming yourself in the sun. My father always said that it helped his stiffness." It was automatic for her to answer in her mother's tongue, and she did it without thinking.

Thana called suspiciously in Etruscan. "Come over to me, girl." Vita walked timidly toward her.

"How do you know this? How can you speak to me as one who knows my family? These words come from my childhood, my spirit. No one speaks this language anymore." Vita explained that she grew up with the language from her mother. Thana studied Vita's face searching for an acquaintance from the past, trying to recall some facial feature.

"It warms my heart to hear these words from you. You must be here as a gift from the gods, sent to me at the end of my life. I can feel my family present in this house again because of you. My father, my mother, so long ago they left me and I dream that I will be with them someday. Each year that passes causes me to forget them, and I force myself to try and remember their voice, their touch, their love." Vita hugged Thana as her heart filled with understanding. No one else in the kitchen understood the exchange in the deceased tongue.

At that moment Calitoria entered the kitchen and walked straight to Aquilina.

"Aquilina, your hair looked lovely last night," she said sarcastically. With her right hand she gave a hard smack to the young girl's face. "Who did your hair?"

Aquilina hesitated knowing that a lie would bring worse punishment, but the truth might harm another.

Vita stepped forward. "I did it."

Calitoria turned toward her and backhanded her across the face. Blood leaked into her mouth.

"Never forget that you are a slave. You do not deserve better. You are not better than me and never will be. So don't draw attention to yourself or any other slave ever with anything better than what I have. In the future, as my property, you will live only to serve me and only if I let you live to serve me." She pivoted and left. Stunned and afraid, all the slaves were motionless.

"Sorry, Aquilina, I didn't know she would be angry." Vita had seen no harm in fixing Aquilina's hair; the problem was that she had done it so well. All were aware that the other mistress of the house, Thana, was still present so they restrained their reaction, saying nothing, fearing more correction.

"*Avaritia facit Bardus*," stated Thana. (Greed makes one stupid.)

Gradually someone moved and all returned to work. The sweetness of the day erased, a new mood set.

"The sun was shining but clouds rolled in from the West," said Vita in a silvery, stupefied voice. Aquilina snorted a giggle.

THE GIRLS CARRIED empty amphorae down the street to the public fountain to collect water for washing. The impluvium had a well that collected rain for use in the villa, but several weeks of dry weather sent them to the fountain instead. At first they carried the water filled amphorae in front of them, then set them down to pull them on the road, then back up in their arms again. They walked on the sidewalk but since wagons were prohibited on Decumanus Maximus, they soon ventured to the street where there was more room enabling them to dodge people walking to the Forum. Outside the Petronius villa, a row of clients wanting to buy or sell something sat on the bench near the front door waiting to see Gaius and Telesphorus about business. The girls walked to the servants' entrance.

As soon as they set down the heavy jugs of water, they left for the Forum to buy fresh fish for the day. A melee of noise and confusion confronted them. Thick crowds made it difficult to weave a path to find the fishmongers. Aquilina searched for the oyster stands offering live oysters fresh from the coast. She saw him, handsome Quintus helping at one of the stands.

"Let's check these first," she said grabbing Vita's hand and pulling her over to Quintus. "What are you doing, Quintus? Now you are a fishmonger and not a gem cutter?"

"Well, not really. I earn extra money helping at the docks shelling oysters. See, we have some prepared for you ready to toss into boiling water. The freshest you will find and hardly any work to do as we have done it for you."

Aquilina's wisdom with money came from lessons of thrift from Lavinia. She knew Lavinia would be angry if she bought already shelled oysters.

"I'll have the ones in the shell. They are cheaper and we have plenty of kitchen servants who can help with the shelling. See, we have Vitalia! She can shell the oysters!"

Vita made a face at Aquilina.

"When do you go down to the docks to help? How much do they pay you?" Vita asked.

"They pay well, but you have to get up long before dawn and work by lamplight. It's hard work. Look at my hands!" Vita and Aquilina leaned over to examine his palms as he held them out. They were raw and swollen with cuts from the rough oyster shells.

"Oooh, you should put some sweat from sheep on your hands to help them heal," said Vita.

"Sweat from sheep, does that really help?"

"Of course it does, I promise."

"Well, when I find some, I will use it," he laughed, knowing it would be impossible.

Vita flushed at his laughter but at least she found her tongue and could speak to Quintus this time. He helped them collect and pay for the oysters and they left his booth.

Vita wanted to peek at all the booths. She saw spices, sandals, writing supplies, wax tablets, and rolled paper. She wished she had some money to buy a writing tablet or rolled paper. Her father taught her to read and do numbers on a wax tablet in Ephesus. She could draw on the paper. It had been a long time since she'd thought about her art.

The girls arrived back home to find the servants preparing lunch. Lavinia handed a tray with cheese, bread, walnuts, and wine to Vita.

"You need to meet with Telesphorus, take this tray in to the tablinum for me. You may ask him about what you will be doing tomorrow."

Vita ambled reluctantly to the front of the villa to the large atrium. To the right was the tablinum where Gaius and Telesphorus were discussing business. Scrolls of paper were laid out on the table and spilled over to the colorful marble floor.

"But how will we pay to feed the sheep if we purchase so many?" asked Gaius.

"At first we will have to procure a bank loan, but as soon as the lambs and wool are sold, we can repay the loan and make a profit. I know this will work for you. It is the same plan I developed with the Calitorius family several years ago," said Telesphorus.

"I am thankful to have you, Telesphorus. My wife did not come with a dowry, but I negotiated for you to come with her instead," said Gaius.

"Yes, but I believe she made that request herself."

"True. I am still encouraged by your Greek education with book-keeping, laws, and the way you are able to organize our business. It is critical that we work together on this before I leave. You will have to know all the details of my property."

Vita entered quietly with the tray and set it down on a small table. She straightened and fussed with the items and poured wine in the goblets.

"At last, the young girl I purchased appears! I hardly recognize you! What is your name?"

"It is Vita, now called Vitalia," Telesphorus answered warmly.

"Vitalia!" greeted Gaius. His booming, raspy voice echoed through the hall. Vita stepped back hoping to shrink into the wall.

"Tomorrow you will go with us to our groves outside of town. We will leave before dawn, and I have asked Lavinia to prepare food for us to take. I want you to help. Make sure we have plenty of water. We will need some for all of us including the horse. A wagon will be brought to the end of Decumanus Maximus loaded with supplies at dawn. You can carry the water jugs and food down in the morning. Telesphorus will waken you."

"It will make me happy to see the countryside," said Vita.

A chance to leave the city and travel up and around the mountain to the groves! I can use this trip to plan my escape to be free again. I can learn where the roads and local towns are. I might even find a place to hide or find food.

After her encounter with Calitoria, Vita could think of nothing but escape. *I will never bow down to Calitoria, but I am smart enough to fool her into thinking that I will,* she thought.

～

LATER, while they knelt in the peristyle garden picking basil, thyme, dill, and coriander for Lavinia, Vita whispered to Aquilina. "I am planning my escape,"

"You must not even think about that. You will be punished. They can legally kill you, or if they are kind-hearted they will brand your forehead, and you will be sent to the farms for hard labor!"

"I don't care. Calitoria will never lay a hand on me again. Tomorrow I will search for a place to hide until I can run away somewhere."

"You are a foolish girl, and she will lay her hands on you again. I will bet on it. It would be smarter for you to learn to be with Calitoria and avoid punishment. You are being so stupid."

"I thought you were going to be my friend," said Vita.

"I am your friend and that is why I am telling you, you are stupid."

～

THE NEXT MORNING Telesphorus knocked on the new slave's door. Vita collected herself and answered, waiting for him to speak.

"Time to start." Her stunning blue eyes with their thick lashes seized him.

"I'm ready," she said misunderstanding his expression as irritation. *Some people are grumpy in the morning. He seemed kind the first night. Perhaps preoccupied with his responsibilities. That's fine. I don't care if he likes me. I'm leaving.*

Vita headed to the kitchen area to gather the bountiful *cena* Lavinia placed on the table and carried it down to the wagon waiting at the end of the street. Telesphorus leaned over the back of the wagon arranging and rearranging supplies. A small niche between grain, cloth, shoes, medicines, tools, and food gave her a place to sit. They were off promptly as the sky began to lighten revealing that dawn would soon follow. Expecting a showy sunrise, Vita pouted finding herself in a gray soup of fog with cold temperatures. As they traveled out the town gate north and east around the mountain, the horse struggled to pull the load up the steep incline. The clouds blanketed the mountainside roads preventing any mapping of the area, destroying Vita's plan to escape. Her equilibrium was compromised as she was rocked and tossed about in the back of the wagon for hours, bouncing against the rough wooden slats.

Approaching mid-day the gloomy fog gradually lifted allowing silvery shapes of shrubs and small trees to appear, then crisp craters and rock formations. The dirt road flattened and turned down a narrow lane covered with brush ending next to a long building. At first, Vita thought it abandoned as no one came to greet them and tall weeds obstructed the doorway revealing a lack of care. The men jumped down and commenced to unload the supplies.

Vita tried to stand to jump out but found her legs unwilling and hard to move. She stretched and looked out at her surroundings; on her left, another stone building with red paint half-way up, and in front, rows of small neatly spaced trees, which must be the olive grove. A mixture of moist aromas filled the air and she breathed deeply to savor the smell. It was a blend of freshly cut grass with something familiar. The sun bore down exciting the crackling insects and cheering the birds into a musical chorus. Telesphorus reached for her waist lowering her effortlessly, setting her out of his way. She turned to wander up a path to inspect flowers which led to an open meadow surrounded by young trees with stacked beehives along the edge. It reminded her of home.

A vision of her father working their hives filled her memory. As if his soul had blended with hers, both of them delighting in the reenactment of a time before: the smell of honey, buzzing bees, her father's presence right beside her reaching in gently to rob their wax. Of course she daydreamed this, remembering how slowly he moved pulling away the

wax drenched with honey. The bees hardly noticed the slight distur-
bance. It seemed they were thankful for the intrusion to help them clean
the hive.

Her father painted ships in Ephesus and used the beeswax mixed
with pigment. Vita helped heat, and clean the wax sometimes adding
the pigment, then her father and other craftsmen would use it to seal the
hulls and add magnificent designs to the Roman fleet.

These moments of missing her parents would attack her without
warning. She caught her breath and held it, shutting her eyes, and
allowed herself to be transported back to that moment. Father was
there. They were together again, so familiar, so much alike. Feeling
secure and comfortable, she remembered the scent of his hair, the feel of
his rough warm hands. She felt his love again.

The sound of soft calling beckoned her around the path where she
found a fold of sheep. Merrily following the circle, she could see a vineyard on the slope with tidy vines supported by sticks. The high sun and
sapphire sky constructed a composition of puffy clouds above and
striped rows of golden brown and green below, encircling boxy buildings of gray and red. She wished she had paper to draw the memory so
that she could take it with her.

This must be close to heaven, she thought.

She trotted back to the wagon when she saw Telesphorus and Gaius
exit the building. Her own stomach was grumbling, so she knew they
would be asking for their lunch.

She followed them into another long, low stone building. At one
end, she could see animals, asses, chickens and oxen. At the other end
were dark, undefined shapes. If one of them had not moved causing the
rattle and clanking of chains, she would have thought nothing of it, but
these were human forms. A stench assaulted her nose, flies and gnats
pestered her eyes. This was where the farm slaves were kept. As her eyes
adjusted to the darkness, she saw several men lying on hay among filth.

"Why aren't these slaves working?" asked Gaius. The overseer plead
their case: they were sick and could not work. Vita thought they looked
like they were starving to death, noticing the bones jutting out from
leathery skin.

"Are they eating?" asked Gaius. He seemed agitated and somewhat
shocked at their appearance.

"Yes, of course. We have grain made into porridge that they get every day. Some choose not to eat. Some don't deserve to eat unless they give a full day's labor."

"Therefore, you are saying they are not eating every day!" responded Gaius. "I have placed you in charge, but I expect you to treat my slaves well. They are valuable property and have cost me a lot of money. I can't afford to have them dying."

Vita was surprised to hear him speak of the slaves as if they were the same as the animals in the opposite end of the building. She expected a different attitude from Gaius, but she didn't know why. He was Roman after all. Maybe it was the gentle way he had guided her through crowds in Pompeii or the life enjoyed by the slaves in their villa.

They exited and Vita was asked to prepare lunch in the red and white building. A woman stood at the hearth stirring a pot over the fire. Her tunic was soiled and she was barefoot. Everything about her seemed faded, her dull hair, her vacant expression. Perhaps she never left the building. Without speaking, Vita set the food items out on the dusty wooden table: bread with olive paste and ground liver, cheese, some walnuts and boiled beets, and a soup made of chicken broth and vegetables. The woman took the terra cotta bowl of soup with the lid on it and placed it near the fire to heat it. The men clamored into the farmhouse and sat down at the table.

"We have plenty for everyone," bellowed Gaius. The women moved their food to a separate table near the hearth. Vita stared at her plate, picked it up, and walked out of the house. She crossed the farmyard and went into the low building again to find the human forms lying on the straw. She knelt between them and handed bite-sized bits of bread and cheese to them. She spread goose liver on the bread and placed it in the weakest slave's mouth. He closed his eyes savoring the delicious nourishment. One of the men wore an iron collar that said, "I am a runaway. Please return me to Gaius Petronius Stephanus." The fresh scars on his back revealed the punishment he had received.

Nothing was lost on Vita. She realized the subhuman existence of slaves. These were *familia rustica*, farm slaves chained together in a group of the lowest class. Collected as war prisoners and sold into slavery, these were once strong soldiers treated as spoils of war, just like gold or silver. They cost less than *familia urbana*, or city slaves, because they were captured on the battlefield and sold immediately to slave dealers. Generals did not want to be bothered with prisoners.

Vita glanced behind her and noticed Gaius and Telesphorus standing in the doorway.

"I thought I would feed your property," said Vita in a soft voice. She looked directly at Gaius, her round innocent face with its piercing blue eyes framed by sienna wavy hair, convicting his heart through her selfless action. Gaius did not miss the message.

He turned to the overseer and commanded, "I want these men well fed with porridge, five ponderi of bread, and figs. If that doesn't bring them back to health, sausage can be given to them in small measures. Make some *posca*, acidified wine mixed with water, to refresh them, as much as they desire. A slave that is well treated will perform better. Telesphorus will be returning in two weeks to check on them. If any of them are dead, you will be flogged or worse."

Vita wondered what could be worse. She followed Gaius and Telesphorus, eavesdropping as they walked around the property planning their improvements. The men meandered back to the wagon deep in conversation.

"We will want to expand the farm house by adding on a large area for a wine and olive press. If we start making our own oil and wine, rather than selling the produce to others, we can enjoy a larger profit. It will take some time and money, but in the end you will be more secure financially," explained Telesphorus. They entered one of the small wooden buildings with bins installed along the side which contained a small amount of discarded sheep wool. "This building will have to be replaced with a larger stone building including a raised floor for sheep shearing. More bins will be needed for the wool, and stalls can be built for the dams and lambs at the far end."

"I want you to work on the cost and amount of time for completion of the improvements," ordered Gaius.

Telesphorus spoke from experience and confidence, saying, "It can be completed within the year with no problem. The cost will take me some time to calculate. You have several clients who will bring competitive pricing for your business. I suggest we visit one of the Herculaneum bankers for the loan or even include Pompeii bankers for competitive negotiations. Markets are strong and growing in the Empire. It is a promising time for expansion. Bankers will be generous with money to lend for a price."

Gaius had some knowledge from running his father's small farm throughout his childhood, however, his feeling of trepidation came from a lack of true experience and real understanding. His father had taken charge of most decisions for the farm and did not teach Gaius the reasons for his choices. In fact, his father had been quite secretive about his businesses. This left Gaius a novice at running a farm, and liable to cause costly mistakes. He hoped to multiply his father's inheritance, expanding the groves and vineyards, letting them deteriorate with age would be nothing but a waste. If he just maintained what they had at present, he would not be able to generate enough income. The risk of failure mauled his thoughts.

"Are we leaving?" asked Vita.

"Yes, Vitalia, load everything up in the wagon," said Gaius. He paused, searching this young girl with his eyes, trying to determine her soul. What was it about her quiet dignity, her sweet gesture to the slaves that convicted him of his dreadful treatment of other human beings? This fragile girl stood before him harboring a power that called him to be better.

"I wonder if I could have some of the discarded sheep wool in the small shack? I know how to make skin softener cosmetic from the wool. I am sure your new wife would like to see the magic I can create with it."

"Yes, I would also like to see the magic you can make from wool," Gaius laughed. "Go ahead, fetch what you want."

Vita rushed back to the shed and scooped up an armload of fleece, wrapped it in her palla tying it with a knot. She loaded up olives and chicken eggs, dried figs, and honey to take back to the villa before they started back down the mountain. It would be dark when they reached Herculaneum.

Chapter Five

W ake up, wake up, I must wake up, Vita thought as she rested in bed that morning listening to the sounds of the city: a rooster crowing somewhere, probably at the bakery, song-birds calling, someone yelling in the street. Loneliness gnawed.

I am a slave. My mother died, my father died. No one will help me. But I am strong, healthy, and smart, and I know a lot for a thirteen-year-old. That will have to do. They taught me to read and work with numbers. Mother taught me to do everything from laundry to dressing brides for weddings. Father taught me about shipbuilding and ports and earning money. This world is similar, but I am not free. Rules that apply to slaves are mine now.

She heard someone moving about downstairs. She slipped on her sandals and tied back her hair, hoping Lavinia would be in the kitchen making it warm and safe.

"I will never be able to get up earlier than you, Lavinia," Vita remarked as she entered the kitchen and wrapped her arms around Lavinia feeling affection returned.

"Oh sweet girl, you are here. For a minute I thought you were Aquilina, you look so much alike. I need you to peel the boiled eggs. You can have one or two to eat with your porridge and honey."

"We brought figs from the farm yesterday. Could I have one of those?"

"You can have more than that, we have plenty."

"I was wondering if I could have some time this afternoon to make a lotion for the mistress that my mother showed me how to make. I think she would like it. It will take some time, and I will need to use the brazier in the side yard, if it is all right."

Lavinia gave her a sidelong look. "Does the master know about this?"

"Yes, in fact he allowed me to collect the ingredients yesterday from the farm."

"You can take some time in the afternoon after *prandium* has been served."

"Thank you." Vita knew that Lavinia was being very kind. Giving her a break from the usual chores would mean more work for someone else.

AFTER *IENTACULUM*, the morning meal, Lavinia told Vita to attend to Calitoria.

"I don't want to go."

"You have to, dear one. Calitoria is the mistress of this villa."

"I don't want to. She is mean. She better not hit me or I will hit her back."

"Oh child, you have so much to learn. I know you were not raised a slave but you must learn quickly if you want to live," answered Lavinia. "Now go. Take the scowl off your face before you get there."

Calitoria's *cubicula nocturna* was situated on the quieter side of the home. Gold and red frescoes covered all the walls from floor to ceiling giving the illusion of three dimensional pillars and carvings. At the far end of the room was a large couch covered with beautiful fabrics and pillows. Cheerful sunlight illuminated the room from a side window contrasting with the disagreeable mistress.

Vita entered to find the mistress sitting on a three-legged stool with her handmaiden standing behind her. Tears slipped down the handmaiden's bruised face.

"Vitalia, could you design my hair in the fashion that the ladies in Greece are currently wearing? I have tried to tell my handmaiden what I want, but she just does not understand. I want it high in the front and full in the back with the braiding like you know how to do."

"Of course I can try." Vita took the comb from the handmaiden and began to comb out what had already been attempted. Her hands shook. The sting of the slap that had left her mouth bloody gave a recurring alarm. After all, the slap was a punishment for fixing beautiful hair.

"You see, many of the women in Greece are using a trick to create height in the front of the hair. It involves cutting some of the hair to be short. We make a roll of hair to get more height in the front. The back will still be long so that we can create a beautiful cluster secured at the base of the neck, and no one really knows part of the hair has been cut."

Vita took Calitoria's hair and pushed it up in the front to show her how it would look.

"Then we use a warm iron rod to curve the shorter strands around the face creating a frame to draw attention to your eyes."

"Oh, I could never cut my hair."

"The hair is not discarded, we make a wrap and use it to insert under your hair to give it height or we can use it in other ways to shape the hairdo," Vita repeated. She knew that hair was very important to women and considered their crowning glory. To cut one's hair was not readily accepted, only men cut their hair and it could be interpreted as being masculine.

"Couldn't we cut some of Talistia's hair to make the wrap?" she asked.

"Since your hair is very pale, an unusual color, it would not match, but I can give you some braiding instead that will be very pretty on you," Vita replied, but she was thinking that Calitoria had asked for the latest styles from Greece. Apparently, that was not really what she wanted. Vita worked with braids and sewed the hair in place with needle and thread. The hairstyle was very flattering to an already pretty face.

"I like it," Calitoria stated as she held the reflective hand mirror up to her face.

"Good, I am glad you like it." *Now is a good time to make a request,* she thought. "I have an idea of something I would like to make for you that my mother used to make for new brides in Greece. I wondered if I might ask Telesphorus for some bits of scroll paper to make storage containers for my gift." *Good strategy,* thought Vita. She could tell that by using the word "gift", Calitoria was intrigued. It was approved and Vita left the cubicula to return to her work in the kitchen.

LATER THAT AFTERNOON, Vita sat in the open side yard with a large cauldron set over the brazier. She poured in some salt and added wads of sheep wool that she had collected the day before into the boiling water.

"What are you doing?" asked Aquilina when she found Vita. She stuck her nose over the pot and said, "No one is going to eat that!"

Vita giggled. "It is not for eating! I am making a cosmetic lotion for Quintus."

"Who is letting you do that? You are going to get in trouble."

"Both Gaius and Calitoria are letting me do it, they both know. I told them I am making it for Calitoria."

"It stinks like a goat!"

"It comes from a sheep."

"Well, it stinks like a sheep! You will have her smelling like a sheep." Vita and Aquilina looked at each other and laughed out loud.

"Shhhhh, we will be caught being bad! What do you do with it?" Aquilina whispered.

"It is magic!" Vita answered.

Vita removed the wool after a length of time, holding the fleece up high, letting the hot water drain into the pot, then continued to boil the remaining liquid until it was almost dry. She had to constantly control the heat of the brazier so it did not get too hot. Finally, a yellow residue was left on the side of the pot. She scraped the substance into a wide-mouthed terra cotta jar and added some olive oil and a little water. She covered the top and shook it vigorously. This cleaned the yellow oily substance of debris causing it to separate and float. Vita took the parchment that Telesphorus had given her and tore it into small squares. She curved it into a cone shape and placed some of the yellow substance inside and folded the top edge down. Vita created more cones for Lavinia, Thana, Aquilina, and Quintus and anyone else she liked, and then she scraped the rest into a small bowl for Calitoria.

"She will smell like a sheep. Gaius won't go near her," said Aquilina shaking her head.

"I did her hair today. I should have braided it into two horns, that would fix her. I could have told her all the ladies in Greece were wearing their hair that way."

Aquilina stifled a laugh which came out in shakes sending them both into uncontrolled laughter, holding their sides until tears came to their eyes.

"Stop," said Aquilina. "I need to stop."

They calmed down while Vita gathered up her supplies and began to think about how and when she would give Quintus the lotion. It was not so easy to get away from the villa with so much work to do. Vita could not slip away without someone noticing. She wanted to see Quintus again. *I will give him the gift and he will know that I care for him. Perhaps he will ask to see me or maybe even caress my cheek.* She fantasized for a moment on that lovely scene.

THE PERFECT OPPORTUNITY presented itself the next morning when the girls were sent to buy fish again. Handsome Quintus was in his usual place selling the oysters he shelled earlier that morning before dawn. Some of the men bought the fresh oysters then stood there and ate them creating a barrier that held her back. She wound her way through to Quintus and asked if he could step to the side of the booth to talk to her. Vita studied the smile she found in his brown eyes.

"I have something for you. I made the sheep sweat. All you need to do is rub it on your hands before going to bed each night. Wrap your hands with cloths while you sleep, and then see the healing in the morning."

He looked at her quizzically, saying nothing, not really understanding. After what seemed to be forever he said, "Thank you," and returned to his booth without even looking over his shoulder at her.

"I can't believe I gave him sheep sweat," she scolded herself as she walked away curling her hands into fists. *What was I thinking, I am so stupid! He will never look at me again without thinking 'sheep sweat'!*

She snuck through the crowd, her head down trying to find a place where he could not see her. Leaning against the wall outside the Forum, she scooted to the ground holding the sides of her head. *I am so embarrassed. He will think I'm stupid.* Her hands dropped to her lap while she reprimanded herself. "This morning when I woke up, all I wanted to do was get my freedom. My goal was to run away. Quintus has nothing to do with that plan, and I must focus on preparing a way out, not on getting this cute boy's attention." She stood up, decided to not think about Quintus anymore, and headed back to the villa.

There was shouting in the atrium when she entered through the servant door and stood next to Lavinia.

"What is happening?"

"Calitoria is filled with excitement because the Balbuses have invited them for a special evening." They both listened while Calitoria squealed with excitement.

"Gaius! We are invited to dinner at their villa, not just us but there will be other guests of extreme importance! I can't believe they included us. Oh Gaius, I just knew that the gods were with us. I prayed to all of the gods and household ancients to make this connection for us and they have. It will be so good for you and your businesses and prestige. I must think about what to wear. I must have a new gown. I will fashion it myself from lovely wool, and we will be the most envied couple. Please can we shop in Pompeii? They will have more choices of fabrics of higher quality and colors."

Elderly Thana commented from her stool. "An invitation to Nonius Balbus's for dinner next week, a *minimus quoque timendum.* (Beware even the tiniest of creatures.)" Then in Etruscan she said, "The woman displays her inner self. There is nothing pure and honest about her. She wants nothing for my son, Gaius, she only wants for herself."

No one else understood Etruscan. Why was Thana using her as a confidante? Vita had instinctive knowledge that told her to be careful, because Thana was not a slave. She held high prestige in the house even though she chose to be with the slaves rather than with her daughter-in-law.

Calitoria pleaded with Gaius to take her to Pompeii the next day so she could start on her costume for the dinner as soon as possible. Vita stopped listening and thought it would be nice to have her gone for the day. Gaius gave in, always wanting those around him to be happy.

Besides, he and Telesphorus could use the trip to find building materials and even talk to some bankers about the expansion to the farm.

Vita felt comfortable in the kitchen with the slaves who had become her new friends and, of course Thana, always present in the kitchen. It was time to present the thoughtful gift she brewed. She handed the salve to those she cared about and gave instructions on how to apply it to their cracked and dry hands and skin.

They laughed at the odor. "You will have to do something about the smell, Vitalia," calling her by her Latin name, Lavinia made a face. "You need to take a lesson from the flowers in the garden, dear one. You can't attract the bees without an alluring fragrance."

LATER THAT EVENING as darkness entered the home, Thana captured Vita's hand and led her to the atrium. Like an invisible thief, Thana managed to pull the reluctant child along the dark corridor. Holding on to an oil lamp, she peered around the corner to be sure that Gaius and Calitoria were absent, then opened the wooden cross-hatched gate that secured the sacred cubicle, and tugged Vita's hand pulling her into the forbidden room. The amber glow of the lamp illuminated ornate frescoes of gold and red and cerulean blue and portraits of unfamiliar gods gesturing to one another. A wooden cabinet and bench were at the end of the room. Thana moved with the lamp toward the cabinet, knelt and carefully opened the doors. Vita gasped at what she saw. Her heart pounded and she felt a rush of energy through her veins until she was lightheaded. Thana reverently reached in with both hands and lifted out the severed head and placed it on top of the cabinet.

"This was my mother."

Vita cupped her hands to her throat holding her breath. Thana moved the lamp closer to the face, and the bright light made shadows dance around the room as if ghouls were rejoicing. Nausea, and then a spirit of grief, entered Vita's body. A moan escaped her lips. She closed her eyes as the sorrow of the ancients laid a weight upon her soul. Blood drained to her feet.

"I think I'm going to faint."

"The spirits of my ancestors are holding your body. You will recover," assured Thana.

Vita forced herself to study the lifeless head. *It's not real, it's wax*, she realized.

The wax form, carved and colored, replicated a human head, with staring eyes, and thin lips as if ready to speak. More heads without bodies sat on the shelves. Vita imagined one as the father, maybe another her deceased husband. Thana caressed her mother's head.

"She was so beautiful and kind. They say I have her eyes. She had such purity of heart, never feeling an evil thought or harming anyone, yet still a mother that guided and corrected her family, raising all of us to be honest human beings. I will never be as good as her. I don't have her nature. I feed the anger and resentment in my heart. I wish I could release these feelings, but I know things that torture me. It is honest to know one's true character and temperament not imagining you are something you are not, but shameful to realize it and feel no control over it. I can't correct it. Sometimes I wonder if she had the same feelings and found victory over them.

"Now, you realize why you are here." She turned to study Vita's face. "You have the Etruscan heart that sees past outward insincere appearance. It is a grave gift to possess. Truth and honesty disguise themselves as friends and are devious slayers of your soul. It will bring you much heartache and you will be alone. You must trust no one. It would be better to be stupid. Your honesty is a lamp that reveals the treachery of others." She repeated it again. "Your honesty will be a lamp that reveals the treachery of others. Beware."

As soon as Thana let her past the gate, Vita ran to her bed. Was it true? Did she have a reason to be here? Was it to reveal some evil secret?

Chapter Six

Vita stepped into the kitchen the next morning and at once discreetly covered her nose with her fingers trying to brush an unpleasant odor away. It was obvious that everyone was using her lotion. She must do something about the smell of sheep sweat. While thinking about how she could change the scent with different spices or flowers, she hugged her Lavinia then sat at the table to help with meal preparations.

"Vitalia, Calitoria wants you to accompany them to Pompeii. Talistia will also be going and Flavius will help with labor should you need him," said Lavinia. Vita put her hand to her forehead and stared at Lavinia with lowered brows.

"You will like Flavius," continued Lavinia as she stirred a bowl of barley flour, water, and fermenting yeast. "He has lived with Thana and the Petronius family for many years. I think he was in his teens when he came. He loves the garden and it is his masterpiece. You can find him caressing each plant, inspecting each petal. He knows the name of every tree and bush there! Everyone loves him." Lavinia closed her eyes picturing a sweet memory.

"One time he built a cage for a song bird that had fallen out of its nest, and he gave it to Thana as a gift. Oh my, she loved that caged bird! When it died she mourned it for such a long time. She doesn't handle anyone or anything dying very well. Flavius always has one eye on Thana, making sure she is comfortable and safe. Vitalia, go to the garden and tell Flavius that he has to go to Pompeii with everyone."

Vita kicked a stone as she entered the sunlit peristyle surrounded by its fluted columns and mosaic walkway. She found Thana sitting on a bench watching a small man hunched over the roses delicately rotating the leaves and petals searching for mites and disease.

Flavius had resigned himself to his status as a slave and found peace and self-worth in it, achieving the high rank of household slave. Being a trusted member of the family and happiest using his hands, he proudly did most of the manual labor around the villa. Clipping and pruning, helping others, content with a safe home, plenty to eat, and time to work in the garden left no need for regret.

His second love was Thana. The pair had an exclusive relationship. Thana depended on him for support and shared her deepest thoughts. Flavius doted on her, anticipating her needs and fetched or fixed whatever pleased her. When Gaius's father died, Flavius felt her grief and despair as his own and watched over her. Together in the garden, they mimicked two devoted doves.

"Perhaps an afternoon in the sunshine would do your health some good today. Let me ask Lavinia to set your table in the garden where the warmth of the sun can share some of its energy," he said to Thana. Compliant like a little girl, she smoothed the fabric of her lap and accepted his suggestion without her usual sharp retort.

Vita caught his eye and blurted out the instructions, "Lavinia says that the family is going to Pompeii today and you must get ready to go with them."

He turned and spoke in his caring voice. "Mistress Thana, it would be best for you to stay home from Pompeii. You know how much walking we will have to do and it will be crowded with sailors and lowly people. Why don't you let me go and get you some of the dried dates you love so much and maybe something else special to cheer you while you have a day of rest right here."

Thana acquiesced even though she loved seeing what the shops were selling in Pompeii. Lately, her stiffness and dizziness made it more difficult to do all that she wanted to do.

~

MEMBERS of the traveling party gathered belongings while the sun still welcomed the morning. They exited the villa onto the street that would take them to the marina. Sometimes they traveled to Pompeii on an access road to go by land to the northwest side of Pompeii, but travel with today's mild weather would be more comfortable and faster by hired boat. It felt damp this morning but the sun already burned the pavement. Vita could smell the sea air with its unique aroma of fish and vegetation carried on the soft breeze. The marina presented a breathtaking view staggering her artistic senses with the teal blue of the sea and cobalt blue of the sky. Seagulls surrounded them with cheerful chatter and screams of happiness before they entered the din of clattering boats and bellowing seamen.

When they reached the dock, Flavius asked Talistia and Vita to hand over Calitoria's bags to be dropped in the boat. Gaius stepped in and turned to reach for Calitoria's hand, correcting her stumble as the craft jostled with its new weight. Once they were seated, the master rower called for cadence. Muscular bodies pulled in memorized strokes responding to the coxswain's chant. Oars danced in synchronized steps across the calm water, gently splashing and pulling them forward. Passengers' bodies relaxed then jerked with the rhythmic jolt of the oars powerful energy. The beauty of the water and the dazzling mountain slopes delighted Vita's soul.

This must be the most beautiful place on Earth, she thought, not knowing that by the end of the day, she would be lowered from this spiritual height to the depths of evil humanity.

She studied the shimmering shoreline laced with luxurious villas which lined the curve of the sea, each one competing for more opulence than the last. Many were vacation sanctuaries for politicians and aristocracy from Rome. Gaius pointed out Emperor Nero's aunt's home and even Nero's mistress's villa. Some homes even harbored banished enemies from Rome. Standard banishment forced them one hundred miles from Rome, so Herculaneum and Pompeii were perfect refuges, one hundred and fifty miles away. The joke was that to be banished to the vacation resorts created pleasure, not pain.

As they traveled, Vita and the other passengers relaxed in the warm sunshine and gentle breeze anticipating the lovely day that awaited them. After a few hours, the sight of elite docks appeared. The rowers slowed to calculate their landing and maneuvered to the pier. Glorious white pillars topped with robed marble statues painted in bold colors decorated the prosperous port of Pompeii. Peddlers ran toward them waving crafted items, tempting them to barter, creating a human barrier to break through. Nothing was lost on Vita as she climbed out of the boat. She made note of every detail. She looked up at the Venus Temple glittering above while Calitoria straightened her hair and dress, lifting her chin and glancing sideways to see who might be watching. Gaius directed the group to make their way toward Venus's Temple where they would split into two groups.

"Flavius, you must chaperone the women and keep them out of the brothel district east of the main Forum; their safety is your responsibility," Gaius directed. "Here are some coins for your purchases, enjoy yourselves, and we will meet at Assellina's for something to eat later today."

Gaius and Telephorus turned toward the Porta Salis to conduct their business and meet up with associates. Calitoria ascended the city steps and headed straight on the main street, Via del Abbondanza, past the Eumachia building and Stabian Baths to the dyer's shop. She entered a small darkened stall with fabrics hanging above and more laid out on tables. Vita, Talistia, and Flavius followed Calitoria stepping across the threshold and entering the shop to study the woolen and flax cloth. Calitoria fingered the many shades of yellow and gold fabric. Shades of brown were abundant and practical but not elegant enough for the Balbuses party. Purple was too expensive.

"I just don't see anything different or special," said Calitoria as she lightly touched pieces of woolen fabric.

"May I suggest something, Mistress? On the steps of the Marine Gate, I saw an older woman selling beautiful fabrics. Since we have all day, we could go back and see what she has. There also could be something at the Forum markets that you might like." Vita stared at Calitoria with an innocent smile. The mistress glared back, squaring her shoulders, searching for impudence but decided Vita's idea might be helpful and agreed. They went back to the Marine Gate.

As Vita hoped, the same woman still sat on the steps quietly bartering with interested shoppers when they arrived. Her fabrics were of superior quality and dyed with exquisite colors. A particularly soft wool of unusual blush pink with lightweight texture caught Vita's eye.

"Mistress Calitoria," exclaimed Vita, "This is beautiful! These two pieces would be lovely with your light hair."

The woman on the steps noticed them and came over to explain the quality. "I clean the wool myself and dye the yarn with rose petals, mint, and lemon. The color will stay true and not fade. Then I weave with a staggered pattern to add the design. "

"I love this. It is so rare. I will have it," said Calitoria.

Vita thought the rest of the day would be spent leisurely visiting the city now that they had accomplished the purpose of the trip, but Calitoria reentered the city gate and began to walk briskly past the Venus Temple and Forum again. Each member followed in a duck line trying to keep up with her.

Flavius questioned, "Mistress, Mistress! You know we must stay out of the forbidden area. Where are you going?" She did not answer and turned south toward the triangular Forum and Doric Temple, then turned east. Vita, Talistia, and Flavius labored to keep up, weaving through the throng trying to keep sight of her until they were stopped by a crowd pushing to enter a gate. Vita squeezed her arms to her side trying to be small enough to press sideways between the bodies as she tracked Calitoria ahead.

The Isis Temple glowed before them in the sunlight, surrounded by a high wall with one entrance. Worshippers filled the paved Temple courtyard. Talistia arrived beside Vita, and they stood on their toes, stretching to see the white Egyptian Ibises strutting gracefully around a central altar burdened with a bloody, sacrificed animal. Two choirs in white robes sang hymns on either side of the wide Temple steps. Vita gazed up and gawked at the tallest black man she had ever seen who stood between the red and white pillars of the Temple. He wore a large white piece of fabric wrapped high up on his chest that dropped all the way to his bare feet. The other priests, men and women, were dressed in the same fashion, all with their heads shaved.

"Talistia, do you see what I see? That statue is moving. Is that man real?" asked Vita.

"I think so. What are we doing here?"

A night time ceremony, Temple of Isis, Pompeii, Drawing by Louis Jean Deprez, 1779

CALITORIA PUSHED to the front of the crowd. Flavius mistakenly thought she wanted to listen to the music for a while.

"Please, Mistress, if you will be staying here, would you mind if I hurry to the market to shop for some sweets for Mistress Thana while you watch this festival? I can meet you at the entrance in a short time." Calitoria flipped a backward hand toward him as she listened to the priest bellow his exhortation.

The priest called for inductees to the cult. Calitoria stepped forward and began to ascend the stairs submissively. Vita grabbed her hand to pull her back in place, but she shook her off and mindlessly climbed up to where the priest stood reaching up to heaven calling for all to come forth. Talistia and Vita followed hoping that Calitoria misunderstood the priest's invitation. Two priests grabbed the handles on the tall wooden door to pull it open. There before them stood Lasennia, Balbus's wife, beckoning them into a darkened hall.

"Did you bring the sacrifice?" she asked. Calitoria pulled out a small purse and coins jingled inside. "Have you been pure abstaining from sex? Have you eaten no meat or wine?" Calitoria nodded and Lasennia motioned her to a waiting room on the left. "Your handmaidens will not be allowed to follow you to your rituals, but they can assist you before and after."

The initiates disrobed and entered a hallowed pool filled with water from the Nile. Talistia and Vita helped Calitoria cleanse herself and dress in new linens. The priest gestured toward the two large statues indicating one as Isis and one as her husband Osiris. Vita listened to him explain that the Mother Goddess resurrected her husband after he was dismembered, offering life after death to her followers. Restoring her husband to life, she became fertile and then pregnant after she put his body back together. Vita's mouth hung open as she gazed at the marble statue painted to look lifelike. Isis wore a painted dress of sheer fabric with gilded ornaments. She held the Egyptian *ankh* in one hand and the *sistrum* rattle in the other. Soft music emanated from a priest playing a lyre, setting a holy mood as light from flickering lamps danced on the walls.

"Isis, the ideal mother and wife, listens to prayers from all who worship her. I invite you to make your prayers known to her," said the priest. The inductees pulled out prepared papers penned with requests and tossed them into a replica of an Egyptian boat. Calitoria tossed in her note and followed them into the next room leaving Talistia and Vita to wait for hours.

"What do you think is happening?" asked Vita.

"I don't know but Lasennia and Calitoria have been together in secret planning something. I was not allowed to listen," answered Talistia.

Two priests finally brought Calitoria back to the darkened room, supporting her as she walked, dazed but euphoric. "I have reached the boundary of death and returned," she cried out. There were red stripes on her back and Vita believed she had been beaten in the secret ritual. The priests and initiates left the Temple and walked down the steps parading into the courtyard amidst celebratory hymns and music. Maidens, including Lasennia, lifted the boat containing all the prayer notes from worshippers over their heads and led the way. Inductees walked in a procession to a rhythmic beat as the priests waved flowers. Suddenly, all were startled as the flock of Ibises took flight in unison. "It is a sign from Isis...a summons. They inhabit the spirit of our ancestors," said Calitoria.

As they left the courtyard, an anxious Flavius ran up to them. "I thought I'd lost you! Where have you been? We should be getting something to eat now. Gaius will be waiting for us at a respectable bar nearby called Assellina's."

He herded them out to the road toward Mount Vesuvius where they faced the congestion of crowds in the city. An air of excitement and uneasiness drew Vita's attention. Clusters of men loitered around them shouting threats at pedestrians. Flavius walked quickly determined to get past them. "There are many more people here than usual," he called over his shoulder.

"Flavius, who are these ugly people?" asked Calitoria.

"Some are from a neighboring town called Nuceria, others are men belonging to trade clubs. Rome recently passed laws declaring some *collegia* illegal, accusing them of seditious agendas and plotting illegal acts against the government. It doesn't look like banning them has worked. While most have turned into drinking clubs, some still take the chance of criticizing the Emperor and the Senate. These men seem to be looking for a fight."

"Why are there so many people today? I don't like it here, Flavius. Can we go another way?" said Calitoria.

"Gladiator games are today. Champions train here in the city and fight in the amphitheater. Have you never been? Their school is nearby. They call it a school, but the gladiators are slaves locked in by the *lanista* who owns and trains them. I think it is terrible. Gaius knows how I feel and does not make me go to the games."

Vita noticed clusters of girls gathered in a more subdued manner stretching their bodies to catch a glimpse of someone famous. Young boys stood in line to buy vials of sweat from their favorite gladiator for a few coins.

Vita's group walked along the sidewalk to avoid the unruly youths, but soon they noticed seven or eight swaggering militants following them. If they walked on the right side of the street, they crossed over after them. If they turned the corner, they turned the same way. Vita looked back over her shoulder as the youths became louder and closer, laughing and yelling insults. She felt terror crawl under her skin.

"Those men are following us! Oh Isis, help us!" said Calitoria. "Quick, Flavius, find this tavern so that we can get away from them." Soon the sign for Assellina's hung overhead. They ducked inside turning to watch the band of hooligans pass on toward the amphitheater.

They were relieved and comforted by the cheerful tavern walls painted red on the lower part and white on the upper with graffiti that seemed to carry the election news of the town along with the names of the waitresses, menu items, and rude comments about the local residents. They walked through a large portal and stood in front of an ample counter covered with mismatched marble and four deep holes or *dolia*. A permanent oven sat at one end. A bronze kettle emitted puffs of steam carrying an appetizing aroma of stew. Behind the counter, four amphorae jars contained fine wine.

Flavius and the women waited to be seated under a bronze wind chime that customers could ring announcing their arrival. Calitoria and the girls studied the chimes curiously trying to understand the decorative shape at the top. Startled, they realized they were staring at a small bronze statue of a naked man with an oversized penis. His hand held a knife ready to cut off his gigantic body part which would ring the bell when pulled.

"Oh," groaned Calitoria, "I have seen more male penises today than I have in my whole life. They are everywhere, on the walls, imprinted in the sidewalk, now hanging from the ceiling, and there was even phallic graffiti at the Temple."

A waitress named Zmyrina called them over to a table set up for travelers in the back.

"Don't eat too much as we will want to buy drinks and snacks when we go to the gladiatorial games at the amphitheater," informed Flavius. "I saw the master and Telesphorus at the Forum market, and they have tokens for seats this afternoon. We missed the slaughter of the beasts this morning and the crucifixions of the prisoners during the recess, but this afternoon's gladiatorial games are sponsored by Livineius Regulus and promise fierce competitions."

"Livineius Regulus! That scoundrel! He has already been exiled from the Senate and now he wants to promote himself here. Treacherous fool," snarled Calitoria.

While they waited for their food, Gaius and Telesphorus joined them at their modest table. Flavius and the two girls moved to the side, but Telesphorus was allowed to join Calitoria and Gaius. All were aware that Telesphorus was treated with a degree of equality unusual for a slave. Calitoria favored him since he was her childhood tutor and they had been slaves together, but now Gaius depended on Telesphorus not only for his expertise in expanding the farms but also to protect his property while he served in Britannia. Apparently, they had had a successful day.

Chapter Seven

T raffic and trade abounded. Thugs and sailors, tradesmen and prostitutes, wagons and carts joined to create bedlam. Leaving the restaurant and stepping out onto the street, Vita existed unnoticed and unremarkable, just a young skinny servant maid, barely more than a child. Her nose inhaled the odor of animal dung and human urine that permeated the city. Street slaves desperately worked their brooms and shovels to clean up the gutter slurry, preparing the city for the influx of spectators making their way to the gladiatorial games. Walking toward the amphitheater, a sailor stopped in her path to lift his long shirt to access his genitals and relieve himself in a pot.

"Why is he doing that?" she asked.

"Urine is a commodity too precious to waste," Telesphorus answered. "It's used by fullers and silversmiths to complete their trade. The urine is allowed to stand until it decomposes to ammonia, then it's collected by the fullers who clean togas and tunics until whitened."

Vita dodged the ammonia-smelling pot, stepping over and around more filth of the city while holding her nose. Herculaneum fought the dumping of litter in the city streets. Posted notices announced fines to anyone using the street as a dump. The Petronius family clearly abhorred the putrid matter thankful that their city valued refinement.

Nearing the amphitheater, the shouting crescendoed. Vita watched groups and gangs of men, innocent eyes forgetting to blink. It seemed a secret scheme lurked in their loud laughter accompanied by shoving and physical aggression by the hooligans. An inner sense told her that these people could be dangerous. Events written on her soul from her capture as a slave taught her that people could not be trusted.

Gaius seemed oblivious to the temper of the crowd weaving his entourage through the throng of humanity to the arches of the arena. Big and strong in stature, he automatically commanded a presence of authority and confidence. Vita's instinct told her to stay close to this pillar of strength. Her eyes darted left and right taking in every detail of the scene. Popular gladiators arrogantly stood on podiums displaying leather gear studded with metal, holding up their weapons proclaiming premature victory. Vendors carried trays with miniature statues of victorious fighters. They shouted in deep gravelly voices of the power that would be transferred to the owner of a figurine. Girls swooned and studied the gladiators' massive muscles giggling and whispering to each other secret desires and crushes. Callers hawked snacks, wine, and food to carry into the arena. Vita ducked to miss being hit by young boys imitating combat contests with pretend weapons.

"We missed the beast fights this morning," Gaius called back over his shoulder. "They are actually my favorite."

"Yes, we also missed the punishment of criminals at high noon. I can't enjoy torture of men even if they are guilty of murder, arson, or sacrilege," responded Telesphorus. "It does no good."

"I don't agree," said Gaius. "But it is true people would rather see the gladiators fight."

The crowd only became thicker as they moved forward. Vita had to hang on to Talistia's garment to keep from being separated. Gaius halted his lead at the entrance, turning to search behind him for the girls.

"Keep up!" he shouted, "or you will be lost!"

Shoulders shoved them as they tried to enter the entrance to the amphitheater, funneling like sheep forward through the dark tunnel. Vita didn't know what to anticipate, but the festival atmosphere was contagious. Calitoria was exhilarated, too. Nearly giddy with delight, she laughed with bright eyes.

"Hang onto me, Gaius, I am being swept away by the crowd." He wrapped his arm around his wife's shoulders protecting her and leading her forward.

"You can't sit with me," he said. "You will have to go high up to the rim and sit in the boxes for the women. Telesphorus and I will sit in the seats closer to the arena. When the games are over, we will meet Flavius waiting at the entrance. Now, head to the stairs to the upper terraces with your handmaidens and find your box." He handed her the tokens with her seat assignments and they separated.

The *spectacula* seated 20,000 spectators and today was full attendance. Built in 70 BC as a reward to the citizens that fought for the Republic, defeating the local Samnite residents, the giant oval was situated in the eastern part of the town nestled next to the city wall. Along the crest, *velarium* swung out over the crowd to protect them from the blistering sun. The awnings covered the private boxes for the privileged ladies tucked near the rear wall. Calitoria seemed confused, glancing at her tokens then searching upward to try to make sense of the seating assignments, not noticing that the rows had carved numbers near the steps.

"May I help? I see where we need to go," said Vita leading her up the steps. It only made sense to keep moving upward as they were causing everyone to wait behind them. Out of breath and dizzy from the climb, they discovered their labeled box. Calitoria perched comfortably in front while the two slave girls stood behind.

The din of voices filled the arena, echoing off the back wall, while masses of people moved to their seats. Vita watched below as factions of friends acknowledged acquaintances, and different groups of all ages separated themselves into their own friendly patterns. Trumpets blared as the Proconsul, political leaders and aristocrats entered from a separate entrance tunneled under the seats which led to the front rows along the low wall surrounding the arena that was decorated with portraits of vicious animals along with local advertisements and political graffiti.

Vita watched Calitoria intently memorizing the faces of the elite as they entered and found honored seats. She studied the women in other boxes noticing hair styles, jewelry, and dress to later mimic their affluent fashions. She surveyed the scene for Gaius and Telesphorus sitting dozens of rows below them. The men waved at her, making note of her location. Vita stepped backward to lean against the wall, dizzy from the height and the entertainment of planned bloodshed.

"Maybe I should have waited outside with Flavius," she told Talistia.

The rivalry between the visiting town, Nuceria, and Pompeii had developed in the last two years, ever since Rome declared Nuceria to be a veteran soldiers' colony and granted free parcels of land to reward retired centurions and legionnaires. The land had been confiscated from respected residents and ancient families that had owned the land for centuries. The supreme right of the Empire unfairly trumped local ownership. The new residents flaunted their wealth and connections to the Empire infuriating the law-abiding, tax-paying freedmen and citizens. Vita could pick out the retired soldiers settling into their seats. Their imposing figures, huge scarred physiques and strutting confident attitudes contrasted with the local hard-working class. Those Nucerians brought their own celebrity gladiators to Pompeii for the challenge.

Equally threatening were the Pompeiian youth and Merchant Marine molded by the hard life at sea. There was a noticeable hypocrisy of the haughty Nucerians that were too privileged to dirty their hands with laborious work and commerce, yet were dependent on the hard-working men of Pompeii for goods and services delivered to their nearby town. Pompeiians had little good to say about the Nucerians, but no one could safely criticize the Emperor and Senate for the injustice of stealing land from local residents. Both sides argued righteous anger and loyalty to their small towns that were now present for some sport to determine who was superior in a gaming event.

Livineius Regulus and his companions stood, drawing applause from the crowd. Already exiled from the Senate in Rome for his bad behavior, Livineius sought to establish himself here as a politician. Dressed in his finest robe and tooled leather, he promoted his career by paying for the Apollo games, matching dozens of pairs of local and celebrity gladiators, many trained in the imperial schools of Pompeii or Nuceria. Vita stood on her toes to peer down to the front row seats and watch them turn and wave. Loving the attention, Livineius milked the crowd for more ovation, beckoning and bowing before them, unaware that before the night was over, he would be blamed for stirring up the local rivalries and plotting destruction with unsavory collegia.

The Lanista, owner and trainer of the gladiators, stood next to him in his rumpled tunic. "Each warrior will cost you 3000 sesterces," he had previously stated.

Livineius cringed and crossed his arms. "That is a hefty price for mere slaves and criminals."

"I train them for agility in offense and defense, I feed them good diets to develop muscular strength, and I house them year-round plus travel expenses. All this costs money. Guarantee my gladiators will not be killed and you can keep your costs down and I can use them again. If you cater to the bloodthirsty crowd and require a fight to the death, it will cost you a hundred times more!" Their agreement had been negotiated and signed in secret.

Trumpets blared announcing the umpire stepping into the middle of the arena. "Presenting Celadus of Pompeii, the *thraex*, fighting the Nucerian, Verus, the *murmillo*. Fighting at the North end of the arena will be Primus of Pompeii, the *retiarius* fighting the *secutor* Nucerian, Rufus." Cheers rang out as powerful warriors swaggered into the arena, rarely armed equally, adding to the suspense and strict rules of combat.

All four opponents paraded around the arena, stopping in front of Livineius in the front row, presenting themselves with a bow. The pairs turned back to the open arena circling each other waiting for the first thrust. Patrons chanted, "Celadus, Celadus!" or "Verus, Verus!"

Celadus, in the regular helmet, had already won the trophy wreath twelve times becoming the Pompeii favorite. For protection, he wore greaves covering his shins and thighs and leather straps wrapped around his arms. He carried a small shield and very short curved sword, the *sica*.

Verus, the Nucerian favorite, held a long rectangular shield and a short sword, mimicking the armor worn by a legionary. He distinguished himself from the thraex by a helmet with a fish-like crest. The crowd went wild, especially those who had served in the Roman army and spent years training in combat with the same tools. They despised cowardice.

The gladiators stalked one another, jabbed at each other with their swords, playing with the spectators, stirring their raw emotions. Metal connected with wooden shields, stabbing at one another repeatedly, while the crowd rose to their feet screaming, "Kill him! Kill him!"

"Nucerian old men!"

"Pompeii cowards!"

Vita was distracted by fans shoving one another in the stands, while spectators raised their fists and encouraged the transgressors. The fight between gladiators became ignored, while the audience waged its own skirmish. Stones were launched across the arena from the crowd, some aimed at the gladiators the rest raining on people in the stands. The umpire raised his staff and pleaded with Livineius to calm the spectators. Instead, he turned to the crowd raising his arms signaling to continue the revolt. The violence escalated as more missiles were hurled at the opposing crowd. Vita pulled on Talistia's shift and pointed to the edge where men jumped over the wall into the arena like scrambling insects. More and more joined the fight, emptying the stands.

Calitoria stepped back against the wall, shaking. Gaius turned his eyes upward scouring the stands for his family as he ducked stones pelting his back.

Telesphorus pointed to the girls high up by the rim and began climbing to the top striding two rows at a time. Gaius pulled his sword and armed Telesphorus with his sheath knife shoving his way upward. Tiny Vita was yanked off her feet and tucked under the arm of Telesphorus, who grabbed Talistia with his other hand. Gaius wrapped Calitoria in his arms. They traced the rim to try for the exits. Clanging swords, screams of men and women, bodies being hacked with mortal wounds made Vita cling to Telesphorus as they headed downward.

Gaius put his arm up stopping them. "They have the exits blocked!" Looking down at the arena floor, they could see lines of men guarding the exits, hemming the victims inside. Vita looked behind her for escape to see desperate people jumping over the back edge of the arena. It was too high to survive such a fall.

Gaius bellowed, "This way!" His sword drawn, he shoved and hacked at those in his way. Pompeiians confronted him, but his training as a soldier was superior. He raised his foot and shoved the offenders down the steps of the arena. The family followed the steps down and ran toward the unguarded elite entrance where Livineius had entered. They ducked through the dark tunnel running to the outside of the amphitheater, then stopped, shocked that the melee had extended into the outer grounds. Fighting pairs were everywhere.

Telesphorus heard Flavius call to them. "This way, Master!" They ran toward him, dodging bodies, running for their lives. Flavius motioned to follow him past the tall umbrella trees lining the amphitheater road to a small stone building. Scrambling behind it, out of breath, hoping to be invisible, they leaned against the cold stone wall listening to the fighting.

"What is happening, Gaius?" cried Calitoria.

"It is obviously a trap orchestrated by the Pompeiians. Why else would they attend the games bringing stones as weapons? The worst part is they think we are Nucerians! No one knows us here! We will wait for the night to cover us and then escape to the boats and head home."

The sound of those dying could be heard a hundred yards away. Vita and Talistia crouched down to hide themselves.

"Surely, we can plead to anyone we meet that we are not from Nuceria. We can convince them that we were only here to do business with their town. We wish them no harm!" reasoned Telesphorus.

"Do you think you are going to have a logical conversation with these murderers? An animal mentality has taken over this town, demons have been released from the underworld and taken over their bodies. Hear the laughter? They are insane! No one will believe us or even care that we are from Herculaneum."

Dusk creeped in slowly with a blanket of darkness that cloaked them with concealment. Gaius peered around the corner of the building to see if the way was clear on the road to the Marine Gate. "Let me go alone to see what is happening nearby." He slipped around the edge and disappeared.

Calitoria began to cry. Talistia's tears began to fall upon seeing her Mistress disintegrate. Vita sat dry-eyed, wary of weakness.

She listened to yelling in the distance. *What if Gaius is captured? Or killed? What can we do? There is no moon to expose us. Maybe we can just stay here,* she thought.

Finally, Gaius returned breathing heavily. "They have the Nucerian Gate blocked with fires and vigilantes, but in the opposite direction at the Marine Gate, no one is on the street. They've left it unattended. Surely, they have no need to block that exit. Nucerians will go east to get home leaving the Marine Gate open."

Flavius spoke. "I spent most of the day in and around the Forum and know it well. We could bypass most of the main road by going through the market without being seen."

"We will have to try. Not a sound from anyone!"

Moving through the black night, Vita leaned forward trying to see the ground in front of her feet and follow the others. She tripped over something that felt bloody and moist. Something told her not to think about the dead bodies strewn everywhere around the amphitheater. *Keep going. Don't think. This isn't real for me.*

Fresco of the Pompeii riot found in the house of Actius Anicetus in Pompeii 79 A.D..
(Public Domain)

Chapter Eight

"Quiet. We are making too much noise," said Flavius. "Earlier this afternoon residents loitered outside. They might still be here."

Silently cutting through the dimly lit Forum, they shortened their path to the Marine Gate. The riot must have spread to the market, merchandise was abandoned everywhere. Flavius picked up a wooden post as his only defensive weapon. Tripping over debris, they moved to the exit, flattened themselves against the wall and waited for Gaius to see if it was safe to continue on the main street. He motioned for them to follow him but after only a few steps they saw a line of four dark figures charging toward them brandishing weapons. Caught! Gaius pulled his sword, Telesphorus struck with his knife. Each of them took on two of the hooligans. The fight was too unfair! Flavius used his fortuitous wooden slat to take out one of the offenders but just as he struck the villain, Flavius was stabbed in the back and fell.

Vita picked up the abandoned trunk of wood and raced forward. She struck a rioter as hard as she could on the side of his knee dislocating his leg. He screamed in pain grasping the contorted limb and fell to the ground. Tiny Vita continued to wage her attack on the legs of the offenders, equalizing the fight. Talistia and Calitoria pulled Flavius to his feet, moving him to safety. Then a final thrust from Gaius's sword stopped the last offender.

Gaius knelt and reached for Flavius's hand. He held it wondering how to move him and the others to a safe place. He hoisted Flavius over his shoulder and turned to lead them to the Marine Gate out of the city, only to stop at the sight of another blockade of timber and fires in the distance. He led them back toward the deserted Forum, past the disheveled market, through the paved colonnade to the hallowed Temples of Apollo and Jupiter. Thankfully, perpetual torches were still burning with low light causing consecrated shadow spirits to dance on the walls as they passed. Vita caught sight of the colorful frescoes of Dionysius and the gods seeming to move as they watched her.

"We must choose a place that allows a quick escape if discovered and yet provides a shield from view."

Gaius hid them in a far corner in back of the Temple of Apollo. It was close to the entrance, and they could crouch behind the base of the statue. Cautiously, they laid Flavius on the ground resting him on his side. Vita recognized his labored breathing and knew his wound was severe. She remembered hearing that sound from her mother as she lay dying. Telesphorus lifted Flavius's tunic to study the injury, but it was impossible to assess in the darkness.

"What do you feel?" he asked, but Flavius could not talk, his mind entirely focused on trying to survive the pain, his side covered with blood. If he could just stay alive long enough for them to find help, they could stop his loss of blood. Vita sensed Flavius's pain. She comforted him, kneeling next to his upper body and stroked his forehead. She whispered into his ear.

"You must be strong and cheat death of its victory. Thana needs you and will be lost without you. Stay with us. You must stay awake. Do not sleep." It was the pain that was keeping him alive. It gave him focus. He shut his eyes but not for sleep; it was to help him endure the suffering.

Gaius turned to Telesphorus. "We are in grave circumstances. I see no way out. I now assume all gates are guarded. If we are found, we will be slaughtered like the bodies we stepped over to get here." Gaius felt responsible to lead them to safety, but his only resource was his trained ability to fight as a Roman soldier. Roman combat was coordinated with others as a well-trained machine marching forward, not as an individual taking on the enemy. There were too many Pompeiians against him. It would be impossible to take on the whole city alone. It seemed hopeless, only a matter of time until they would be discovered.

Then Telesphorus spoke. "There are businessmen here that know us. We could ask them for help. The banker Jucundus knows us. We were just with him today. He knows that we are from Herculaneum and could speak for us. He may take a chance and protect us. That is our only hope. We need someone who can vouch for our citizenship of Herculaneum."

There was no time to consider the moral wrong of this attack on Nucerians. No time to blame the Emperor who cast favoritism on Nuceria by gifting stolen lands to favorite veterans. No time to give forethought to how it might jeopardize Jucundus's life in his own hometown by asking for his help. It might be cowardly to claim safety based on neutrality of the greater injustice taking place, but self-preservation was instinctive.

"Everyone respectable in Pompeii is hiding behind their walls tonight. I doubt Jucundus would even open his door to us," said Gaius. He thought for several moments. Perhaps that was not true. Maybe Jucundus would help him. He said, "Let me go alone to his house. It is nearby on the road to Stabiae. If I am alone, I might be able to go unseen. If I don't return, stay hidden until daybreak, then try to buy your way out of town with payoffs to the rebels." He handed Telesphorus his leather bag filled with coins, certain he would not survive the walk in the streets. Telesphorus still wanted to try to reason his way out of this mess, and maybe the money would help. Truly, that was a futile idea as well. It would just be stolen before they were killed.

Gaius looked at each of them memorizing their faces. Torn by conflicting emotions, he felt he should stay to protect them. Visions swept through his head of gangs slaughtering his family. Perhaps, it would be the last time to see each other. He held Calitoria for a moment in his arms savoring her warmth and softness, then slipped away. Vita watched his shape pass across the open space and down the colonnade in the darkness.

"Be very quiet," warned Telesphorus.

Behind Apollo's statue, the fugitives crouched, trembling with fear. An eternity passed. The wind whistled, Flavius coughed, till a new sound alarmed them, a thump followed by silence. They listened with their eyes closed, holding their breath, trying to increase their senses.

Footsteps on cobblestones. No, Vita thought, *It's my imagination.*

Now a scraping of small rocks crunching. Vita felt energy surge through her body starting in her back and shooting through her arms. She bent low slowly peering around the base of the statue far enough to see the open Forum. Then a shadow moved. *Was that the figure of a man? Are there two of them, three?* She strained her eyes to clarify the darkness. They moved again, getting closer. Vita pulled back and turned to Telesphorus. He could tell by the fear on her face that she had seen someone. Flavius moaned and twisted on the gravel. Calitoria clamped her hand over his mouth.

The figures, alerted by the noise, ran toward Apollo's lifeless statue. At that same moment, the quick-witted Vita scurried to her feet and ran out from behind their hiding place in full view. She stopped long enough to make sure the figures caught sight of her then ran across the colonnade, dashing like a mouse scurrying for its life. Making as much noise as she could and waving her arms as she ran, the figures paused to watch her as she passed through the torchlight.

"It's just a young girl," one said, dismissing her as without value. Listening and searching the darkness for more movement, they waited. Everyone held their breath. No one made a sound. No one moved. Satisfied that the Forum Temple remained empty, the predators turned and left.

Vita shrunk low inching her way along the inner wall until she reached their hideout. Telesphorus looked at her with disbelief. Could this be the worthless waif who lived with them? Had she just saved their lives again? First, clubbing attacker's legs, now, risking her life for theirs? Did he owe his future to a quick thinking slave child? He extended his hand to Vita. She reached out and accepted it, stepping over Flavius, and seating herself next to him. He kept her hand, clutching it to his chest, unable to express his affection. He studied Vita's naive eyes and held her gaze. It was as if he saw her for the first time, or that she suddenly mattered to him. He owed her his life. He embraced her pulling her into his warmth, resting his chin on her head, savoring her scent.

It had been so long since anyone besides Lavinia had touched her, an emotion filled her that could only be described as joy mixed with trust. Embraced, she yearned to belong to someone who cared about her.

"What made you do that? What made you risk your life for us?" he asked.

How could she utter words that were unspeakable? She didn't care if she lived or died. Death only meant the end of the struggle day after day after day. Death meant the end of the grief and the repetitious visions of watching her parents die and leaving her so alone. Death would end the pain of her broken heart and release her from the life sentence of slavery and sadness. Death was the easier choice.

Calitoria heard the comment and watched the gesture. A wave of jealousy flushed through her. *Don't elevate that slave girl to any status above her true inferiority. Don't adore her. Telesphorus is mine.*

ALONE, Gaius moved unseen through the streets. Slipping into a recessed doorway or crouching behind a bush, he measured his way to the banker's house. Lucky to travel without encountering gangs or villains, he moved swiftly and silently. His soldier instincts, resurrected from their joyous burial, came naturally. He truly wanted a peaceful life without killing and war, and here he was, near his hometown, fighting for his life against enemies he passed on the street earlier in the day, and sat side by side attending a sporting event, a celebration of games and life. He fought a cynical distrust of humans creeping through his intellect, making permanent notes on his brain that human nature was evil. *Can anyone be trusted ever again?* he thought.

Gaius moved up Stabiae Road using darkness as his shroud until he found Jucundus's villa. It was the same place he had been earlier in the day borrowing funds for his farm expansion. He pressed his ear to the heavy wooden door listening for movement and voices. Upon his knock, all became quiet inside.

"Jucundus, it is Gaius Petronius Stephanus from Herculaneum. I need your help." Gaius waited while hushed voices held discussion inside. Soon, the massive door opened slightly and Gaius slipped through, followed by the sound of the bolt being thrown behind him.

His eyes slowly adjusted to the low lamplight revealing a crowd of suspicious visitors returning his stare with narrowed eyes. Groups were seated on the floor of the wide atrium talking in cautious tones: Centurians, businessmen, slaves, families, children, all sequestered for safety in Jucundus's elegant villa.

"Hello, Gaius, welcome. We are fortunate to be able to give you safety."

"Thank you for opening your door. I know it is not without risk to your life and business in Pompeii to help me," Gaius acknowledged, knowing that the earned trust and position in the city that Jucundus fostered could be destroyed by choosing to harbor the outsiders.

"I have chosen to do what is right, not what is good business," answered the banker.

"I have greater need than my own safety. I left my family hiding in the Forum. One wounded slave cannot walk on his own, and my own wife is hiding there from the monsters that chose to slaughter innocent people in this city. Hell has opened up its gates and spilled into the streets today."

Jucundus called to his trusted house slave. "Philadelphus! Join me! I will take a few slaves and go to the Forum. I am the only one who can safely roam the streets while the gangs still hunt for more Nucerians. They recognize me. Find Menipus and Dionysus and tell them to bring oil lamps and weapons."

"I am going with you," said Gaius.

"I forbid you. You might add danger to our rescue." replied Jucundus.

"My family is protected by me. I will not hide here in a cowardly way!"

"Then cover your expensive garments with this robe so you will appear to be one of my slaves."

Vita waited quietly with her arms wrapped around her folded legs, sitting behind the statue. She listened to Flavius's labored breathing until the sound seemed to scream in her soul.

"Telesphorus, I think we need to get Flavius help now. He seems to be getting worse. I know the sound of death rattles. We don't have much time. Is it true that you know where the banker Jucundus lives? We could each help carry him through the darkness to safety."

Telesphorus was not eager to reveal his fear to walk the streets where he might have to fight should they encounter warriors, and since he was the only healthy man in the group it would surely fall to him to defend them. He was not trained with the combat skills that Gaius possessed, he was a tutor, an accountant, an intellectual.

"Let's wait here for Gaius to return. He told us to stay."

"But if we can get closer to Jucundus's residence, it will speed our rescue and Flavius will have a chance to live. There are four of us who are healthy. We can each carry an arm or a leg." Vita pleaded with her eyes hoping that he would choose the braver course of action.

Telesphorus hid his shaking hands.

"You are a man of valor. You are strong," said Vita.

I'm afraid I can't do this. I prefer hiding but she thinks I am a man of valor. I am not. Then God spoke to his heart, *I will be with you.*

"Let us go."

They gathered up their belongings and each member scrambled to grab an arm or a leg lifting Flavius as gently as possible. Four holding him made the cumbrous task easier as they shuffled toward the entrance to the Forum. They turned to Stabiae Road. Again, Pompeiians bore down on them. There were eight of them with weapons and torches.

Telesphorus, forced to be in charge, mustered all of his courage. "Proceed forward boldly toward the mob. Flavius, don't make a sound," he commanded. The command was without need as Flavius was unconscious. Pain and loss of blood had taken him into a deep sleep. The two groups moved forward, each with their own purpose until the men of Pompeii shouted for them to stop. Telesphorus's intellect churned as he struggled to think of a plausible explanation for their appearance on the street.

"Let us pass to the funeral pyre," he shouted. "We carry a Nucerian's body that litters my mistress's residence."

One individual extended his foot and kicked Flavius's body. Vita held her breath hoping that Flavius would not react to the kick.

Calitoria stepped forward. "I want this filth out of my home before it begins to smell," she added with natural arrogance.

"Fine, let them pass," said the obvious leader motioning for the mob to part in the middle of the street. "Women and slaves are no threat."

Telesphorus proceeded forward without hesitation yanking Flavius's arm with him, dragging the group forward. Daring not to look back, they advanced past the mob.

Gaius and Jucundus were coming straight towards them. Gaius caught sight of them and ran to collect the injured Flavius. The slaves helped to lift the heavy body onto his shoulders.

THE SOUND of the heavy wooden door being bolted behind them caused the group to thank Sales the goddess of safety and Fortuna the goddess of fate and good fortune.

"Thank you, Isis!" added Calitoria.

Vita said nothing but observed that Apollo was not thanked. After all, he did nothing for them in her eyes. She wondered how and why the gods should be thanked when one member of the group was dying, they had found their own safety, and how could any of this be good fortune? *Are the gods playing games?* She halted her criticizing thoughts afraid the gods might punish her in some way for questioning.

Vita's vision quickly adjusted to the darkness. Huddled groups were everywhere, men, women and children. Hushed and muffled moans crept through the hall. She surveyed the room until she saw a familiar friend sitting on the bare floor against the wall. It was Quintus. At first, she just stared at him while tears gathered in her eyes, confused that he could be in this place. She looked harder thinking maybe she was simply wishing it was him. He motioned her to come to him then patted the marble floor gesturing for her to sit beside him.

Vita walked forward keeping steady eyes on his handsome face ignoring all those around her and nestled next to him. Quintus lifted his left arm and wrapped it around her small shoulders and held her close. Safety! Oh, the delight of human contact. The warmth of his body felt like nourishment to her soul. The touch of affection that she once knew with her father and mother, the human need to be held—such a reprieve from her inner demons of loneliness, fear, and longing for this life to be over.

. . .

Fig. 246. — Portrait herm of Caecilius Jucundus.

Bust found in Jucundus's villa 79 A.D.

Chapter Nine

Vita slept fitfully next to Quintus dreaming of her mother and father. In the dream they still lived together in her home. All was calm and secure and felt normal. In the dream her mother prepared bread in the kitchen. Her father tinkered at the table carving a doll for her. Neither parent looked at her, busy with their own activity. In the dream, Vita moved slowly toward her father and touched him recognizing that he was real. He turned to question her.

"There you are! I have been looking everywhere for you. I was lost and you were gone and no one would help me find you and you didn't come for me! I cried out for you but you didn't answer. Where have you been?"

He stood and opened his arms to hold her. She looked at his face but it seemed different, still him, but younger, healthier. They held each other. Vita felt his warm, familiar body and the softness of his shirt on her cheek as his love flowed through her soul healing her hurt. He said nothing and turned to let her go. A crowd waited that he knew, but Vita did not recognize any of them. *When did they come?* she wondered. He pulled away and left her arms empty again.

As he turned to leave, he said, "I love you. I will help you as I can from here. It's time for me to go again. Live, Vita, my sweet daughter. Live."

∼

CHAOS WHIRLED AROUND HER. Lifeless adult bodies were placed in parallel rows in a room next to the atrium. Two small bodies with dark brown hair were near the door. Someone's children had been slain. A woman got up from her chair and went over to the door of the room gazing in disbelief at the children, shaking her head slowly, comprehending the loss resting before her. Too many dead, too many injuries, too horrible to understand the events of the day. The woman tilted her head back and moaned with eyes closed. A man, maybe her husband or brother, turned toward the sound and jumped up from his seat to put his arm around her. She leaned into him as they both stared at the lifeless bodies.

Vita noticed a trail of blood across the floor that led to the injured. A surgeon worked frantically to tend to their wounds. She wondered if Flavius was being helped. Curious, she stood up and walked over to where Flavius still suffered. His wound had been stitched, but his color was the same as cold ashes. She pulled back his torn tunic to examine the severity of the injury still oozing blood that captured her hand. She wiped the red sticky mess off on her stola. The stain announced the imminent death of an innocent.

"Flavius, I am here with you," she said as she took his hand. "It will be all right. You can get better. Keep trying. There is so much to do in the garden and Thana is waiting to see you. It won't be long until we can get you home again."

She didn't cry as she delivered this message. She believed in her own power to make it all right. It was the child in her speaking. The child that couldn't believe bad things happen. The child that hopes all things good. The child that can't predict bad or understand evil.

Flavius never hurt anyone. He is so kind. So why is he the one dying? she wondered. *Why can't just the bad people die?* Negative events were being written on her soul that would change her forever. Her childhood was swiftly being lost.

∼

DAWN WAS BREAKING. Quiet murmurings had given way to shouts. No one had slept through the night and tempers flared. Everyone had a different idea of how to escape. Jucundus's bald head could be seen in the middle of the indignant citizens. His gruff voice compensated for his short stature.

"We must have a plan. We can't just go into the street with weapons. Your women and children are here and can't be left behind or taken into the fight! The young rebels have been drinking and celebrating all night. Perhaps, drunken stupor could make them easy to outsmart."

Vita noticed Calitoria sitting nearby with other wealthy women while Gaius and Telesphorus could be seen in conversation with a Senior Centurian named Publius Alfenus Varus. Carrying prestige by reputation and wealth, the Centurian had been a member of the Praetorian Guard, and was a respected leader from Nuceria, well-connected with power in Rome. He took charge of the group.

"We will make them pay for this slaughter! The young rebels with their illegal societies and Livineius Regulus the instigator of this attack, shall be forced to take responsibility!"

"They should die! We can form a mob of our own and come back here to wipe them out!" shouted another. "We all know enough wealthy soldiers with countless slaves. If we add other Nucerians indignant about this massacre and come back, we can kill them all just like they slaughtered us!"

"They should be stripped, beaten, and flogged! How can we not retaliate? Look at what they have done to us!" pleaded a mourning father as he pointed to his dead children.

Varus tried to calm the anger. "First we need to get out of Pompeii and back to safety. We don't know how we are going to do that yet. Then we can plan our strategics for revenge, which could include a return attack. I am not saying that we should be passive and accept this, but there may be even better ways of holding these people accountable. We can find out exactly who planned this attack. It could be that it wasn't supposed to be a murderous assault but became a mob, out-of-control, feeding on itself."

"You really believe that this wasn't a planned war on us? Then why are all the city gates blocked? Why were they all armed at the Gladiator

Games? They not only had their weapons, they carried in rocks to throw at us! They had us trapped like swine!" yelled another.

Gaius held back his comments until he felt he had something to contribute. "We can use the local authorities to take this to Rome and find justice there."

They all laughed at him. "Who are you? Some coward? Justice with these barbarians? You know that no authority is going to care about this slaughter. Senators just want peace so they can stay in power."

Varus held up his hand. "Wait. There are many of us here that still have friends in the Senate. If we pull Rome into our retaliation for this injustice, we stand stronger than if left on our own. This area is the Roman politicians' playground. They will not want us destroying it with war and strife. It might be best to follow legal channels of retaliation as Gaius suggests."

"It takes money and power to go through the Magistrates. Most of us are ordinary citizens and have neither."

"We could take out loans against our farms or ships or properties," said another.

"I could administer contracts for loans," said Jucundus.

"Of course you could," sniped one citizen sarcastically. "Then you could skim a profit from all of us! How dare you try to make money off this horrific event where my children have been killed and my wife attacked!" He lunged toward Jucundus, clasping his hands around his throat, taking him to the ground. Two men pulled him off. Choking and gasping for air, Jucundus rolled to his side, while Gaius helped him to his feet.

"Jucundus took us in or we would still be on the streets hiding. Leave him alone!" reminded Varus.

Jucundus massaged his throat and apologized. "I only meant that I would help."

Cinterus, a silversmith from Nuceria, spoke up. "I have no money for lawsuits! Grinding through political channels will get nothing done. I think we should gather all our slaves and colleagues and come back and slaughter them the same way they did us! We have enough to surround this town. No one is going to do this for us. The Empire craves peace! Well, they should wipe out these butchers instead of making war with barbarians that are so far away that they pose no threat. The Empire should take care of their own citizens first, and if they won't we will!"

"We need to find out what is going on in the city. Perhaps, Magistrates and soldiers have already taken over and secured tranquility," said Varus. "I was hoping news of the attack would have reached Nuceria by now, and they would be here to rescue us. That still might happen, but if not, we might be able to save ourselves at nightfall, by sneaking out to the Nucerian Gate," said Varus.

"I think I should go out into the city and see what is happening," said Jucundus. "I was born in Pompeii and most recognize me and call me by name. I would not be attacked."

"We need to know what is happening outside this villa. Jucundus is our only chance," said Varus.

"I'll go immediately." He took two of his trusted slaves and slipped out the street door.

VITA ROSE from her spot by Quintus and stepped over bodies to check on Thana's beloved Flavius again. She recoiled as she touched his arm and found it as cold as the stone floor. He was dead. Vita gently loosened the bag from his waist that contained the perfumes and dates he had purchased for Thana and tucked it in her belt. She walked over to Gaius.

"Flavius is no longer living."

Not believing her, she watched as he went to Flavius's body and touched him. Vita went back to her spot by Quintus.

"Is he dead?" asked Quintus.

"Yes."

"Was he someone you cared for?"

"He was kind to me. My master's mother was very fond of him, and she will be heartbroken."

"Do you like your master and his family?" he asked.

"I have no attachment to them, but I am owned by them, for now."

"You are very young to be thinking of your future without them or even your own freedom."

"I will be free someday. You will see," she declared. "Are you free or a slave?"

"I am free. I want to become a voting citizen but I will need money and a wife and children to be written on the city tablets. I have a plan to do that."

"What is your plan?" She was curious now.

"I am learning the gem trade, in fact, I came to Pompeii to buy gems. I am also saving money to have my own shop someday. I rise early and work as a fishmonger in the mornings. I remove pearls from the oysters I clean, and my payment includes a portion of the pearls. I also bargain for imported gems at the market, and my teacher pays me if I negotiate well for him. The gem trade is good in Herculaneum. Tourists have money to spend, and they like the jewelry I design." Vita admired his maturity as she gazed at his profile, then he asked, "How long have you been with Gaius Petronius Stephanus and his family?"

"A short time but I am not staying. I am planning to run away. I won't be running to Pompeii after this. I hate this city." There, she had shared her secret with him.

"You can't run away. They will find you and flog you. It is a simple idea that has been tried before. The Empire does not tolerate runaway slaves," he scoffed.

"I was not always a slave; my father was a citizen in Ephesus. I am a slave because I am an orphan. I am going to be free again. You will see."

"Well, you are a slave now and you better not run away and get flogged. If you are flogged, you will be scarred and never free. That makes you a slave forever in the Empire," he warned. "It would be better to have a plan for your freedom. I will help you. Do you like to work?"

"I want my freedom. I will work for my freedom," she answered.

"When we return to Herculaneum, if we get out of Pompeii alive, you will ask your master if you can earn money for him at the seaside and clean fish with me. He will allow you to keep some of the money. It is a good business for both of you. He makes money and knows you will work harder for him if he lets you keep some. It will not take away from your duties at the villa because it is before the sun is up. When you have earned some money, I will show you what to do next," Quintus said confidently. He did not really know what to do next but was sure he could figure something out. It was especially difficult because she was a girl. Females were not welcome at the seaside.

"Perhaps you should pretend to be a boy when you come to the port to help me. They won't pay you if you are female. They won't even let you on the docks. Tuck your hair in a cap, we will make your name into a male name. Change Vitalia to Vitalis, and you must wear male clothes. You will have to be clever and convince your master to allow this."

Vita thought it was possible to do everything that Quintus told her. She knew her position in the family had gained in respect after saving their lives twice the day before. Gaius watched her breaking an attacker's leg, and Telesphorus gazed astonished at her self-sacrificing run to save them from being found in the Forum. Yet she must keep her long-term plan for freedom secret, or it would not work. Besides, how delightful to spend the early hours of the morning with Quintus, who was very handsome and now her friend. More than that, she admired him.

"Yes, I will do it," she told him. Satisfied to have a plan, she tucked herself under his arm, leaned her head on his muscular shoulder, and gratefully shut her eyes.

THE DAY PASSED SLOWLY. No one came to rescue them. Gaius paced near the door, his hand rubbing his forehead, while Calitoria slept on the floor. The Centurion from Nuceria occasionally walked over to the wounded to check his son's injuries. Vita watched two men move Flavius's body to the adjacent room of the dead. Planners for revenge plotted in their corner, slaves tended to masters, injured still suffered.

Jucundus and his slaves returned bringing with them a local junior Magistrate, Licineius Romanus. Before, his charismatic personality got him appointed and on the way to a bright political future. Now, his authority and ability to govern weighed inadequate. The men gathered around him as he entered, hopeful for good news of a rescue.

"It is difficult to say who is really at the bottom of this riot. For some time, I have been investigating the local clubs and trade groups making sure that they are not gathering illegally and are complying with registering their members. They must follow rules or they are fined and banished. Our city council gives us authority to police these clubs and collegia. Mostly, they are groups getting together to drink and promote their trade and have a good time, but recently we have heard of suspicious activities involving seditious behaviors and even deeds of violence. The underclass groups, such as the actors, undertakers, gladiators, and deserters, are probably our villains in this riot, but some of the Magistrates witnessed our respected clubs involved in promoting the gladiator match yesterday, hoping for violence. There are illegal groups outside the city, the Campanians, who have been accused of violence and murders before. They want to destroy the Republic. Pampered sons of elite citizens that have vacation homes here like to roam the streets at night causing trouble from time to time. We don't know who started it and impossible to prove anything."

Varus interrupted, "It had to be a coordinated, planned killing of revenge. It didn't just happen. You should be able to find out who planned this. You should have been able to stop this before it started."

"I did my best to try to bring order during the outbreak, but it was impossible without soldiers from the Empire, and no one to enforce the peace," he continued. "We will get to the bottom of this. Livineius Regulus backed these games to buy his political future and the senior Magistrates, Grosphus and Gavianus, supported him in this gladiatorial match with the Nucerians. I just don't know what else I can do to control the powerful takeover of the city by these groups." Romanus shook his head helplessly.

Varus, former Praetorian Guard and Senior Centurian, spoke with measured anger. "You don't know what to do. You stand before us knowing that every family here is suffering the murder of a loved one or suffered grave injuries, and tell us that you don't know what to do. In other words you are going to do nothing! This slaughter will not go without punishment and will be noted by the authorities in Rome. You will all lose your political positions in Pompeii if justice is to be carried out!"

Another Nucerian, Vitruvius, not gifted with rank or wealth, spoke to Licineius Romanus. "Can you give us any protection to leave the city and return to our homes?"

"I cannot assure you anything right now, but I can tell you that the Nucerian Gate is guarded by the rioters and leaving by that route is certain death. You have a better chance to leave the city through the north Herculaneum Gate. I know there are others hiding elsewhere in the city who would join you. Perhaps, if you organize to leave at the same time, you would have each other's protection by being in a group."

"I say we leave by the Herculaneum Gate at dawn and continue our travels straight to Rome! Let us present our dead and injured at the steps of the Senate and appeal to them for justice! They can't ignore our plight if we present ourselves to the Empire and beg for punishment of Pompeii!" said Varus.

It is the best way." They all agreed.

"I can spread the word to the others hiding in Pompeii to leave at dawn," said Jucundus.

"Then that will be our plan. We leave at dawn with all other Nucerians injured and hiding. We will leave through the Herculaneum Gate and go straight to Rome and demand justice," said Varus.

Romanus left quickly, worried about the loss of his political future. Jucundus went to spread the word to the others that were hiding in nearby villas.

Chapter Ten

Those hiding in Jucundus's villa chose not to travel back to Nuceria. Instead, they would leave by the Herculaneum Gate at dawn, carting their dead to Rome to protest the violent slaughter.

Vita sat quietly in her corner next to the boy that she hoped cared for her. She watched Calitoria and the other women kneeling in a circle lighting votives and chanting to the gods for safe travel. At the same time, veteran soldiers called on Jupiter or Apollo to protect them. Those who worshiped the goddess Isis, with power over life and death, pleaded for her to save the families. Little charms and miniature statues were clutched in tight fists. Telesphorus stood separately with the banker Jucundus. They were both Jews and had their own separate appeal to their God, Jehovah. The hum of memorized prayers comforted her.

Children in the villa fussed. Mothers held their small bodies comforting and reassuring them. Innocent eyes had witnessed bloody bodies and heard the violent screams. Vita thought it sad to watch their childhood lost forever, stained by the images of killing. Each mother suppressed her own fears, to turn and comfort the children as they whined for attention. She wondered how the women summoned the courage to comfort the clinging children. Perhaps the dead bodies of other children laying on the floor in a separate room brought a thankfulness to their heart that they still had their children.

Would the small bodies be taken to Rome with the others? Would Gaius take Flavius's body home or leave it behind? Would he send it to Rome with the other bodies? After all, Flavius was a slave, not a citizen. He did not deserve a funeral.

VITA AWAKENED the moment she heard someone stir deep in the night. Groggy from lack of sleep, she could see figures moving about the atrium packing satchels. Children protested. She lifted Quintus's arm that wrapped around her waist as they lay on the mosaic floor and dragged her woolen palla around her shoulders as she stood.

"We're moving. Everyone is getting ready to leave," she told Quintus.

Someone had decided that it would be safer to use the cover of night to leave the city. She hurried over to the Petronius family to gather belongings. Flavius's stiff body joined the stack of dead bodies layered like logs on a wagon outside, their arms laced together forming a knotted pile of testimony to protest the inhumanities they'd endured. Thankfully, a tarp was flung on top covering their faces and reducing the metallic smell of blood. The woman who mourned the death of her children cringed at the sight and cried out in agony. Her husband's arms wrapped around her, muffling the screams in his shoulder as he explained that the wagon of bodies was needed to make the protest in Rome. She wanted revenge for her loss. This gave her anger focus and calmed her.

The group formed a dirge behind the wagon as it hcadcd towards the Herculaneum Gate. Vita turned to search for Quintus in the group. He didn't wave but their eyes spoke the fear they both felt. A light drizzle glazed the cobblestones. Silence surrounded them except for the rattle of wagon wheels drumming the march. Vita's feet chilled, wet and numb. Her palla collected the rain soaking her shoulders, and she shivered, maybe from cold but probably from fear.

More fugitives silently joined them as the death march passed villas on the Cardo Maximus. Tradesmen, soldiers, and families, they now numbered nearly a hundred.

When they passed the salt market, the sight of the Herculaneum Gate beckoned them to come closer. If they were to be attacked, it would be near the gate. Talistia gripped her mantle at her throat with both fists, but continued to walk forward. Vita reached out for her hand to comfort her. Gaius and the veteran soldiers encircled the women and children, clutching their weapons, waiting for an ambush. All eyes focused ahead on the moonlit gate. It appeared unguarded. They climbed over a blockade of debris from the previous night, moved forward passing smoky fires whimpering their last flames, shoved away wagons, barrels, and abandoned bloody weapons to open a path. An eerie silence hung broken by the rumble of more wagon wheels counting the cobblestones and hundreds of cautious footsteps grinding in the gravel. As the last cart of corpses passed through the Hercula-neum Gate, they knew they were safe and transported their cargo of righteous protest to the Senators of the Empire.

"The gods favor us! They have responded to our need! Now the gods will avenge the murder of our families," proclaimed Varus. "We will demand that the Roman Senators punish Pompeii when they see our dead families!"

Gaius decided that Flavius's body needed to stay in the wagon and become part of the burning funeral pyre on the steps of the Senate, to convince Emperor Nero and the Senators that punishment for the Pompeiians was their demand.

The Petronius family walked along with the others, their tired bodies trudging forward. Shock and disbelief of the last days took a proper place, suppressed in memory. Calitoria forgot fashion, hair undone, dress disheveled and soiled. Gaius reflected the warrior, his beastly arms still wearing the blood and wounds from combat. In contradiction, he gently held Calitoria's hand. Telesphorus, tall and lean, wore his usual furrowed brow of concern as he placed one foot in front of the other to journey home seeking rest and safety. Vita and Talistia trailed behind. Vita, marred in her tattered tunic striped with Flavius's death stains, felt joined in these lives like family but quickly rejected this confused emotion, perturbed at herself for allowing any attachment to those who owned her.

Finally, they reached the road to turn west to Herculaneum, and separated from the traumatized group. The Nucerians had been the target of the riot, so Gaius chose not to go to Rome. He wanted to find sanctuary for his family and aimed for their villa, leaving the prey to register their protest.

When they entered their villa, each separated to blend back into the rhythm of the home. Vita went to the kitchen to prepare food, Talistia accompanied Calitoria to help her wash and dress, Telesphorus sought the comfort of his office and papers, and Gaius walked purposely to his mother to tell her of Flavius's death. Nothing seemed changed at home and yet everything had changed.

IT HAD ONLY BEEN a few years since his father died leaving Thana a widow. They mourned the loving, loyal man together with unspoken sadness, only theirs and private. Sometimes they would speak in hushed tones in the garden about their loss, finding that memories still brought sadness and grief but always hoping that someday those memories would bring comfort. Grief was always a heartbeat away for Thana, still, she learned to step around the chasm of heartbreak to survive. She lost everything when her husband died—friend, lover, confidant, the other half of herself, half her flesh, substituted now with the care of her son. Her mind betrayed her with suffering while she tried to wear a mask of sanity.

Now, Gaius must deliver the news that her dear Flavius was gone forever. He found her weaving, an activity she enjoyed. The counting of stitches and rhythm of the shuttle brought peace. Even in her confused mind, the memorized ritual existed permanently. She stood at the warp-weighted loom that leaned against the stone wall supported by two tall poles throwing the shuttle, counting aloud.

"I have something difficult to tell you, Mother," began Gaius. He paused wondering how to continue. "Pompeii had a violent riot while we were there." He thought it best to be very honest with her about what had happened. "We were caught in the middle of the slaughter and had to fight for our lives. In the attack, Flavius was injured and died from his wounds yesterday."

Thana turned and looked at him intently, searching his face for understanding. She had just been with Flavius, and he was healthy and alive. It was impossible. They were just words. There was no body to touch to make it real. Surely, he would be back and walking in the garden any minute. *Not again,* she thought. *Why is it that those I love and love me are always taken from me?"* The shock prevented tears from falling. She studied her son, confused, that more of her life had been erased. Gaius gathered her in his arms and held her.

Thana relaxed in his embrace, until she realized it was his fault. She shoved him away. "You have not assumed your role as *pater familias* in this family! If you had sacrificed to the gods, these troubles would not have happened. It is your duty to pray and sacrifice daily to bring favor and benefits from the lares and gods. They care not for us because you care not for them. They walk among us in disguise, and you know them not! How can you deny their existence when we see them in the moonlight, feel them shake the earth and rumble with thunder in the hills! I have sacrificed but it is not enough! *You* must sacrifice. You must call upon them for favors. You must give them the attention that they want. You should have pleaded with the gods for favors."

Thana covered her ears and started to shiver.

"Gaius! One walks among us! Minerva transforms herself into my ancestors. She knows secrets and is wise. She has come to help us!"

"Who has come to help us? Who is this god among us? This is old woman talk! I am not responsible for Flavius's death or the riot in Pompeii!" countered Gaius.

She leaned closer and whispered, "I suspect the new slave Vitalia is one. She is a god! You watch. She has powers. She is not just a girl!" Thana's eyes were wild as she swept her arms out across the villa trying to make Gaius see what she saw.

He knew Vitalia had saved his family from harm in ways no child should have been able. Perhaps his mother was right. Perhaps Thana was able to see the god masquerading as a slave girl. He owed his life and the lives of his wife and family to the young girl.

"If she is the goddess Minerva, why is she here? I rely on myself. I have never devoted myself to honoring the gods and asking for their attention and good favor. I don't believe in it. So, why is she here?"

"To reveal the secrets and truth that are hidden in this villa! You have made your own choices and relied on yourself, that is true. Sacrifices to the gods have been neglected. You opened up this family, allowing treachery. Now, she comes to uncover deceit that you can't see," said Thana.

"What are you talking about? How do you know this?"

"I see it clearly," said his mother.

Gaius accepted ideas of jealous gods needing attention, trained from birth by his mother, but he grew to ignore such belief, only participating as required. Perhaps he should believe in the power the gods had to offer. Especially, since the goddess, Minerva, could be living with them.

"Forgive me for my neglect as the head of this household. I understand. If only I worked harder to devote myself to prayer and sacrifice, we could benefit from the gods' protection. From now on they will be offered spelt and grapes and first fruits of the season. We will give honeycombs and black beans from our tables to them. We will attend the public festivals and number our steps according to their needs of attention and earn their favor."

He owed his life to this suspicious slave girl knowing he should treat her with care but not arouse others to know of her deity, keeping that mysterious knowledge guarded in secret. No more would he allow penalty from the gods for his disloyal acts retaliated upon this family. He wondered if that was the deceit his mother meant. After all, he had a right to bargain for the gods' favor as much as anyone. He would memorize the prayers to accompany his sacrifices spending time daily pleading for protection and prosperity, lighting votives, and offering oaths, weaving a closeness to the unseen world.

"I will go now to ask for the gods' protection of our family." He left her to visit the sacred ancestral room near the villa entrance. He knew he must give to get their favor, and he would begin today. As he passed through the atrium, he noticed the slave girl Vitalia drawing water from the impluvium. He paused to study her. She was not powerful in stature. Her garments were common, her hair pulled simply back against her head with no ornamentation.

Could she be a god in disguise? Could she be Minerva? She seems intelligent beyond her years and her countenance is strong and calm.

He leaned forward and squinted to see if he could collect an aura about her. Vita caught him watching her and settled her gaze, piercing his eyes to discern what he wanted. This was even more unsettling to Gaius. It was as if she looked through him reading his thoughts. Her blue eyes seemed to glow, a sure sign that she was Minerva. Quickly, he looked away and entered the lares room to offer sacrifice.

Vita finished collecting water from the impluvium and delivered it to the kitchen slaves. Lavinia, occupied with cooking, too busy to comfort the young girl, did not notice the devitalized spirit she wore. Desperate to heal herself and erase the bloody images engraved on her mind, sure that she would not be missed, Vita stole away to the quiet of her room in the servant area upstairs. Images of lifeless bodies and dear Flavius, gray and cold, churned relentlessly in her mind. *How can life go on so normally after death and murder?* She tried to comfort herself by thinking of Quintus with his strong body warming her. She remembered his offer of help and how to gain her freedom. *I must get away from here,* she thought. *Telesphorus and Gaius must let me work at the docks. I will buy my freedom. I want my family back, to have mother comfort me and see father again, to have my life as before, if that could only be possible.*

Panic shook her heart as she tried to remember her father's face. Of course, she remembered his dark hair and blue eyes but how were they set? She grabbed some parchment and charcoal and sketched his face full on and then from the side. She smudged out the jawline knowing that it was wrong but what was right? She covered up the nose and tried to remember how it looked, then sketched some more. Finally, she had a likeness on the parchment that felt correct. Satisfied, she hid it behind an amphora in the corner of her room, fearing that if someone found it, they would take it or ask questions. This was her own private sorrow that would not be understood by anyone else. The likeness of her father, etched firmly in her memory again, still existed. She looked up to the heavens and cried out to him, while tears dried on her cheeks. "Where are you? Don't you know how sad I am? Don't you care?"

She gathered herself and rose slowly to gaze out the upstairs window. She noticed a young girl walking past holding her father's hand. Transported, she felt her own father's hand in hers, so warm, tough-skinned but tender.

"People die and then you go on...and live...and pretend that nothing happened," she whispered.

Chapter Eleven

C alitoria's voice echoed throughout the villa as she called for Gaius. Stopping at the tablinum, she found Telesphorus working on figures for the expansion of the farm and the loan obtained from Jucundus.

"I'm tired of looking everywhere for Gaius. Have you seen him?" she asked.

"No, I haven't seen him but I have been working here for quite some time. I am so frustrated with the farm. How can we expand our land and develop our farm when our government allows rebels and murderers to prey on our own people in the Empire? If we move forward with the expansion, it could all be taken away from us by rebels or even the Republic, if they so choose. Aren't there enough enemies attacking the Empire without our own people attacking each other? Enough! I have seen too much bloodshed and anger. God will have his vengeance on those responsible. Innocent people and children died for nothing." He seemed to be talking to himself.

"You should pray to the ancestors for guidance at the family altar. They will hear you," she said.

He shook his head.

Telesphorus never entered the sacred room. He was Jewish but felt no reason to practice his faith. With no family, books and education were first and foremost in his life. His tall, lean body returned to its previous position hunched over parchment and tablets. Raising his hand to massage his brow with his thumb and forefinger he thought, *Focus on numbers and supplies. Avoid the other nonsense of people.*

Calitoria turned away knowing she could never reach him when he retreated from life. She wished he was different so he could comfort her in some way after the chaos. She needed him. He was a friend. Just a few words would help, but he comforted only himself with his numbers. She left silently to find Gaius.

He was kneeling in the sacred room lighting candles to the dead ancestors and his father. *I don't know,* he thought. *Do the gods control our world? Can they take on human form? I thought they were just stories that old people told.* He waited for the small god figurines Thana had placed on the top shelf to speak to him. His gaze lingered on the figures painted in the frescoes next to him.

Calitoria stood in the doorway watching Gaius. "What are you doing in there?" she asked.

"I am asking the gods and lares for help and protection, nothing more," he answered. He took her hand and kissed it. "Everything will be right now."

She hugged Gaius, holding him tight, not to give him affection, for that did not occur to her, but rather to rejoice that Isis existed among them. Calitoria received her conversion to Isis just days before and accepted this with hope that the goddess Isis entered her home. Gaius misread the response as love and held her tightly.

"We will be all right now. The gods care about us now, and I am sure we will receive their attention."

THE NEXT MORNING Gaius dressed and walked past the impluvium. Looking up, he felt distressed to see rain pouring through the rectangular opening to be collected and fill the cistern below the floor. Gaius had plans for the day that rain interrupted.

"I am going to the Baths this afternoon," he told Telesphorus. "It will be the best place to get news about the Nucerian protest in Rome. Some of the Roman political leaders are vacationing in town. They may know something of matters in Rome and be willing to speak. I would love to be in Rome and watch the funeral pyre burning on the steps of the Senate forcing Nero to do something." He paused to savor the thought.

"He will probably do nothing," said Telesphorus. "I heard from the Nucerians at Jucundus's villa that Emperor Nero has been in Neopolis since the death of his mother, Agrippina, with no sign of returning to Rome immediately. They said he is rehearsing for his preferred career, that of actor and creator of the arts. Such an embarrassment to have our glorified Emperor cavorting in costume as a lowlife actor. The Senate will have to decide on its own what to do about Pompeii, if there is to be a punishment. I would be surprised if they stopped the celebration of gladiator games, absolutely the right thing to do. They know Nero loves the games, and they are afraid of him."

"Balbus has invited me to his Elite Baths which is the best place to find any of the pompous Senators, those damn fools," said Gaius. "Fools they are, but they might know what Nero intends to do about the riot. I also want to discuss events with my friends, Q. Tamudius Optatus and M. Vinicius Proculus."

"The Senators may see the riot as unrest and move to enforce calm." Telesphorus tilted his head back, vacantly staring at the ceiling thinking out loud. "Nero has battles securing borders and expanding in Britannia. He can't afford the chance of civil wars. In fact, the Senate could agree that this petty rivalry would expand unless peace is enforced.

I also heard from the Nucerians that Seneca and Burrus, Nero's favorite advisors, tried to silence Nero's popular mother, Agrippina, for the last few years, and now she is dead by command of her own son. There is so much corruption in Nero's court. They said Nero wanted to be rid of her because she was too powerful. That is why she lived near here in Baiae. The Senate worried about her self-proclaimed position of power and popularity. Agrippina couldn't accept being banished, so she was stirring up trouble, maybe to take over the government. Then Nero had her killed. The Senate has to be afraid of Nero," said Telesphorus.

"Could be just gossip," confided Gaius. "But Nero should give credit to his mother's political genius for getting him the position of Emperor! She is the one that had Claudius adopt him as his son. She is the one that probably had Claudius poisoned so Nero could be

Emperor! Rumors say that she was behind the killing of Claudius's real son, Brittanicus," said Gaius.

"No, I think Nero had Brittanicus killed," Telesphorus disagreed. "Agrippina was making threatening statements to have Nero removed as Emperor. She was going to endorse Britannicus as the true heir when he reached manhood. Who knows who killed him? It makes sense to me that it was Nero," said Telesphorus.

"You know all the political gossip today. Quite a conversation you had with the Nucerians. We will never know for sure. But we do know that Nero and his advisors saw Agrippina as a threat. She publicly made seditious remarks. I think she thought her direct lineage to Caesar could let *her* take over. She wanted Nero dead after her mistreatment! She may have been plotting to kill him. Beware the power hungry. Strange a mother wanting her son dead," Gaius mused as he leaned against the wall with hands on hips.

"More strange to have a son wanting his mother dead. Degenerate behavior from both. Thou shalt honor thy father and mother," judged Telesphorus.

"So, Nero had his mother killed. It is normal behavior for political or economic gain. No one stands in Nero's way now except Seneca and Burrus," concluded Gaius. "I am off to the Baths to hear more about Rome and what is happening in the Empire. I want to know if there will be punishment for the horrible massacre in Pompeii."

GAIUS PREPARED for his assignment with his legion in Britannia. Telesphorus worked on the farm expansion. Calitoria and her hand-maiden constructed a lovely pink gown for the gathering at the Balbus home. Vita continued as kitchen slave until Gaius called her to the tablinum one afternoon.

Vita stood quietly waiting for Gaius to look up from the wax tablet where he was studying the contracts for developing the farm. He sat back and stared at Vita. "Telesphorus told me that you would like to work on the docks each morning. He believes you are wanting to work for the cost of your manumission."

Vita wondered if Telesphorus purposely gave away her secret. *Whose side is he on? He is a slave too. Surely, he understands I need to be free.*

"It is true that I want to work on the docks. I have made a friend who will help me start as soon as you give me permission," she answered. Vita knew it was not the time to talk about her freedom. She laced her hands behind her back as she felt a rush of emotion that made them shake.

"You know that women and girls are not allowed on the docks."

"Yes, I have a plan to present myself as a boy."

Gaius suppressed his laughter, looked away, and was silent for what seemed to be an eternity. *Minerva masquerading again?* he thought.

He stared at her while considering permission. *Working the docks would bring more money into the business of running the home and farm. Vitalia could keep just enough to motivate her to work harder and I'll keep the rest for myself. Maybe I can hire out other slaves to make even more money. This skinny slave girl could pass for a boy. She is not recognized by neighbors yet.* He studied her form searching for deity.

"We call you Vitalia, you will have to change your name and you won't keep all the money. Do you know that?"

"I will call myself Vitalis, the male form of my name."

"Bring Telesphorus your pay as you receive it. I will inform him that he will be in charge of you while I am in Britannia. You will have to continue with all your household duties that you currently hold and play the female the rest of the day."

Gaius gestured for her to leave and watched her curiously as she returned to the kitchen. *Who is this creature? One who has magic and intelligence. She appears as a young waif without family or history. First, she is a young girl, and now she will masquerade as a boy.*

Vita could not wait to tell Quintus her news. Their plan was actually going to happen. Her stomach fluttered. The thought that every morning she would be with him fulfilled a fantasy of falling in love with him.

However, this day she must work in the garden. Since Flavius was no longer living, all the slaves had to help take care of the beautiful flora, herbs, and vegetables that made the garden useful. Lavinia needed the produce and herbs for cooking. They grew figs, cabbage, lentils, and other vegetables next to the statues and rosebushes symmetrically arranged for beauty and calming the mind. On her hands and knees, digging in the dirt, she whispered to her best friend Aquilina that she was going to work on the docks before daybreak each morning.

"You asked them if you could do more work, you crazy girl," she laughed.

"It is to earn money to buy my freedom," Vita stated.

"You have good fortune, Vitalia," she commented wistfully. "I wish I had some future to work for in this life."

"You will. We will think of something that will give you opportunity," answered Vita.

"In a way, I am not sure I want to be free. I feel secure in this domus. They give me a home and food and clothes. I have friends here. It is my family."

"Not me. I need to be free. I was free until I was brought here. You don't know what that feels like. I had my parents, and we had our own home. We worked together and loved each other. The bond of a real family is a comfort. As a slave you could be sold at any time and lose all of this security that you think you have. It is only because I am an orphan that I lost my freedom, and I know there is no security unless I am free."

"There is no security anywhere. You just don't know it," stated Aquilina.

"Yes there is, Aquilina. There are laws in this Empire. People have to obey the laws of Rome."

"You will see that laws can't replace what should be in the heart. People can be evil. They look after their own good, not yours. Look at what happened to you in the riot at Pompeii and Emperor Nero just had his own mother murdered. Where is the security in all that! This life is my best option. I'll stay here, I'll die here."

"What has happened to you, Aquilina? So young and already done with hope."

Aquilina sat back shaking her head at Vita. "The gods choose whom they favor and whom they discard. I am discarded by the gods. At least I know this and expect nothing, so that I can't be hurt. This is the best life I will have." She went back to scraping the soil.

"Aquilina, you give the gods too much power," said Vita.

"Hush, the gods will hear you! Maybe we should stop talking about the gods."

There was silence between the two friends until Vita finally asked, "How did he kill his mother?"

"Who? Nero? You haven't heard yet? He had her banished to Baiae to keep her from interfering with his love life, his decisions, and his place of authority. First, Nero had his engineers design a boat for her. It was quite a boat. The canopy was designed to include a lever that could be pulled, dropping the canopy on top of Agrippina.

"That would not kill somebody. She might be hurt but not killed."

"What if the canopy was filled with lead?" She paused looking at Vita with a smirk, and returned to digging out more weeds. "The gods were with her though. The lever was pulled, the canopy dropped, but she was saved because the back of the couch prevented the canopy from smashing her. Her handmaiden was killed, but Agrippina crawled out, jumped overboard and swam all the way to shore. She is quite a heroine in Baiae. So, Nero had to come up with another plan. No more attempts to make it look like an accident. He dispatched someone to murder her! His envoy broke into her home announcing their orders to kill her. Performing hateful irony and to show that she knew her son was behind it, she requested to be stabbed in the womb where her evil son was conceived! A bloody mess it was."

"Doesn't anybody care that our Emperor killed his own mother?"

"Nero told the Senate that she was a traitor planning to have him killed so she could take over the Empire. Maybe she was. The Senate approved," Aquilina said.

"How do you know all this?"

"Oh, I listen! When I'm serving, at the Baths, at the market, even here at home. People talk and pay me no mind. Plus, I have a good friend that lives in Puteoli which is close to Baiae. He tells me the news when he comes with his master to the market. He says that people are still lined up on the coast of Baiae protesting Agrippina's death. Brave and scary to go against Nero. So much for your Empire laws, Vitalia. They are made but if you are privileged they can be ignored. Justice is not for those without power, and you are without power," said Aquilina.

It was a warm, beautiful day. They tried to maintain what Flavius had started, two olive trees placed on either side of a center path with pomegranate bushes, rose bushes, and myrtle to be used by the family. On their hands and knees weeding and trenching the onion plants, sweet marjoram, and bay laurel for Lavinia's kitchen, Vita suddenly rolled over on the cool earth to lay flat to gaze up at the sky. The fluttering leaves on the olive tree made a kaleidoscope of light and color to amuse her.

"Do you think that Luna, the goddess of the moon, really naps in the olive tree?"

"Of course! You can see the silver moon glow on the leaves at night," answered Aquilina.

"You seem so sure. To me it is just the beauty of the tree and what is natural."

"You better roll over and get back to work before you are caught by Calitoria. I hear she is not too happy with you, and she will probably be thankful she has a reason to beat you."

"Why? What have I done?"

"She told Thana that Gaius and Telesphorus are giving you too many favors, like you are something special. She said you are a slave and should be treated like the human property tool that you are, not like you have manumission."

"Telesphorus is a slave, and he gets treated with favor."

"Well, she brought that up. She said he is intelligent and provides a need to the family and you do not. I'm just warning you to be careful. Now get up before you crush the rosemary plants. Thana uses them for incense to the gods."

THAT NIGHT VITA dreamt that she was living with her family again. It was a different house, more grand, but without locks on the doors. People kept coming and walking through the house taking things. Her father was there somewhere but he was not helping her keep the people away. She tried to lock the doors but the locks were always missing. Strangers kept coming and she tried to push them out. She tried yelling at them to leave. Nothing was working. Then Quintus appeared in the dream and said to try pushing the furniture in front of the doors. They worked together to shove heavy chests and beds and chairs against the doors. Finally, the parade of thieves stopped.

The dream left her drained and saddened. She wondered why her father wouldn't help. She felt he should be doing something. She laid in bed confused. How was she going to have a safe future and take care of herself? She'd always thought that her father was on the other side of life and was somehow taking care of her.

Unable to go back to sleep she waited for Quintus to come before dawn. She heard his call, like a screeching peacock, signaling his impatience. She scurried downstairs and opened the heavy door.

"You better think of a quieter bird to imitate when you come for me. Obnoxious peacock screams are only going to wake the neighborhood and family," Vita remarked annoyingly.

"I wasn't sure you were awake and would hear me."

"I heard you, silly boy, and so did everyone else on the street." She rolled her eyes at him. He smiled his white smile back at her.

"Let me help you with your hair, and we can stuff it in this cap." They struggled to pull and pile her thick tresses, tied and pushed, but the hair perched atop the cap like an umbrella tree over her head.

"Here," she said, "Give me your knife." Vita grabbed the knife and began to saw off the bottom half of her long hair. She then pulled, tied, and pushed her hair back into the cap.

"There," she said. "That will work."

Quintus raised his eyebrows and stared at her. "Well, that was quick." His shock not only reflected the ease she displayed of using his knife, but the shock of short hair on a female. The Roman mark of femininity was gone. Vita looked up at him.

"What?" She shook her head and squinted at him.

"Won't you regret doing that?"

"Not today!" she commented over her shoulder as she turned to skip to the docks. Quintus had to run to catch up with her.

"You don't even know where you are going. Follow me." He darted in front of her to assert that he knew more than she did. "Now if anyone asks your name..."

"I know, I have already figured this out myself. I am Vitalis, a young boy slave of the Petronius family. I want my pay in coin not in food."

"And I will show you how to clean oysters. It is the lowest job and you will start there. If you have a question ask me, otherwise don't speak. You sound like a girl. You may be able to fool them but you can't fool me. You are a girl," he pompously stated.

"I am just like you. I am just female," she retorted.

"Best not to talk to you today. You are a bee looking for someone to sting." He walked the rest of the way in silence.

They arrived at the docks and slithered through the crowd of ruffians and sailors to find the baskets of oysters imported from several miles up the coastline at Lake Lucrine. A combination of salt and fresh thermal waters created a lovely flavor for these oysters. New methods of cultivation using ropes with artificially heated basins kept the oysters alive through the winter, developing a lucrative business for the owners. The rich would not think of having a dinner party without oysters. It was considered a strong aphrodisiac for sexual conquests, channeling Venus, the goddess of love. Also, visiting soldiers thought oysters gave them power to win on the battlefield. The costly catch would bring ready cash at the market.

Vita and Quintus took their positions at the baskets and began cleaning the shells of debris. Since they were cultivated oysters, they were not as dirty as wild catch, but the sharp gnarls cut into their hands. Some were handed off to have a knife inserted into the shell to break it open. The meat was harvested and tossed into ironware to be presented at market.

"Faster, you little men with soft pitiful phallus!" shouted the filthy boss. Vita listened to the language of the docks and tried to understand the slang. She guessed that someone was always bigger and more erect than another and some were accused of having female parts when obviously they didn't. She easily ignored some of the insults aimed at her with a blank expression, lacking understanding of the male slang.

The first day took its toll, but Quintus assured her that she would get used to the work. She mopped her bloodied knuckles and palms with a rag and wrapped it around her hands to stop the bleeding. She could feel them throbbing and watched them swell and turn red.

"Tomorrow, wrap your hands before we start cleaning the oysters," suggested Quintus as he looked down at the painful cuts.

"Now you tell me!" *If I didn't adore you I would hit you,* she thought. "Do you like me, Quintus?" Vita asked. She didn't know what made her say it. Maybe she was so tired that she let her guard down. Of course, he must like her a little, or he wouldn't be helping her or caring about the cuts on her hands.

"Yes, I like you most of the time," he answered.

"Do you like me as a girl?"

"You are a girl and I like you."

"Do you think I am pretty?" Quintus stirred something unknown and newly awakened in her.

"Your hair is too short, you're too skinny, and you're way too independent for your own good. But your eyes talk to me in a kind way and I like that."

This must be a friendship to Quintus and nothing more.

"Well, I think your teeth are too white and your..." She had to stop because she couldn't think of anything awful about him to equally hurt. He was perfect in her eyes. "And I like the way you look at me, too. Pick me up tomorrow at the same time, and just whistle a soft tune, not that annoying squawk of a peacock. I will be ready and hear you." With that she ran ahead and slipped in the door of the Petronius villa.

Chapter Twelve

A s Vita entered the servant's door, she was snatched by her hair and thrown to the ground. Calitoria shoved her in the back with her foot.

"Where have you been? You smell of fish!"

"I have been working on the docks. I was given permission by the master."

"Don't talk. Get up and get to work!"

Vita went straight to Lavinia who was immediately handed her a large bowl of olives to pit. Lavinia gave a look of caution. Calitoria laid one more backhanded slap to the side of Vita's head as she left the kitchen.

"Why does she hate me so?" she asked Aquilina.

"It is just the way it is," she replied. "We are slaves and that is the way it is for us. I don't think she hates as much as she knows she is to treat slaves that way."

"I think she hates," said Vita.

Although Vita had heard rumors that Emperor Nero called for compassion towards slaves and they should be given medical attention when sick and there was responsibility of slave owners to treat slaves as family, Calitoria laughed at such suggestions. Vita could not help but think Calitoria's controlled anger carried a deeper meaning. The way she controlled her abuse to times when the Master and Telesphorus were not present betrayed her.

~

IT WAS time for Gaius and Calitoria to have their evening with Balbus and Lasennia. The pale pink gown was finished. Talistia had used her weaving and sewing talent to roll the neckline and artfully cross-stitch a design over the edge. Two large golden clips secured the long stola at the shoulders allowing Calitoria's lovely neckline and arms to be visible. A gently tied belt sparkling with golden studs dropped from her slim waist. No one else would have the soft color or intricate woven pattern of the fabric.

Calitoria called Vita to her large bedchamber to design her hair. It would take most of the day. She wanted an elaborate and structured style reflecting the sophistication of the Roman Empire. Vita used a light wax to secure a row of identical curls across Calitoria's forehead. A purchased wiglet placed underneath her blonde hair, stitched in place with thread, added height and depth. Vita deftly combed Calitoria's long blonde hair over the wiglet and braided it into several long thin braids. She wound them together in the back securing the bun tightly with a jeweled comb.

Calitoria's fine features reflected the domination of the Empire over its conquests in northern territories. Her natural hair, pale as sunbeams, the envy of all, announced Germanic descent. In years past, prostitutes were required by law to bleach their hair to label them. Women ignored the law. The popular whims of the ladies' sense of style and desired elaborate hairstyles, sometimes blonde, sometimes a red henna dye from Germanic manufacturing, could not be controlled by a law.

Calitoria looked beautiful, but some of the local ladies whispered that Calitoria had been a slave. Her unusual light-colored hair came from her parents who were captured slaves of the prestigious Calitorius family in Herculaneum. Calitoria ignored the whispers and relied on Gaius's prestige and heritage to validate her status. She acted the part of the class she wanted to acquire.

Gaius entered the bedchamber. "Calitoria, are you ready to leave? I want to pray to the lares before we go and want you to join me."

They entered the lararium adorned with family images and statues of gods, Jupiter in gold, Venus in marble, smaller gods in bronze, but the hallowed family gods prevailed most sacred. Calitoria knelt at the shrine lighting lamps, offering garlic, while Gaius bowed, reciting memorized requests. Calitoria added her petition for social opportunities to receive influence and power in Herculaneum.

Vita and Talistia prepared to accompany Gaius and Calitoria to the dinner.

"Talistia," said Vita. "I think we should wear fresh tunics and pull our hair straight back tied with a leather strap."

"But you know how to braid and curl hair. Why can't we dress up? The Balbus home is so elegant."

"I don't think we should try to impress anybody tonight or even think we will have a bit of fun. The mistress wants to be the center of attention. We are only going in order to make her look highborn, rich enough to have slaves attending. You have been here longer than me. You know how to stay out of trouble. Stop and think, Talistia."

A hired bodyguard named Severus waited in the atrium. There were always rumors circulating about gangs and violence making the streets dangerous at night. Even Emperor Nero had enjoyed preying on unsuspecting victims in his youth, dressing as a slave with his friends to amuse themselves attacking strangers. As a young teen himself, inheriting the throne, harming unsuspecting tourists and citizens was a right the Emperor enjoyed. All witnesses were killed.

If an upper class family expected to be out after dark, the former gladiator was hired to protect them. Majestic, he towered over Gaius, his muscular body reflecting years of training and combat, wearing scars and wounds that made Vita's stomach hurt. She watched him stand with legs apart and hands on his hips, chest out. *His muscles are so huge he can't put his legs together. He looks like a rabid hound that has been beaten and chained his whole life. With that mane of red hair, he must be a former slave probably captured and used as a gladiator until he won his freedom,* she thought.

❧

THE PETRONIUS FAMILY stepped onto the street for the short walk to the villa, Severus in front, Gaius and Calitoria, Vita and Talistia trailing behind. A soft breeze from the sea ruffled their garments while the setting sun cast a golden hue to all it touched.

Welcomed by their host to the Balbus home, they passed over the threshold following the ritual of stepping with the right foot first and touching the frame acknowledging the gods of home and family. Vita's eyes reached up to marvel at the ribbed columns with filigree at the top and then down to the beauty of the glistening mosaic floor. Swinging between the columns were cherished reliefs in marble that told of a story she would have to review later. A small inscription caught her attention. WHO DOES NOT KNOW HOW TO DEFEND HIMSELF, DOES NOT KNOW HOW TO SURVIVE. Another said, EVEN A SMALL DANGER BECOMES GREAT IF NEGLECTED.

The home rambled past the usual atrium and impluvium with a maze of additional rooms and ornately decorated frescoes to either side. Incense burned a pleasing scent to cover the odor of the adjoined stable with its separate entrance into the villa. Privileged family and guests sheltered their horses near by, unlike the rest of the community that had to use the public stables. Another separate entrance led to the Elite Baths owned by the Balbus family for invited prestigious individuals. Passed down from famous father to famous father, this was an inherited home overlooking the sea.

After friendly greetings, slaves offered simple bites of fish and meats along with wine from local merchants. As Calitoria surveyed the room, she was dismayed to see so many other residents of Herculaneum in the atrium.

"I thought this was a dinner invitation to us and a few elite guests, not the whole city! I see that everyone who wants to call Balbus a friend is here. Some do not even have status to vote in elections and they are here. Even our neighbor Lucius Venidius Ennychus is here with his wife, Livia Acte. He is such an unlikeable man. I don't care what he thinks he is, he is a Junian Latin and has no real social status. He is just a freed slave trying to be a Roman citizen, and he thinks we don't know he was a slave. I don't know where he found his wife, Livia. He says she is a freed slave, but she acts like a woman beaten into submission. Look at her, with her shoulders rounded and her gaze only at the floor."

Gaius ignored the gossipy comment, whether true or not.

They wandered through the large atrium greeting their neighbors and clients. Calitoria stopped to spend a few moments with her new friend Lasennia. She stood with the wives of two distinguished citizens, Q. Tamudius Optatus and M. Vinicius Proculus.

"Calitoria! I have not seen you since the day of the riot in Pompeii." Lasennia grabbed Calitoria's hands and held them in her own. "We had such a meaningful experience worshipping Isis, and then to have it ruined by so much horrible death and violence. Such a tragic day! Rome must punish those responsible. I heard that your slave girl saved your lives twice with incredible bravery. She is such a young girl. You must be so very thankful to have her. Where is she? I want to meet her," gushed Lasennia.

"If you mean Vitalia, she is here behind me. But it was Gaius and me that saved us. I was surprised at myself taking on part of the fight with a club. Unfortunately, one of our slaves was killed."

The other women gasped.

"You must have been so scared," stated Lasennia.

"Of course, we all were. I comforted each member of our family and kept them from harm as best I could."

"Gaius shared your experience with my husband at the Baths a few days ago. I am so pleased that the gods favored you and allowed your escape." Lasennia was not entirely fooled by Calitoria's lie. She would ask Balbus to repeat the story he heard from the head of the Petronius family later.

Calitoria's countenance never wavered. She nodded to the other women and smiled. Lasennia changed the subject to speak of her son and current pregnancy. She reigned over the other women: a handsome family, prestige, beauty, respect, and an exquisite home.

"Please visit the rest of the villa and be sure to see the view of the coast upstairs."

While Calitoria and Gaius climbed upstairs hand in hand, Vita and Talistia stood near the wall of the atrium waiting to serve. Talistia looked to her side at Vita's profile. Vita stared straight ahead with no expression.

"Vitalia, the mistress has changed the events of the Pompeii riot. I was there. I saw what you did while the mistress and I cowered in the darkness petrified with fear. I nearly laughed when she said she swung the club! She was only concerned that she would make it home with her parcels which we managed to hang onto and carry out of the city in spite of the violence and killings. One could say that is a costly dress she is wearing tonight. It cost the life of Flavius."

Vita stared straight ahead. *Is that my fate? Will being a slave cost my life?*

She didn't know, but one thing was certain. Emotions needed to be suppressed. *Talistia is a handmaid. I cannot trust her. Anything I say could be repeated. I will not correct or speak of the truth ever. If Calitoria is caught in her lie it will be from Lasennia who got the true story from her husband.*

To comment to Talistia would put both in a place of jeopardy should they be questioned. Vita remembered her new understanding of the relationship with her mistress. The bruises were still sore. There was no one to speak for her or to protect her. No one would even feel that truth for a slave was important. *This is what it feels like to be alone and abandoned,* she thought.

～

GAIUS AND CALITORIA delightfully explored their friends' home, admiring the superior craftsmanship.

"Look at the portrait of Venus and Mars. I saw something similar at the home of the politician Albuscius Celsus in Pompeii years ago. Could we do something like this in our villa?" questioned Calitoria.

"Soon we can. I want to work on the farm expansion now. It will give us enough money to do the work on our villa that you want eventually."

They continued strolling through the rooms, stepping up higher and higher until they reached a room overlooking the Mediterranean Sea. The sunset welcomed them with a beauty that could not be copied with paint on walls. It was a gift from nature that filled their souls. The rippling water stole the colors from the sky above glittering with satisfaction in its success. Directly below them, torchlights lined the marina making the evening even more romantic.

"Oh, to be Lasennia and Balbus and see this everyday must be wonderful!" Just as these words were uttered, friends of the host and hostess joined them to admire the home and sunset.

"Yes, it is beautiful, but it comes with a price," volunteered an elite neighbor.

"What do you mean?"

"Lasennia lives with her mother-in-law like a guest in her own villa. There is endless strife between them. Permission to live or breathe only comes from the matriarch, and Lasennia must step cautiously. I wouldn't be surprised if Lasennia can only eat and piss with authorization. I wonder how long she can endure. Have you met her mother-in-law, Volasennia, yet? A powerful woman, with a scowl that could kill Hercules!"

"Not yet," said Calitoria.

"I have known her somewhat," answered Gaius.

"She is here tonight, dominating the activities. You will see her. She says that Emperor Nero might be joining us with Poppaea. Only Volasennia would try to tell Nero what to do, where to go, and think he should do it. Of course the Balbus family has mingled with royalty and Emperors since before Julius Caesar, so it is common for them to connect. You know that the Emperor is in love with Poppaea Sabina of Pompeii, don't you?"

"Really! But he is married to Octavia Augusta," exclaimed Calitoria.

"Doesn't matter to him. Octavia is a political marriage. There are no children. I am told that Emperor Nero has a sensitive side that leads him to desire Poppaea. She has inherited her mother's beauty, but not her sensibilities, and is attentive to Nero even though she is married.

"Poppaea's mother was the most beautiful, wealthy and distinguished woman in all of the Empire until she committed suicide after being accused of infidelity. So beautiful that she wore a veil to cover her face when she traveled the streets of Pompeii in her *palanquin* hoisted on the shoulders of four slaves." She paused. "I am using the same cosmetics that she used," she said as she brushed her cheek with her hand.

Calitoria thought of her own beauty and how it could compare.

"Volasennia would never endorse a relationship between Nero and a woman who was already married," the woman continued. "She believes he should honor his own marriage and respect it. It would not be uncommon for her to speak her mind to the young Emperor. She might try to remind him of his unfaithful behavior tonight. It was the same with Nero's mother. She did not like the relationship with Poppaea Sabina or the slave girl, Acte, before her. Now his mother is dead. Kings always see threats. To stay in power you must make your enemies disappear. Volasennia should be careful. If Nero makes a visit tonight, there could not be a more exciting evening! I don't want to miss anything. We should get back downstairs."

"Do you think Nero will really come tonight?" Calitoria asked Gaius.

"No, I happen to know that he is performing on stage in Neopolis and has been for several days. Some are worried that he is neglecting the Empire to pursue his career as an actor. Such nonsense! How could he believe acting is more important than being Emperor?"

Calitoria wanted to agree with the disparaging view Volasennia held of infidelity but the opposite attitude was very familiar. She respected the attempt to establish a social script of behavior for marriage but she knew men. She had witnessed too many with a lack of respect for women. Some agreed with Volasennia that marriage needed to be upheld as an ideal state for the good of the family and the Empire. Some scoffed at marriage unless money was to be gained.

Calitoria knew she must marry to change her status from young maiden to mother. If she didn't produce a child, she could be discarded and sent back to her former family. She must protect her position with Gaius.

"Tonight I will be yours," she said as they walked from room to room, hand in hand.

Returning to the atrium, they found guests being served delicacies. The food was perfectly seasoned and satisfying. Lasennia and Balbus did not have to impress their guests to gain position in Herculaneum. There would be no use of expensive and rare foods or gifts to the guests to try to influence. It was their purpose to give to the town, instead, supporting the theatre, sports, and the needy.

As they entered the atrium, the scene before them told the story. Balbus was holding court with several neighbors who wished to gain status to vote. They would boast of their education, wealth, and family. Most were citizens who wanted to participate in religious activities and elections. They promised to vote for Balbus and work for any elected officials he endorsed.

"I should go over and be with the men and Balbus. You should go and speak with the women," Gaius told Calitoria.

She surveyed the room and her eyes fell upon a group of women in a circle. She walked up to them with her radiant smile that dissolved when she saw Vita in the middle.

"I wanted to meet the little slave girl who saved the Petronius family when they were in Pompeii!" said Lasennia. "I am so thankful you were there and so courageous to put your life in danger for them."

Vita said nothing but other voices filled in the details of how she distracted the murderers and even joined in the fight to protect the family.

"You are so small and cute!" Her short, chopped, pulled back hair drew curious attention. It was unfortunate that Calitoria entered the circle at that moment. She nodded to the ladies as if she was created by the universe offering something unique then captured Vita by the arm, squeezing a little too tightly, leading her to the door.

"Go home! Rodent!"

Chapter Thirteen

⟶⟋⟍⟋⟍⟍

There was no moon to light the way and no lights nearby. Should she turn left or right? Vertigo took over and she thought the earth shifted. *I feel so dizzy. I hate being so confused,* she thought as she tried to clear her head, hands touching her temples. *I think I turn left to go back to the villa.*

Vita could still hear the voices of the Balbus's gathering behind the door. Hesitating on the step, she considered going back in and asking how to get home. "I'm sure we came from the left and turned into the doorway here." Speaking to herself aloud made her feel like another was guiding her. A shadow moved along the wall. "Maybe something is there to capture me." She moved a few steps forward to distance herself from the night demon. "I should run but I don't know which way. Where is the street where I turn?" She decided to go to the first street and turn away from the sea. Now the stars were visible. "If only the moon would light the way." She pushed her hands forward to keep her feet from stumbling.

As she shuffled cautiously, Vita heard voices in front of her, men's voices. Searching for light to beckon her, she hoped that the voices could tell her which way to go. She knew her villa was across from the markets. Everyone knew the market in the city. She could ask the men and then she could find her way to the villa but their tone marred her hope. The voices had a threatening sound.

How horrible to be caught alone at night with no understanding of how to get home to safety! Vita crossed the street to flatten herself against a wall. She searched in the black night for a better place to hide. The voices were becoming louder, and now she could hear their feet scuffling. They carried torches. A moment ago she was hoping for light, now she hated it.

I can't find a place to hide! They are too close for me to move. They will see me. The men held their torches high, drunk with pleasure and bravado, young hooligans with no maturity of mind, looking for trouble. Vita's heart raced. She felt energy flash through her body but she stayed paralyzed against the wall.

Perhaps they will pass and not notice me.

She closed her eyes waiting, foredoomed light! Maybe they would be so interested in each other that they would not see her.

They are going to pass. Their imposing, sweaty bodies took over the street. Vita counted, *one, two,...six, eight men passing,* when one straggler yelled, "Hey, look what we have here! Boy or girl, I cannot tell. It doesn't matter. We like them both!" He laughed and reached out to fondle her short hair. The others turned around abandoning their swagger to stare at her.

"A slave for sure. I don't know her or him though. I wonder, who do you belong to? What master do you serve? Are you a eunuch? Made for pleasure? I will make you give me pleasure!" He traced her hidden breast and grabbed her around the waist. She pushed with both hands on his bare-skinned chest. Stale breath smothered her mouth as she twisted and turned. Surrounded, another put his hands on her to pull off her short mantle. Another tugged her sash and was attempting to tie her thrashing hands behind her. Someone fondled her legs. She vowed not to cry. She would bite and fight instead.

"Wild like I like them," said one.

A deep horrible growl came from the underworld, a demon from beneath their feet.

"What the *cacare* is that?" questioned one, speaking with Roman plainness.

"Spirits of the dead?"

"The gods!"

Again the earth groaned louder. Explosions in the distance detonated as the earth shook. Stones toppled from the walls. A rhythm of movement beneath their feet drove them to bow down to the surge. Brave hooligans now fell to the ground on their knees screaming like children to the gods. "Stop, be merciful!"

Doors flew open pouring occupants into the street. Mothers clung to crying children.

"Why are the gods so angry? Who has offended them? What have we done?"

Fathers sheltered their loved ones, hovering over them, protecting them from falling debris. The street filled with panicked residents repenting as they clung to the ground.

As quickly as it started, the quake suddenly stopped. The wind whispered ghostly sirens in the stillness. Vita stood straight up still wearing the cords binding her hands behind her. A gang member pointed at her and shouted, "This is a chosen one. This is a god! Only one who is loved can command the gods to protect them." They backed away leaving her in the center of a vacant arc.

Grabbed from behind she turned to find Gaius hovering over her.

"I found you!"

He untied her and scooped her under his arm as if she weighed nothing. Gaius was so distressed by Vita's disappearance from Balbus's home and the shaking of the earth that he ran with soldier strides. Calitoria, Talistia, and the gladiator trailed behind.

When they reached the villa, they found Thana exiting the lararium. She had asked the ancestors for their guidance when the earth shook knocking figures off the shelf onto the floor, and they spoke to her. It was a sign; her life was in danger. She could only assume that it had something to do with Calitoria, the only one who wanted her to disappear so that the family would no longer have her, the matriarch, as mistress. Thana's eyes were bright with fear and settled on Gaius and Calitoria.

"I told you the gods were angry with us! Can't you see that they are powerful? Now you will believe me."

"Calm down, Mother. We are all fine. The earth shakes often." He put his arm around her shoulders and held her. "You see, all has returned to normal. Everyone is home and safe. Let's get you some sweet wine and let you rest for the night. You will see that in the morning, the sun will still rise and the birds will still sing their daily song. Lavinia will have your breakfast for you just as she always does. You will forget about this by morning. You will go back to your weaving and finish the beautiful work that you have started. That is so important to us. Rest now."

Thana trembled as if shivering with cold staring blankly at the floor. Gaius led her back to the kitchen area settling her on her favorite stool.

"The dead spirits have spoken to me. I can't understand but I must not ignore them. Someone is going to die, I know this."

Gaius stood beside her massaging her shoulders and asked Lavinia to pour a cup of heated wine. She poured the drink sweetened with sapa into a silver drinking cup. Thana wrapped her distorted fingers around the two handles and sipped slowly, savoring the comfort it provided.

"I hope you didn't add too much water. I like the way the dizzy feeling helps me relax," said Thana.

Lavinia saved the sugary syrup made from boiling wine in her lead kettle especially for Thana. Every morning she would enter the kitchen ready for her cup of mulsum and every evening she ended her day with another cup. Lately, she had requested a cup at midday as well.

Vita watched Thana drink her wine, startled by her strange behavior. After all, Thana had shared secrets with her. Being a confidant had responsibilities of caring and protection. However, the spirit room with its effigies and the way Thana spoke to them made her think the old woman might be unbalanced.

Thana neglected her cup and set her eyes on Vita.

"There she is. I see their spirit faces in you. I have received utterances from the ancients. They prepare me for danger and unavoidable harm," she said. Her eyes widened as she spoke in her childhood language knowing that Vita was the only one in the room who could understand.

Gaius knew some of the Etruscan language but had discarded the need to learn or remember it when he was young. He saw no reason for it and felt it was ancient and unpopular. It was for the old ones. He knew more Latin and Greek as his education demanded. He knew enough of the words to realize she shared her premonition, and Vita understood his mother when she answered her in the same tongue.

"Danger is avoidable. We can save ourselves by preparing for it.

Perhaps, that is why the gods have shared this with you," answered Vita in Etruscan. She patronized Thana in a way because she had no belief in stories of gods and their strange ways.

Thana paused considering Vita's logic.

"That could be," she answered. "I would still need to know what danger is coming after me." At that moment, she thought she saw a dark ghoul move past the doorway. She stared in that direction but it was gone. Thana climbed off her stool, reminded of the pain in her legs and feet, and stumbled over to the doorway and peered left then right.

"Mother, why are you searching there?"

"I saw one of them."

"Come with me and find your bed for the night. It is late. There has been too much excitement for you." He led her through the peristyle to her chamber and watched to see if she settled down.

"I want to talk to Vitalia before I go to sleep. Please."

"Of course," said Gaius turning immediately to find the young slave girl helping Lavinia.

"Vitalia, my mother would like to speak to you. You seem to be able to calm her. Go to her now." He followed and stood outside his mother's door to listen. What power could this young slave have over his mother?

"Vitalia, I want you to take me to Hercules at his Temple tomorrow. I need to make sacrifices to him immediately. I need to ask him what danger is after me." Thana spoke in her mother's tongue.

"Yes, tomorrow. Now you must rest. You know you have been upset since Flavius died. You must try to think of the good things you have. Think of the beautiful garden Flavius left for you to enjoy, the beautiful cypress trees and fragrant oleander. Think of the way the birds come to visit the flowers and trees and the way the sun feels on your face when you sit in the garden with your handwork.

"You know that Gaius will be leaving for Britannia soon. You should make him warm socks to take with him. It is not so warm in Britannia as it is here. He will be very cold. Tomorrow we will buy wool. You can start making socks for your son," said Vita as she stroked Thana's head. Her sweaty brow revealed how terrified she was.

"Yes, tomorrow I must help Gaius prepare for his trip," she answered in a drowsy tone. Already the wine was calming her.

Vita softly stepped out of the bedchamber and closed the door silently only to bump into Gaius's tall frame.

"It is remarkable how you can handle my mother. I didn't understand what you said but I know it made her feel better. What did she want?"

"She wants me to take her to the Temple of Hercules tomorrow."

"Well done. You must take her tomorrow. Now all of us must get to our beds to rest."

Vita made her way up to the second floor to her room. By lamplight, she decided to sit and sketch to calm herself. She drew charcoal faces from the night on pieces of scroll. The images were horrifying. They were ones she'd imagined while stumbling in the darkness. Some were the men who taunted her before the earthquake. She put them on paper and pulled the lamp close. One by one, she carefully let the flame set fire and extinguish the images. Ashes fell to the stone floor and the images vanished. *Gone,* she thought.

Chapter Fourteen

Quintus's daily call for Vita came before sunrise. His delightful whistle carried a melody mimicking the songbirds that loved their olive trees in the garden. No one would suspect it was a boy trilling, but in truth, songbirds would never be awake without the summon from the sun. Her masquerade as Vitalis, the boy who worked mornings at the docks, fooled everyone and bolstered her friendship with Quintus. Each day began with her plan to see him, and each evening fed a strange hunger to see him again.

Quintus witnessed the earthquake the night before and testified to her that he believed Hercules started it. He proudly recounted a story, as they walked home from the docks.

"Hercules killed a nine-headed hydra and even held up the world for Atlas for a while. He wrestled and defeated ferocious beasts with strength beyond any power known to man. He is the son of Zeus and has power over the underworld and Olympus. Even as a baby, he strangled two snakes sent to kill him by his stepmother. She drove him to madness, and he accidentally killed his wife and children."

Vita looked at Quintus, with his joyful smile and warm brown eyes in awe. After all, he was the nicest and most wonderful boy she had ever known.

"I'll have to think about that. You mean he still exists?"

"Of course, he is a god."

"Where does he live now?"

"Well, half the time he is in the underworld, and the other half he is with the other gods living in Olympus," he answered with chin high.

"Where is Olympus? I'm supposed to take Thana to give Hercules sacrifices today."

"Well, I don't know where Olympus is. I think it is in the clouds, but the old Temple of Hercules is near your villa. That would be where you should take her. I will point it out on the way back this morning."

"So much to learn about this god, Hercules," said Vita. "How could he accidentally kill his wife and children? I will have to figure out this religious way of thinking. Maybe it can save me from Calitoria. Maybe having the strongest man in the world on my side would be good."

"Why? Is your owner hurting you?"

"Just Calitoria," Vita answered in a hushed tone and didn't want to say more, even though the treatment was becoming more of a constant rather than incidental in her life. Quintus studied her with concern, but they both knew that Calitoria had every right to beat her.

AFTER THEIR MORNING at the docks, Vita stopped by the tablinum in the villa to deliver her coins to Telesphorus. It was still early in the morning and he was busy reading, so she sat on the cool mosaic floor, leaned up against the wall, and waited quietly until he looked up at her. This young girl had his heart. He only had to drop his eyes on her face to feel affection for her. Vita reached out towards him with coins to put in his hand.

"What are you reading?" she asked.

"Part of the Torah."

"I don't know what that is. Are you learning something?"

"Yes, God's will on Earth."

"God's will on Earth? I am visiting Hercules's Temple today with Thana. Hercules is a god. Thana is going to buy his attention and safety for the family."

"That is different from what I am reading. I am reading about the

God of my people," Telesphorus explained. "My God is the God that loves us. I have ignored Him until now, but because of our difficult time in Pompeii and nearly losing my life fighting horrible men, I have decided to see what God says about life and death."

Vita sat and thought about what Telesphorus said. She felt comfortable sitting with him, a nice young man, gentle in his heart, always analyzing his way through everything rather than acting impulsively, every comment and thought weighed against its consequences.

Finally, Vita spoke. "I know some things about death," she said softly. "I know that in this life when people are mean and want to kill and hurt others, it should disappoint God or the gods. I hope that gods or your God hates the bad things people did to us in Pompeii and other things that have happened here, too."

Telesphorus looked down at the young innocent maiden. "I hope that is true, Vitalia. You have a good heart. I hope you don't change as you grow up."

Telesphorus counted the share of coins for the family and dropped them in a box. He proudly opened a separate box and deposited Vita's share. His loving smile lingered after she turned to walk away.

It wasn't long before Thana was ready to go to Hercules's Temple. She clutched a parcel, wrapped and tied in linen, full of lentil cakes for her sacrifice, and Vita carried it on their very slow walk. Thana favored her right hip, and both of her feet complained as she walked awkwardly on them.

"Everything must be done properly for the sacrifice and prayer, or it will be no good. In fact, it might draw more harm from the gods if they are offended," instructed Thana.

This early in the morning, the wind was soft on their faces, and the heat of the day had not yet arrived. Vita cradled Thana's arm to steady her along the cobblestone sidewalks. Thana curved forward to examine her steps, treading cautiously along the stone grooves.

"So many people in line before us! I told you I wanted to get here early. A little shaking of the earth and everyone in town wants to sacrifice to Hercules," she fussed.

Thana and Vita took their place behind residents holding their sacrifices of fruit, cakes, vegetables, bread, and small animals. With so many waiting near the sacred Temple, city slaves had to maintain order. They strolled up and down the line demanding silence.

"I don't know if my lentil cakes are good enough," whispered Thana after the Temple guard walked past. "Others have brought nicer things that might buy more favor. I wish Gaius had come with us with something better to lay at the altar."

Thana's thoughts suffocated her with doubt that her purpose would succeed.

"Gaius's lack of respect for ritual sacrifice is so exasperating. He neglects his responsibilities as religious leader in our home, preferring to spend time on his farm and finances. Maybe he will do better now that bad things are happening."

They shuffled forward in small steps, patiently anticipating their admittance, while the sun rose higher and stronger on their backs. Finally, they reached the entrance to the Temple. Hesitating on the steps in the cool shade, Vita peered past the huge columns and altar to examine brightly colored frescoes. One, of a bare Hercules struggling with a lion, and another with a wild boar on his shoulders as if hurling it to its death. She studied the detail of the face, the sculpturing of the heroic body using different shades of the same paint creating shape and form. Another image with Hercules seated wearing fabrics with the illusion of soft folds. *How could this be when it was painted on hard stone? How did the artist do that? It looks as if the characters were alive caught in a moment.* Paralyzed by their beauty, Vita felt Thana yank her arm past the frescoes to the immense statue of Hercules seated under a radiant brass arch.

A rambling tune from a flute player filled the hall to abate combative evil spirits. Incense burned an acrid odor on a black tray next to the statue of Hercules. The priest floated close in his floor length tunic with head and face covered by a dark hood, no evil sights or sounds to distract him.

Thana bent forward to kiss the feet of Hercules and deliver her prayer. The priest recited the words, and she carefully repeated them, straining to be absolutely correct because Hercules could easily be angered. All citizens were obliged to maintain good relations with the gods, and all gods were tolerated by the Empire.

Thana's passionate prayer was about giving the cakes to Hercules so that he would save her family from harm and destruction. She raised her hands with upturned palms and asked for deliverance from the evil she felt existed in their home. In return, she vowed to pay homage to him in her daily prayers if he would do this for her. She wept as she spoke her promises. The moment of prayer and sacrifice abruptly ended as the Temple slaves nudged her out to the street and the next worshiper moved forward in line.

Thana and Vita staggered into the bright sunshine shading their eyes. Thana righted herself and inhaled deeply with satisfaction, convinced her tribute as a citizen of the Empire had been rendered. She noticed tables at the exit covered with amulets, rings, and prayer statues for sale. Her greedy fingers sifted through the objects, and she bought two items, a ring for Gaius to wear for protection while he worked in Britannia and a miniature female wax statue. She secreted the figurine inside her leather pouch so no one would see it. Vita raised her eyebrows. *Looks a little like Calitoria*, she thought.

"There, now Gaius will be safe in Britannia," said Thana as she patted her pouch, convinced she had garnered all the gods' favor. She turned to limp home to her garden where she could spend the rest of the afternoon sipping her sweetened wine dozing on her bench. Then, socks for Gaius would be constructed by her arthritic hands knitting for hours, as an act of love for her son, on that tranquil bench.

Vita walked beside her noticing that Thana had appeared reasonable this whole day. No phantoms followed or leaped out of corners. *Thank you, Hercules.*

~

CALITORIA AND AQUILINA had been gone all day. When they returned in the late afternoon, Aquilina was sent to her room upstairs next to Vita's. After a slight peck on the door, Aquilina opened it with a broad smile.

"Hello, my friend," said Vita. "I notice that Calitoria has you helping her more and more, and I am assigned kitchen duties for most of the day. It is too bad. I know that you love cooking and would rather have my position."

"It is all right. It may change again. You never know. Where did you go today?"

"I helped Thana make sacrifices to Hercules. Where did you and Calitoria go?"

"I am sworn to secrecy. I will only tell you that we visited Lasennia. I can't tell you what we did there."

"I hate when you do that. Now, I am so curious."

"You and I know that if I tell and am found out, we will both be severely punished, and it will ruin your chances of earning money for your manumission and my chances of learning the trade of the kitchen," Aquilina warned.

"You have told me enough for me to suspect what she was doing with Lasennia. Remember, I saw what was happening in Pompeii at the Isis Temple. What is Calitoria doing now?"

"She is napping, trying to rest to stay fertile for conception before Gaius leaves," said Aquilina. "He will be gone for two years, probably not allowed to visit home during his assignment."

"Aquilina, can you ever keep a secret? Now I know exactly what happened at Lasennia's."

"Well, I guess we tell each other everything. I know you won't say anything. I see your face sometimes and know what you are thinking. I just hope no one else can see it."

CALITORIA'S PRATTLE about the moon being full and when her menses stopped were daily comments. She required Aquilina to give her a nightly report on the exact shape of the moon. "I forbid the clouds to arrive!" she would shout as she walked through the atrium. She needed a full moon. She stopped drinking wine and required Gaius to do the same. Sober couples increased fertility according to midwives. It was especially important for the mother to be sober during conception so that the child did not receive her foolish behaviors into his soul. Calitoria ordered Talistia to give her nightly massages with olive oil and herbs to help her desire her husband and encourage fertility.

Surprisingly, Thana and Calitoria had found something to agree upon: Thana wanted an heir for Gaius and Calitoria wanted a child to elevate her importance in the home. Thana put aside the female statue she had purchased from the Temple to save for later in case she needed it. She forced herself to muster some affection for Calitoria and the young woman was responding. Calitoria asked Thana for advice on conception.

"You must wear this amulet around your neck at all times," Thana instructed. It was a small carving of Juno, goddess of fertility. Calitoria also kept her small statue of Isis close by and continued to give coins to Lasennia for delivery to the Isis priest whenever she went to Pompeii. Thana visited the master's bedroom nightly to place herbs and charms under the bed, honoring every trusted ancient Etruscan custom and superstition of reproduction she could remember.

GAIUS PLANNED a trip to Pompeii for business before leaving for Britannia. A new slave was needed to replace Flavius, and financing for the loans with Jucundus needed to be finalized. Calitoria cringed at the thought of returning to Pompeii even though it had been months since the riot. Gaius hired the retired gladiator, Severus, to join them for protection, which made Calitoria willing to go.

"Has Rome responded to the Nucerian's complaint of the entrapment and slaughter of innocents yet?" she asked Gaius.

"Yes, I heard at the Baths that after months of discussion in the capital, and having the Consuls brought in for recommendations, the Senate has finally passed their judgment and punishment on Pompeii. They had to act. I guess the wagon and funeral pyre for the victims burned for two full days in front of the Senate steps. Pompeii will not be allowed to have Gladiator tournaments for ten years and Livineius Regulus has been banned from the Empire. The magnificent arena will lie abandoned to crumble and grow thistle and weeds. Quite a surprise, because Nero loves the sport, and the games are becoming more popular than ever. Rome has been adding more and more forms of entertainment, partly driven by Emperor Nero's lust for violence and bloodletting. We will have to wait and see if the ten years will be enforced or gradually forgotten."

"Did Nero agree on the judgment?" she asked.

"Hard to say. I think not. I heard that he passed it to the Senate and they passed it to the Consuls and they passed it back to the Senate. Nero is still absent from Rome pursuing his acting career and coupling with Poppaea, his new love."

"If Nero is not in Rome, how can he function as Emperor? Now, I am worried about your service in Britannia. Will the Legions have the guidance and supplies they need to protect you and the other Roman soldiers? Will the towns that are being constructed be safe for citizens and their families?" she asked.

Gaius was careful with his answer. He knew he had said too much already. He also knew that Calitoria was bound to hear rumors from friends while he was gone. It would be best to plant the seeds of confidence rather than doubt.

"The Roman Empire is the strongest and most powerful on Earth, Calitoria. No one can conquer us. It is true, over and over again, that Romans can do anything. We work together and govern together to accomplish the magnificent. The gods are with us, the gods favor us. Nothing can come against us that we can't overcome. It is the same with us, nothing can come against us that we can't overcome. With you loving me the way you do, I have the best life."

He calmed her doubts and took her in his arms. The masculine strength and stature of this man, with his arms around her, made her feel safe. It made her realize nothing would harm him while he was away. She knew the power of the Empire would take care of him.

THE NECESSARY DAY trip to Pompeii was a great day for the slaves when Gaius, Calitoria, the red-haired gladiator, and Telesphorus left. This time Vita did not have to go. She and Quintus secreted a plan to find each other in the afternoon and spend the day at play. After she finished helping Lavinia and gave her the usual hug, she spun out the door to find Quintus at his gem cutter shop. As her eyes fell on her best friend, all cares and sad thoughts were forgotten. His tan face and perfect smile caught her heart once again. For several weeks, she had not seen him in the daylight. The sun was not even up before they finished working at the docks. She stood watching him move about securing the shop and felt her body quiver with a fluttering sensation. He was more handsome than ever.

"I have an idea," he said grabbing her hand, heading out toward the edge of town. "I know a great place where we can swim. The sun promises a very warm day."

When they arrived at the cliff, they cautiously maneuvered their way down through the sharp, black rocks, clinging with hand grips, to a small beach. Quintus directed the activity having frequently visited this spot with his friends. He shed his clothes and hung them on a jutting rock. Without waiting on Vita, he waded out into the water until he was able to float on his back and yelled back to her.

"Hurry up, funny face!"

Vita shed her clothes and waded out into the water. The sun scorched her shoulders. She lowered herself into the cool water, shocking her hot skin. Closing her eyes, she moaned with delight. Quintus called her again. She dove to demonstrate her best swimming and moved out next to him.

"Where did you learn to swim like that?" he asked.

"My father taught me when I was very young in Ephesus."

Quintus was somewhat surprised that she was so sure of herself in the water. He dove down into the azure sea and disappeared long enough that Vita began to be concerned. She swiveled and searched for him in the soft waves as she tread the water, then felt him tug at her legs, sending her into screams. He surfaced beside her like Neptune rising from the watery abyss. Then down again he disappeared to blow enormous bubbles under her. As the bubbles erupted, he surfaced to get her embarrassed reaction.

"I did not do that! You did!" she squealed, splashing him in the face.

They swam out far enough to look back at the shore. Floating on their backs, they could see the rise of the cliff. Even the rocks dazzled with beauty and seemed to send out sparks of sunlight. White clouds meandered with rainbows at their scalloped edges against the deep cerulean sky. The two friends reached for each other's hands as the waves pushed and pulled, knitting their emotions together. Was it the beautiful day, or the friendship at the docks, or the chance to belong to someone lacing this knot together?

"Someday, I will make you a ring with a stone that will make you remember me forever," he said looking down at her hand.

After swimming all the way back, exhausted, they lay alone on the beach without a boss to tell them what to do and how to do it, without prying eyes from a slave owner or fellow slave, while the sun continued across the sky measuring time. Quintus pulled out a leather bag harboring some figs and walnuts. He passed the bag first to her so she could reach in and take what she wanted, then he riffled some out into his own hand.

"Are you planning on some kind of escape from the Petronius family?" he asked.

"Yes, that is my goal. Even if Calitoria did not hate me, I want my freedom. Are you still willing to help me?"

"If I can," he answered.

"You are already helping me, but it is going very slowly. I will need to find something else to earn more money."

"You are young and have time to develop some skill. Do you have any ideas yet?"

"No."

"Maybe something will find you when you are not looking for it." He paused to consider options, then without coming up with any suggestions, he said, "We better return home before it gets any later."

They pulled their clothes off the rocks and dressed and began the slow ascent up the steep cliff. Quintus reached back for her hand to help with the precarious footing until they reached the top and headed back to their assigned lives.

～

THAT NIGHT VITA had a visit from her mother in her dreams. She felt her mother caress her forehead and stand by her bed.

"I am so sorry for the strife you are enduring. I wanted you to be happy. There is nothing I can do to stop the persecution. It is going to get worse." Energy passed from her mother's hand to Vita. "I will be with you through the strife, but I can't do anything to stop it."

Fully awake, Vita remembered the dream. The warm comfort of the visit and the love she felt remained but a wave of alarm enveloped her, to think her life would be getting worse and there was nothing to stop it. Hopelessness entered her, but she dusted it off. *I can't see how it could get worse. Anyway, I know I can overcome anything as long as I belong to Quintus.*

Chapter Fifteen

The precious poetry of Homer rested on Telesphorus's lap. He squinted, bowing forward to devour the reading material. His long finger traced the poetry emphasizing the importance of each word. He was like a sailor longing for the sea, a critic craving enlightenment.

He frequently borrowed scrolls from a local private library, by invitation only. An opulent villa, originally belonging to Julius Caesar's father-in-law, it housed a variety of books and a coveted collection by the moral philosopher, Philodemus. This esteemed sage implied a nonspiritual alternative with no God or gods in his theology, believing the cosmos arose accidentally. Telesphorus occasionally joined meetings at the villa in a special room designed for lectures, with rows of chairs in a semicircle. He listened to scholars explain this philosophy, as he silently challenged their assumptions. He tormented himself with conflicting thoughts of God, the God of his people, the Jews, contrasting the book of Genesis with these Epicureans, who questioned if there were any gods. They focused on seeking pleasure.

The owner allowed him temporary use of the scrolls hoping Telesphorus would establish a local school for elite males, a popular idea for parents and an intriguing idea for him. He could charge a tuition for each student. Many parents recognized that their boys must pursue military prowess for Roman excellence, followed by a formal Greek education. All this to remain upper class. Telesphorus, an educated Greek, only had to become a Freedman to create a school. He contemplated the cumbersome parchment rolls littering the floor around his feet. His favorite, Vita, sat in the corner of the tablinum watching him, partly for the company, but also hiding from her tormentor. Today, she sketched Telesphorus's face shape, shadows, and studious expression on scraps of parchment that he'd discarded.

Telesphorus cupped Vita's face in his hands and said, "Hello, my little friend, Vitalia. How was your day?"

"Hold still! I am just finishing. Did you know your eyes do not match? One is not quite like the other, but together they make a pleasing face, now, that's a miracle. What are you thinking about? You have a distraught expression."

"The Rabbi in town told me about Elijah, a fascinating man whom the God of Abraham, Isaac, and Jacob chose to reveal Himself through. During that time, there was an evil king named Ahab who had a controlling wife, Queen Jezebel, who hated Elijah. When Elijah warned the people to stop worshiping false gods and idols, she sent soldiers out to kill him, and he had to hide. He became very depressed about his situation, but God sent angels to take care of him while he was hiding. It is a distressing story."

"How did the angels help him? Did they destroy Jezebel? I'm hoping for the destruction of a vile wicked woman." Telesphorus gave her a side glance of correction.

"The angels fed him and made him strong because they knew he had a long journey ahead of him, but they did not get rid of Jezebel. God gave her many chances to repent but she wouldn't. God gave Elijah encouragement and revealed that the future belonged to God, so he should not worry. Others could take over Elijah's position as God's prophet. It wasn't all up to Elijah."

"Hiding can work," said Vita as she tucked her head. Telesphorus looked at her, and they both laughed as he realized what she meant. "But you can't hide forever. I wish God would have gotten rid of Jezebel," she added.

〜

GAIUS PURCHASED a new male slave captured from the kingdom of
Armenia in the Parthian Empire. The family Calitorius originally
purchased the slave but found him to be difficult and offered him to
Gaius. The war in Armenia was ongoing, but this slave had been taken
when the Romans attacked the second capital of Armenia, Tigra-
nocerta. The slave never spoke to anyone so they named him Certa after
the city where he was captured. Vita and Aquilina tried to befriend the
dirty, gaunt man who stood in the atrium.

"What is your name? How old are you?" Aquilina asked but with
no answer.

"Maybe he speaks another language?" said Vita. She asked the questions in Etruscan, then Greek. He looked at them never opening his
mouth. "I don't know any more languages."

"Are you hungry?" He nodded his head.

"Well, he understands that." Aquilina brightened and scurried to
the kitchen for some bread, olives and mulsum. Vita stood waiting,
listening to Calitoria shouting in the atrium.

"Another problem you are leaving me before you exit for Britannia.
He is so skinny and short I don't see how he can help with the heavy
work around here. You know that I only have these small girls to help.
They can barely carry the water jugs, and the wine amphorae are even
heavier." Gaius grimaced. She decided to stop her tirade.

It was true. Certa was skinny. He did not appear to be very strong
and was shorter than both Telesphorus and Gaius. Vita wondered if she
would have to give up her space upstairs so that he would have a place to
stay. She was correct. That very day she was told to move in with
Aquilina. The girls couldn't be happier to share a room. They sat
together on their wooden pallets fluffing pillows and covers.

"What do you think is wrong with him?"

"Probably the same as me: loss of his freedom, no more family. I
think he will run away."

"You always think slaves can run away. He has the look of a slave. He
might get to the end of the street before someone brings him back, and
then he would be in worse circumstance," said Aquilina.

The young girls clung to each other with a shared alliance in their
circumstance. They seemed to trust each other beyond a friendship,
spirits joined in the harmony of youth with forgiveness, laughter, and

support, rather than the stale adult life of judgment, criticism, and impatience. Aquilina accepted the life dealt her and continued to dream of being an accomplished cook. It was something that might actually happen for her. She could be hired out to earn extra money. The kitchen had her heart, warm from the glowing coals in the dome-shaped oven and the love of Lavinia. The other fought against it. Vita yearned for freedom.

They finished moving Vita into Aquilina's room and headed downstairs. Thana was on her stool, as usual, enjoying the commotion, savoring the scent of meat frying and the sound of eggs boiling rapidly.

"I want to learn how to make bread like you," Aquilina told Lavinia. "Gaius likes your bread better than any other. How do you do it?"

"It is better than any of the bakeries in town. My flavor is better and unique," bragged Lavinia. "I have my own bread starter that I feed every day and I add a little honey."

"Please teach me, Lavinia," said Aquilina.

The girls waited next to the rough wooden table eager to help, but Aquilina was the chosen one today. She took a towel mimicking her mentor and stood erect waiting for orders. Lavinia stifled a smile and filled a scoop with a large amount of flour and dumped it on the table.

"Now, open up a circle in the middle," she instructed.

Aquilina folded her knuckles on her right hand and smoothed out the middle and surveyed the perfect circle she made. Lavinia poured some of the starter in the open area. Aquiline began the rhythm of folding the flour in from the sides with both hands. Lavinia brought over salt water from the sea and a bit of honey to add a little at a time. The mess became sticky, and Aquilina jumped back and held up her hands in panic.

"How do you keep this stuff from sticking to your hands!"

"Just keep folding in more flour and be patient," said Lavinia.

Soon the mixture became more manageable and stuck together in a soft ball. After rubbing with a little olive oil and covering it with a moist cloth, Aquilina gave it a loving pat just like Lavinia always did and set it in the corner next to the hearth, the warmest place in the kitchen.

"Now we must let the little one rest and grow," said Lavinia.

"I think I did pretty well," remarked Aquilina.

"Well, yes, you did. But you have the dough in your hair and on your belly!" Vita laughed and pointed.

Aquilina looked down at her stomach, sticky hands raised, surprised to see her belly covered with flour. Lavinia raised her hand to her mouth, covering her smile. There was dough and flour all over the girl, and her hands were crusted with the drying goop.

"You are wearing bread!" said Vita. Even Thana began to laugh.

Aquilina came back to knead the bread and let it rise again. Soon, it would be round and plump on the board with a heavenly scent. Eight triangles lightly carved in the surface displayed sections, and twine wrapped around the outside provided a handle for carrying after baking. Lavinia made her mark on top assuring the return of her own loaves from the baker in town.

"I don't want the baker switching anything on me! I can always tell when he tries to do that. I bet he would like to get starter from my bread, so he can claim it as his. Now, go both of you to the baker's!"

A short walk to the baker in the morning sun warmed the girls with joy.

"Walk slowly," said Vita. "There is no hurry. I like being out in the sun and on our own."

"Maybe someday I could have my own bakery with several ovens."

"Maybe! That would be the best thing for you. You could become the best baker in Herculaneum! In the meantime, this will be another chance for us to get away for a while," said Vita, yelling back over her shoulder as she hurried to the baker's to drop off the bread.

"Hey! This is not a race! You said walk slowly."

They stopped by the market on their way back. Vita searched the crowd for a glimpse of Quintus. She stretched on her toes to see if he was at the fishmonger's booth. Disappointed, she decided he labored at the gem cutter's in the village practicing his art of creating jewelry.

They had been told to find new clothes and shoes for Certa, the new slave, and Lavinia suggested they find a shaving knife for him.

"Maybe we will be able to see his face when he is done shaving," Vita giggled.

"Or maybe we will wish we could not see his face if he is ugly!" countered Aquilina.

"Oh, you are terrible," cried Vita as she poked her with her elbow.

They easily found the sandals and tunics, since there were no choices, only the standard leather sandals and coarse tunics for slaves. Vita noticed bright colors in the adjacent booth, and she saw ground pigments for painters. Drawn like the hungry for food, she needed to study them. Cheap red ochre and hematite pigments, already ground to a coarse powder, beckoned from large containers. Small terra cotta bowls housed vermilion made from cinnabar. Vita leaned over and lifted the lid of a covered bowl containing pure crimson color shipped from Hispania to get a closer look.

"Leave it! Sunlight will damage the color!" shouted the vendor.

She dropped the lid and moved on to look at the other supplies available to artists. The vendor guarded bowls of yellow iron ore to make shades of gold and yellow, sea snail shells to be ground for making precious purple, copper and numerous roots lined up in bowls like soldiers. These could be heated or mixed to create new colors. Vita wondered how to use them.

"Come on!" urged Aquilina jerking on Vita's tunic to break her away. "Let's go pick up the bread and get back to the villa!"

Vita paused. "I will have to be happy having my black soot and charred sticks for now, but someday I will draw with these colors."

THAT EVENING VITA sat in Telesphorus's tablinum, as usual, but was more intent on drawing and dreaming of the colors she needed to match the eyes and hair. She quietly sketched Certa's face from memory.

"What are you drawing tonight?" asked Telesphorus.

"The face of the new slave. What are you reading tonight?" she asked him.

"I'm reading about David tonight."

"You should read to me," she said.

"Keep thy tongue from evil, and thy lips from speaking guile. Depart from evil, and do good; seek peace, and pursue it. The eyes of the Lord are upon the righteous, and his ears are open unto their cry. The face of the Lord is against them that do evil, to cut off the remembrance of them from the earth. The righteous cry, and the Lord heareth, and delivereth them out of all their troubles. The Lord is nigh unto them that are of a broken heart; and saveth such as be of a contrite spirit. Many are the afflictions of the righteous: but the Lord delivereth him out of them all. He keepeth all his bones: not one shall be broken. Evil shall slay the wicked: and they that hate the righteous shall be desolate. The Lord redeemeth the soul of his servants: and none of them that trust in him shall be desolate."

"All I hear is a lot about troubles and evil and unhappiness. Why do you want to read that?" she said.

"You hear the troubles that we can expect; I hear the righteousness of God and His deliverance."

"It is all sadness. You can be in sadness all the time if you think about your troubles. I don't see God helping me with my troubles. They are only getting worse." She held up her drawing to inspect it, tilted her head, and began to sketch again.

Telesphorus looked upon Vita, who showed bravery and intelligence. He knew of her loss of freedom and family. He knew of Calitoria's attitude towards her. Sadness showed in her eyes.

Vita continued, mostly talking to herself. "Sometimes the sadness and grief are too much to endure. So I have to decide to not think about it at all. It doesn't go away with time, but time makes it easier to push it into a box and hold those feelings there because they hurt too much. Sometimes the feelings make me fall into the box and then it is hard to climb back out." Tears welled in her eyes and she looked up at Telesphorus. "See, here they come now. They are only a thought away. The sadness is too much to bear."

She stared at him, blinded by tears, and blinked heavily to squeeze them back in to continue her drawing, but the tears stayed. She brushed them away.

"Private hurts are not to be shared with others. They don't want to hear them."

"I want to hear them. I care about you," he said.

She expected her friend to make a comment like, "You will get better," or "It is time to get over it and move on," or "Everybody has troubles," but he didn't. It would be an insult for him to answer this wise child with an inane remark. So they spent the rest of the evening in caring silence.

Chapter Sixteen

It rained during the night. The cobblestone pavement, washed of grime, was left cool and clean. The smell of damp earth signaled the new day. Quintus arrived as usual before dawn with his whistled melody. Vita joined him and moved through the streets toward the docks. Their daily routine had forged a solid friendship, but Vita felt more toward Quintus than friendship. She wondered if Quintus cared for her even the smallest amount.

"Where are your sandals?" he asked, realizing that Vita had a cautious step this morning, wincing as she encountered small sharp stones.

"Calitoria took them," she answered.

"But why?"

"She thinks I don't know that she did it. She crept in last night during the rain and removed them from the side of the bed. I don't know why. Maybe to stop me from going to the docks, maybe to make me look stupid when I can't find my sandals, maybe to show she can control me."

"What will you do?"

"I will continue to do everything as normal, without my sandals."

Quintus shook his head. "When does Gaius leave?" he asked.

"He leaves tomorrow. Telesphorus will travel with him to Puteoli where Gaius will board his ship. I think Telesphorus wants to see him off, but he also wants to hear a Jewish man speak, named Paul, who is in Puteoli."

Quintus was worried. He predicted that things would be worse for Vita when Gaius left. Especially, since he would be gone for a year or two.

"Quintus, I want to tell you something," said Vita in her soft voice. "I care for you. In fact, I think I love you. You are such a good person. You are so kind to me. I don't even care that you think of me as a child. Inside, I feel the same feelings that a grown-up has towards someone they love. When I am not with you, I long for you. You are always in my thoughts and always in my heart. I just want to be with you forever."

He reached over and pulled off her cap, letting her shaggy hair fall. He ruffled it gently but said nothing. Her words held too much emotion for Quintus. He already knew that she loved him, he had for some time, but she was just a girl masquerading as a boy named Vitalis, a friend.

LATER IN THE DAY, everyone in the villa helped Gaius prepare to leave. Thana tearfully gave her son several pair of warm socks she had knitted. She added parchment to his bag insisting that he write to her and gave him a ring to wear to gain favor with the gods. Lavinia packed olives, bread, and wine for their trip. Calitoria made sure her husband packed his *sagum*, a red woolen cloak worn by Roman soldiers, for cold weather in Britannia. Telesphorus and Gaius studied details of the farm and vineyard construction that was already underway.

The kitchen slaves gathered around Lavinia asking questions.

"How will we be protected from thieves or poverty without Gaius?"

"Will Telesphorus take his place, or will Calitoria be in charge?"

AT DAWN THE NEXT MORNING, Gaius and Telesphorus left for Puteoli. Soon after, Lavinia and Aquilina began preparing the morning meal. Talistia helped Calitoria dress for the day, and Certa, the new slave, transplanted herbs in the garden. Someone knocked on the kitchen door, and Lavinia answered it thinking it was a client selling some food.

"Where is Vitalia?" asked Quintus as soon as she opened the door.

"What do you mean? We thought she was at the docks with you," answered Lavinia.

"No, I came by this morning as usual and whistled for her. She is always ready and waiting for me, but she never came down so I went on to work at the docks. I guessed she must be sick or the family required her to do something else today."

"Aquilina, do you know where Vitalia is?" questioned Lavinia.

"No, she was gone when I woke up. I thought she went to the docks with Quintus."

"I'm sure she is here somewhere. You go on to the gem cutter's, Quintus. We'll find her," said Lavinia.

"I'll come back tomorrow morning to pick her up. Tell her I missed her," he answered and left.

Chapter Seventeen

"I knew she was a goddess," said Thana as she brushed away some invisible dark shadow. "She is magical. She transformed herself. I prayed to the family ancients to send someone to save us and they sent her and now she is gone. Maybe she traveled to Britannia with Gaius to protect him. She might have transformed into a winged creature or a goat or a bull!" She raised her eyebrows and caressed her throat.

"I have looked for her everywhere," said Aquilina. "I can't ask Talistia. I don't want her to tell Calitoria." Aquilina began to cry. "Maybe she got rid of her. She could. She could sell her! What can we do?"

Lavinia thought out loud. "Maybe she ran off with Quintus. If she did she will be branded as a runaway. Quintus surely knows that. He would not encourage it. We should check with him again. She may have told him of plans to run away. Aquilina, go to the gem cutter's and ask Quintus if he knows anything. We must find her before Calitoria misses her."

"Unless she killed her!" shouted Thana with eyes widened.

"No. She could just be hiding somewhere," said Lavinia to calm Thana's outburst. "Maybe she went to Puteoli with Telesphorus and Gaius. Nobody knows whether they took her. Let's wait to tell Calitoria until Telesphorus returns. We will all feel silly for thinking these horrible thoughts when Telesphorus and Vitalia return together. Perhaps Calitoria knows Vitalia went with them and that is why she hasn't been looking for her."

Aquilina walked to the gem cutter's store front where Quintus sat at his bench grinding stones. Wearing a look of concern, he stood up and walked out to see what she wanted.

"Vitalia is missing. Did she say anything to you about going anywhere? We think she might be in Puteoli with the master and Telesphorus." Before Quintus could respond, she blurted, "I know she wanted to run away. No one else in the villa knew that but me. She always planned to leave, but never would she leave without telling me. We are good friends."

Quintus searched his thoughts and shook his head. "Maybe she knew she was leaving. She told me she loved me yesterday. I didn't say anything in return. I disappointed her. You think she ran away?"

"I'm afraid it could be something worse. Things have not been safe for her in the villa. The mistress..."

"I know. Vitalia told me."

He rubbed his brow looking to the heavens, trying to remember if she had said anything. Thoughts raced through his head confusing him.

"As soon as I can get away, I will go down to the docks and to the beach and anywhere else that I think she could be. I'll find her," he told Aquilina.

"Thank you, Quintus."

As the day passed a slow feeling of dread took hold of their hearts. It was hard not to imagine the worst things that could have happened. Yet, no one spoke aloud those thoughts. They kept encouraging each other to think that she was well and safe.

"Get on with your chores," said Lavinia. "If anyone hears anything, come find us and let us know."

~

AQUILINA FINALLY SPOKE WITH TALISTIA. "Do you know where Vitalia is? Don't say anything to Calitoria because we don't want her to get in trouble, but we can't find her."

"No, but something funny is happening with Calitoria. She usually has me go with her everywhere, but the last few days she has been making local visits without me. She left today then came back all flushed and excited. I think she might be seeing the Gladiator, Severus, maybe to hire him to accompany her to Pompeii. Whatever it is, she holds a secret," said Talistia. Then she added, "But I do know something about her plans for Vitalia when Gaius is gone. I was listening outside of Severus's place a few weeks ago. It is horrible. I can't tell you. I know her too well. She would kill me. I am so afraid."

Aquilina went back to the kitchen to tell the others.

"Do you think Calitoria sold her? Or killed her?" asked Aquilina, more frantic than ever. "Vitalia is a slave. No one would do anything. Has Quintus come by? He was going to look for her. Maybe she ran off with Quintus, and he is just pretending to look."

Thana had a theory from her perch in the kitchen. "I don't trust that new slave, Certa. He never speaks. He is a criminal to the Empire. Maybe he is a murderer and he killed her!"

"Now we are speaking about things we do not know," said Lavinia. "The most likely scenario is that Vitalia got up early to go to the docks with Quintus, but Gaius and Telesphorus decided to take her with them to Puteoli. Telesphorus likes her. He is also a valued slave who has the master's ear, so maybe he persuaded Gaius to take her. Maybe he asked for her company so that when he goes to listen to the Jewish Rabbi, Paul, he would have her with him. You know he likes to talk to Vitalia about his thoughts and studies. She is a friend to him." She paused satisfied in convincing herself. "None of us were awake when they left today, so how could we know?"

Silence saturated the kitchen. Lavinia returned to her cooking then stated, "We are going to wait, and we will see her when Telesphorus brings her home."

Chapter Eighteen

Hope is a wonderful thing. It lifts the dread. It heals the spirit. It makes one feel powerful. It makes one predict good not evil. It makes waiting possible. A suspended space of existence in good, rather than facing the probable future of horrible and worse. This described Lavinia's existence frozen in hope. Everyone decided Vita must be with Telesphorus.

Quintus came by the villa each day. Hopeful, but unable to wait, he reported frantically searching everywhere and finding nothing. He checked with the slave traders in Pompeii to see if she had been sold. He searched the brothels, questioning girls and owners. For days he scoured the streets of Herculaneum, forcing himself to be visible if she sheltered in disguise as a runaway.

Then came the evening when the thick, heavy front door of protection opened, and Telesphorus walked into the atrium, dropping his bag and removing his cap. The slaves and Thana ran to welcome the return of their beloved slave child. They waited for Vita to follow him through the threshold.

"What is going on?" asked Telesphorus feeling an atmosphere of fear and dread.

They watched while only the diminishing light of dusk passed through the doorway. No one followed him. He stood motionless.

Everyone tried to peer past him, hopeful that the young girl straggled behind. They waited. A vacant awareness settled in the pit of their stomachs. Aquilina covered her face and began to weep, no one else made a sound, they only stared.

Thana spoke first. "The slave girl, Vitalia, has disappeared. She has extinguished her earthly body and returned to her home with the gods, she has vanished to the spirit world," she stated with a grand gesture toward floating phantoms, smiling with eyes bright, gray hair wild like strands of frayed rope.

Calitoria, entering the atrium from her room, heard Thana's announcement. Surprised and shocked, she began asking the needed questions. Telesphorus stood baffled by the scene he was witnessing.

"Well, where is she?" he asked incredibly.

"If she has run away, I will find her and deliver the punishments myself," said Calitoria.

It seemed that these two suspects genuinely expressed pure innocence. Lavinia felt a deep sadness permeate her body. She felt weak realizing there was no way to find Vita now, and all the theories of her whereabouts were ended. Now, Telesphorus and Calitoria would repeat the frustrating search in all the same places. Grief replaced hope.

Imagine, reader, how horrible the thoughts can be when someone you care about or love, is absent whether by choice or evil. Could Vita have chosen to disappear without even saying goodbye after so many have loved her and cared for her? It would be easy to be angry. Could Vita have been harmed? Taken? Was she being hurt by someone? Visions of torture and unspeakable atrocities invade the mind. How could they know? How could they help her? Would Vita choose to cause them so much worry and hurt on purpose?

Lavinia believed that Vita would never have been so cruel to those who had taken her in as family and cared for her. She believed Vita was dead or unable to return, too kind and caring a person to purposely cause such tremendous sorrow to anyone. Either way, hope was gone. The hurt streamed unbearable.

Calitoria, usually a person only caring for herself, seemed overwrought with worry. The household watched as she searched and questioned and tried everything to recover the slave girl, astonished to discover a woman could disappear and no authority would track her or even felt she was worthy of finding.

"Just buy a new slave. You know you never cared for Vitalia," said Telesphorus. "It would do no good to complain to the Roman courts. They are overwhelmed with similar complaints of runaway slaves. It would be an arduous process and only if you can prove that she committed some crime. Go back to taking care of the villa and the slaves that you have. Go back to being a wife. Forget about the slave girl."

IN THE DAYS THAT FOLLOWED, Lavinia and the kitchen slaves and Talistia became more and more fearful. If one of them could be taken and considered an expendable human being, then staying close together was their only security. Telesphorus knew their fear and called them all to the atrium.

"I believe we should never allow any of our female family members to go anywhere without a male escort. You must be accompanied by myself or Certa or we will hire the former Gladiator, Severus, to go with you. If you must shop or travel, you must have one of us with you. If you are working elsewhere or visiting someone outside of the home, you must take one of us with you. Stay inside the walls of our villa for all your daily activities. Continue to garden, cook, weave, clean, and work as always, but you must be careful. A female can easily be overpowered and harmed," he said.

Everyone left the atrium understanding why they must be careful, but it would be a change that made them feel some of their freedoms had been taken away. They gathered in the kitchen to prepare the evening meal.

"It's funny how Certa, the new slave, is now such an important member. I'm not sure he is so reliable. He is nicer looking with his bath and haircut, but he still hasn't spoken a word," said Aquilina.

"I would rather they teach us to defend ourselves with swords and knives or even poison than treat us like prisoners," said Thana. "Women need to know how to defend themselves. I want to go to the Temple by myself. I want to visit my friends without taking the arrogant giant Gladiator with me. I'm sure we won't bother Telesphorus with our trips here and there. He has so much to do managing the clients and doing his numbers. He will not be available to us. And Certa! Who can trust that enemy slave! This won't last long. I'm going to do what I want."

Lavinia finally spoke. "We will do as we are told and hope Vitalia will return to us. We must not think of the horrible things that might have happened to her." Her voice broke at the end as she bowed her head to choke back tears. "Besides, if we had knives and swords, they would just be wrestled away from us."

"Yes, and then the attacker would use our own weapon to kill us," shouted Talistia.

"Why, Talistia! I don't believe I have ever seen you so angry," said Lavinia.

"Well, I am angry. We are all fearful for our lives now, and I think there are some people in this villa that know more about what happened to Vitalia than they are saying. Or maybe they are just upset that they weren't the one to cause her disappearance, and they are really glad she is gone. Maybe Vitalia ran away before someone did something to her," said Talistia.

"Hush! You must never say anything like that or even think it. Never, never, make any more comments about it. Don't forget your place." Lavinia stared sternly at Talistia then glanced to the door. It was enough to cause Talistia to break down.

"You are such a fragile, little girl," said Aquilina. "It only takes words to slay you!"

"Girls, enough! Talistia, get back to your weaving. Aquilina, you have bread to prepare. Get to work," ordered Lavinia.

Chapter Nineteen

F our Days Earlier

GAIUS HELD his helmet under his arm as he watched his belongings being loaded on the Imperial ship. Impressive, wearing his leather and bronze garment with segmented armor, he stood straight with angular jaw, muscular arms and legs, defining a Roman soldier of personal courage, honor, and integrity. His hand-tooled baldric hung diagonally over one shoulder with an attached sheath cradling his weapon, all inherited from his father. His woolen tunic dropped to his knees, dyed with crimson madder by his mother for her beloved son. These cherished items cemented the tradition of serving the Empire throughout generations. He proudly wore a new heart-guard breastplate purchased especially for this assignment.

As a commander, he supervised the arrival of military supplies from Alexandria and transferred them to naval vessels going to Britannia. The harbor at Puteoli, central to commerce in the Empire and one of the largest ports close to the Appian Road, had a perfect coastline to accept goods. The port of Puteoli distributed products from the Mediterranean and Egypt daily during the clement months. Necessary grain for the people of Rome and the surrounding Empire filled the ships with deliveries that included the soldiers stationed to protect the borders.

Gaius supervised the loading of grain on the naval ships, capable of carrying 400 tons, headed to his destination, Britannia. He also needed to collect building materials, including heavy stone ingredients to create concrete completing Emperor Claudius's Temple in Camulodunum. The former Emperor, now a god to the Romans, needed a proper place of worship for his deity. Gaius's assignment: to supervise the engineers, construct the roads surrounding the Temple area, and complete the Temple.

It should take a week to collect and load the supplies. In the meantime, he would enjoy a trip to the healing sulphur baths in the city and then travel to Baiae, a nearby city to explore. Telesphorus stood beside him on the pier.

"I know I am here to assist you," he said, "but I would like it very much if you would come with me to hear the Jewish man named Paul speaking in Puteoli. Some of his followers called Christians have offered me lodging, and I am sure you would be welcome, too."

Telesphorus studied Gaius's face to see if he was willing to join him, but Gaius long ago decided to cancel out extraneous thoughts in order to focus on his assignment in the army. His aloof face revealed nothing. This was the man that became a Roman soldier to fulfill his requirement to the Empire, his other persona, separate from the caring family man.

"Those are my belongings!" he shouted as the handlers interrupted his thoughts with the urgency to claim his bags. His dark mood lifted as he began to survey the port of Puteoli. "This city really is quite beautiful, if you can ignore the stench of sulphur from the pits."

Gaius looked out over the harbor with its wide piers held in place by stone arches anchored under water with concrete that Puteoli produced, the same *pozzulana*, volcanic dust, he would be taking to Britannia for the construction of buildings, the same lime burnt from limestone to add to the mix. Add the marble statues holding sentry, glittering in the sunlight, and you had a scene that displayed the genius of the Empire.

Giant ships with their oars at rest were anchored out in the bay while smaller vessels worked to transport goods from ship to ship or ship to land. Hundreds of men, some poor, some slaves, some foreign, labored to work this pivotal port, with its industrial coastline, for Rome. Sea birds cried and begged while seamen shouted and did scut work under the burning sun. Most of the goods came from Egypt and the Orient culminating their voyage here, then the ships would reload with Roman amphorae filled with olive oil, wine, garum, cedar logs, pozzulana, marble, and whatever commerce demanded to return home. While this activity provided a reverie of noise and chaos, the added arrival of tourists eager to visit the hot springs and neighboring cities added fuss and pother to the soup.

"I will take you up on the lodging offer, but I am not sure I want to listen to your religious oracle. I have duties to enough gods paying loyalty and homage. I don't need another," Gaius finally answered. "Still, I need a place to stay. The closest inns are filthy and debauched in Puteoli, catering mostly to military. I am sure your friends will provide better food and a clean bed and maybe some peace. I will come at least for tonight."

Wall Painting from Stabiae, 1st Century

AFTER GAIUS COMPLETED supervision at the docks, Telesphorus led him to the nearby Christian community where he heard that a Centurian named Julius was holding the Rabbi, Paul, prisoner. After asking a few shopkeepers if they knew where they would find the Christian brethren, they found the area easily. Everyone seemed to know that Paul was in Puteoli. Gaius and Telesphorus overheard his name mentioned here and there as they walked. Some groups spoke of his knowledge of God, some spoke of his teachings of Jesus the Messiah.

They stopped to join a group of men, intending to ask for directions. Easing into the group, they did not interrupt the discussion. One man said Paul was chained arm in arm with a Roman soldier and was pausing here on his way to prison in Rome. Another said that Paul must be afraid to go to Rome, that being on trial could only mean the end of his life.

"On no, he says he needs to go to Rome," said a man who appeared to know him personally.

"Well, he will surely be stopped and imprisoned there. How can that be good for the message of Jesus to be spread?" the other answered.

"He thinks that Rome is the place to start. Before he was crucified, Jesus told his friends to spread his message to the ends of the earth. Paul comes from a family of commerce, so he knows that Rome is filled with people from every country who will return home with the message of the Messiah and the teachings of Jesus. That is how and why his goal is to reach Rome. Ha! It is ironic that his arrest is causing the Empire to fund the trip!"

"He will wait on Emperor Nero to judge him. Now that is ironic! Nero, who just had his mother murdered not far from here in Baiae. How can an evil man judge a righteous man?" said another.

"Hush! Someone might hear your sedition and report you!" They glanced suspiciously around them and then their eyes fell on the new strangers standing behind their group, Telesphorus with Gaius, who was wearing his soldier's uniform. Fear registered on their faces as they all turned to study them. One of the men bent down and drew a curved line in the dirt with a stick. He stood up expecting a response from Gaius and Telesphorus.

Telesphorus bent low and drew a corresponding curved line under it. He took advantage of their sudden silence to interrupt and make inquiries.

"Greetings to all of you. We are searching for a Christian Brethren family. Do you happen to know of my friend from Herculaneum, Marci Helvii Erotis? He is here staying with relatives. The family came to hear and see Paul, and we would like to join them. Do you know where they might be staying?"

The men refused to speak, turned their backs, and walked away.

The one who seemed to know Paul stayed.

"You know Marci?"

"Of course, I know the Helvii family. I can take you there. I am going that way now. They live very close and are honorable people. I am Gnaeus and I came from Baiae to hear Paul speak."

"The city seems to be quite excited that Paul is here," remarked Telesphorus as he followed Gnaeus toward the Helvii home.

"Yes, if you have not heard him speak, he will change your life. He speaks of Jesus and a new life, a new way of living, a new hope to be with the true God for eternity."

"What is his profession? Is he a priest or psyche? Who appointed him to speak to so many? How is he qualified?" asked Gaius.

"He is a man that was chosen by God. He was not one of the first followers. In fact, he was sent by the Jewish authorities to persecute the remaining believers after Jesus was crucified. You must come and hear his conversion. Only he can explain.

"Here is the Helvii home. They are part of the Craestus Brethren, also called Christians. It is good that I have met you. I will leave you here," said Gnaeus.

They followed a long blank wall and rattled the knocker of a wooden door that gave no hint of the villa behind it. A towering slave opened the door motioning for them to enter. Passing from the bright sunshine to the dim villa, their eyes needed to adjust before they could see the many guests sitting on the floor of the atrium. Marci Helvii Erotis came to greet them.

"I'm so pleased you came," he said with hushed tones. "You both are welcome to join us. We are listening to one of our brothers speak about the teachings of Jesus. We should be finished soon and be able to make you comfortable."

The two men, Gaius in soldier uniform and Telesphorus in homespun tunic, sat on a bench to wait. Soon a beautiful voice began a melody, barely changing in pitch, singing words familiar to Telesphorus from his readings in the Torah. The melody continued to repeat words from the ancient writings. Then a man stood up to speak. He quoted scriptures about the Canaanites. He spoke of Joshua when God told him to exterminate his enemies. He then spoke of Jesus.

"Jesus said the opposite. He said to show mercy to your enemies, to be merciful and not judge them, not show vengeance. Why has God changed His message? Is there no longer evil in the world? No, there is still evil. The difference is Jesus. He came to do God's will. He made our final sacrifice," said the old man who paused in his pacing.

"All have sinned and fall short, which makes us separated from God.

The price for sin is death, but God has no pleasure in the death of anyone. Jesus took upon himself God's judgment for all who have sinned. He knew his mission and purpose. He took our punishment for us. We are no longer separated from God. Jesus came to save the world through him."

He sat down and bread was presented. They each passed the loaf and broke off pieces. Someone spoke some words. Gaius and Telesphorus sat back in the shadows and watched, unable to hear all that was said. Then wine was presented and shared.

More words were read and more of the beautiful singing, then the meeting was over. Several members came up to greet Gaius and Telesphorus. No one seemed discomfited. In fact, an air of tranquility filled the place as soft laughter echoed in the atrium.

"Are these people speaking about a new mythological god I have not heard of?" asked Gaius. "They act like he is a person not a god."

"So sorry to neglect you. As you see we are fortunate to be able to host the meeting today," said Marci. He called for a slave to take their belongings and called for a basin and water. Marci bent down with towels and began to wash Telesphorus's feet.

"But Marci, why are you doing this? You have slaves. It is their job to welcome us and cleanse us."

"You know, Jesus washed the feet of his brethren. He said we are to serve others. It is my blessing to serve you."

He shifted over to wash Gaius's feet. Gaius stood abruptly, stepped away and waved him off.

"Tell me, Marci, there must be a cost to join your group?" asked Gaius.

"Oh yes, you would think that." Marci searched the soldier's face. "It will cost you everything. Everything you have been and will be. It requires your life. You will want to change the way you have lived, the way you have loved, the way you are in the world. The cost is your life. You will become a new person with the Messiah in your life." Gaius examined this man who humbled himself as a slave to wash his feet.

A slave girl with delicate features and soft brown hair came to remove the basin and towels. She captured Gaius's attention and he began to stare.

"You own a very beautiful slave. What is her name?" asked Gaius.

Marci faced Gaius carefully constructing his answer. "Her name is Vestia." He paused again and then explained. "I know it is customary in Roman society to provide slaves for your pleasure if you are a guest in the home but understand that all of my slaves and the slaves of my family members are followers. We treat them as family. Just as I would never offer my sister for pleasure, I would not offer Vestia. She is part of our Craestus Brethren family. She is my sister in Jesus the Messiah."

Gaius nodded, although he truly did not understand. He felt he had trespassed in some way. None of his friends thought of their slaves as equals in family.

"She must be a freed slave?"

"Not now. That will be her decision. She is cared for in our family. It might be something in the future for her," Marci answered. "Come around and let me introduce you to the others."

Gaius and Telesphorus met many men and women. Some were local residents, some had traveled from farms, some were from distant cities. All seemed to exhibit a confidence or firm trust in what they believed and why they were there.

"So, you have come to Puteoli to hear our Paul speak," assumed Marci's wife Korinna.

"Well, no. I am here to prepare and load materials for the settlements and soldiers in Britannia. My companion here is curious to hear Paul speak," said Gaius.

"We are happy to have you with us," said Korinna. Marci came up behind her and put his arm across her shoulder.

"I must steal my wife away for a moment. Some of my new friends do not believe that I was a winner in the public festival games. I used to be quite a runner and they seem to be doubting my abilities, probably because of the roundness of my middle. Korinna you must come and witness for me," he laughed.

GAIUS SPENT time at the Helvii villa in the evenings. Marci would sit with them and talk about how he viewed life and his responsibilities to God, himself, and others. Gaius and Telesphorus had never known a friend like him. It was intriguing to know someone who knew what he believed and why. He constructed his life governed by self examination and following what a man named Jesus taught. Gaius never considered being a better person according to a god's commandments. All the gods he knew were aloof and selfish, not loving. Their legends were hard to believe and did not require any reform of self.

On his last morning at the Helvii villa, Gaius dressed in his full uniform. He gathered his belongings and met Telesphorus at the door, eager to slip away secretly. The sun was not yet entering the sky as they stepped out on the street. Marci noticed and hurried to stop him.

"I must give you our Blessing before you leave. May God be with you and prepare a safe path for you. May God send you ministering angels to protect you from harm. I and my family will include you in our daily prayers."

"Thank you. I leave my family and financial responsibilities in our friend's hands. Telesphorus, I trust your judgment. The farm improvements are to be continued. There shouldn't be any clients that have needs or services that we haven't already discussed. If a problem comes up, you can write to me in Britannia but it could take months to get a reply, especially during the winter when sea routes may be closed, so most decisions should be yours to make. You are my good friend and a good man." Gaius turned toward Marci. "I want to stay in Britannia and finish service and then retire to a quiet life with my family and friends. Good fortune to you and may the gods favor you."

With those words, Gaius turned and left Telesphorus standing with Marci. Telesphorus wondered if he should call him back and reveal the secret he was hiding. It felt wrong to know something so important and not tell his master, but the words sealed his throat.

GAIUS RETURNED to his old familiar ways, living, soldiering, and worshiping as before, but he could not forget his experience of a culture filled with attitudes and behaviors of a group set apart. They earned a respect from him like no other. It created an imbalance in his mind when he compared them to the Empire's traditional philosophies of Apollo, Mithras, Hercules, Venus, Isis, or the deity of the Emperors. There was something very genuine about them, a peace that was solid. A man called Jesus gave his life for others. This, he understood, because soldiers gave their life for the Empire. They said this Jesus's life was a sacrifice paid for others so they could spend eternity with their God. However, he had been taught from birth to seek the gods' attention for good fortune, not eternity. He was more comfortable with those thoughts. Yet, what if they were right?

Chapter Twenty

Gaius returned to the Puteoli docks to find an early morning gray mist blanketing the vessels and buildings. Although the sun had lightened the sky, the moist haze still obliterated the harbor. They would wait to set sail.

He squinted, straining to see the large trireme at anchor, embraced by fog, ready to leave for Britannia. The other smaller bireme and accompanying safety ship, erased by the mist, must be somewhere ready to leave. He could hear voices of seamen and passengers, but without visible bodies, they haunted as apparitions in another dimension. Gaius walked toward the boats transporting elite soldiers out to waiting ships. Through the thick fog, he could only guess their existence.

A small silhouette of a human figure stood motionless on the dock. The shape reminded him of Vitalia, the favored slave girl he left behind. The shortened hair, the slim body, the tunic were all the same. He called out to her, "Vitalia?" The figure turned and seemed to stare directly at him then disappeared into the mist. He stepped forward to go after her, pausing to wonder if he had seen anything at all.

It couldn't be Vitalia. Mother thinks Vitalia is a goddess able to transform and appear and disappear, but it could not have been her. Just a touch of homesickness passing through me making me see things, he thought.

Gaius waited until the sun gradually revealed the bireme, trireme, and a quadrireme, loaded and waiting. A favorable wind would assist the tiers of more than three hundred oarsmen to power the warships up to nine or ten knots. It would take one or two weeks to reach Britannia depending on the weather.

Gaius and six supervising soldiers climbed in the transport boat. They would replace the retiring architects and surveyors currently developing the city of Camulodunum, designated the capital of Britannia, a town for retiring soldiers with theatre, Forum and Temple. As they rowed toward the waiting ships, one soldier named Pontius shared the latest news of the area.

"Have you heard of the unrest in Britannia? The Iceni tribe united some of the neighboring tribes as a force against Rome. They have always fought each other until now but have been united by a queen, named Boudicca, against us. I hear that she is horribly ugly with bright orange unkempt hair and a heinous face."

"How is it that she unified the barbarians?" asked Gaius.

Pontius answered, "Some Druid magic. Some say she has an evil temperament. After her husband died, who was a client king of the Empire, she went into a rage. All Celts are not really human. They are degenerates."

"There must have been a cause to get them to unite. Especially, if they have fought each other for years," remarked Gaius, remembering his conversation with Balbus.

"You would think they would see the advantage of being a part of the Roman Empire and become Roman," Pontius sharply responded.

"Do you think the queen is really that ugly? Look how the Romans still talk about the defeated Egyptian queen, Cleopatra. They say she was hideous to your sight, but how could she have been? She got both Julius Caesar and Mark Antony to fall in love with her. Power requires beauty in a woman," said Gaius.

Another soldier named Dracus interjected.

"Queen Boudicca's tribe hoped for peace by applying her husband's will, which called for half of the Iceni kingdom to go to Emperor Nero and the Roman Empire and the other half to be kept for the Iceni Tribe. Decianus, the royal procurator tax collector, and the Governor decided that the client king's treaty was null and void after his death and moved into the Iceni territory taking it as land for the Empire. He sent soldiers and slaves to confiscate valuables and treat it as any conquered people. The Iceni had no way to retaliate as we confiscated all their weapons years ago."

This news was unsettling to Gaius, worse than he thought.

"Did they take them as slaves?"

"Well, you know some soldiers get carried away with their victories," he laughed. "The usual rape, pillage, burn. You have to show your superiority and some soldiers have a bit of a licentious soul. It was an opportunity to increase the wealth of the Empire and show who is in charge now." Dracus shrugged. "And yes, we took slaves, even some of the royal Iceni family. Of course, we sold them."

The group boarded the Roman transport trireme and began the voyage north. The afternoon sun cleared the sky to a beautiful blue with a crisp wind behind them. Each day, Gaius leaned on the railing astonished by the beauty of the uninhabited coast. The wind played with his hair as he stood near the bow breathing the salty air. He watched sea gulls follow the wakes of the ships, circling the masts and diving for food. *Neptune must be the favorite god to rest in the beauty of the sea,* he thought. *These days have such pleasant weather and sunshine.*

Days passed. The farther north they sailed, the more the sea scorned the passengers, causing the men to weave an unsteady dance to stay upright while insulting them with ceaseless cold, drenching rain. Gaius summoned endurance as he longed for his mild climate at home.

After weeks, they reached the designated landing point to transport supplies to the coast. It couldn't be a worse day to arrive, with tempest wind and low hanging clouds. Pontius squinted through the driving spray, hanging onto the ropes as the ship rolled with the swells.

"Can't we wait for a calm sea before we transport soldiers and supplies?" Gaius inquired of the captain and was met with laughter. Apparently, this was the expected sea for this area.

Gaius needed to oversee his cargo and hoped that nothing would be lost to the seas below, especially the statue of Emperor Claudius secured on the ship. He surveyed the ragged cliffs, wondering how they would transport the heavy equipment and supplies to the top. Ominous figures lined the crest. They were being watched by men in carts and on horseback, certainly not Romans.

"Never mind them," said Pontius as he turned to see what Gaius was watching. "Crazy Celts. They are always here harassing and spying. They can do nothing."

AFTER A FEW DAYS unloading the ships, Gaius and the others found time in the city to locate their living arrangements.

Camulodunum governed Britannia, all commands originated from the soldier settlement. The officers from the arriving vessels trudged through the main street, their boots sucking in the mud of the saturated ground as miserable rain continued to fall. Even in wet weather there was activity everywhere. They passed recruits practicing military pace, a crucial part of fighting in the field to maintain ranks in the presence of the enemy. Other soldiers were practicing with weapons made of wood or wicker against stakes six feet tall, building strength for battle. The group located the barracks and sought refuge in a nearby tavern for a good meal. When the door shut behind them cutting off the damp chill, a roaring fire welcomed them, luring them to a table in the crowded eatery.

"Is the weather always like this?" asked Gaius as they found seats and a table in the corner.

"It doesn't always rain, but it is cold and even colder. You probably want to buy some leggings to warm your ass!" Dracus laughed as he slammed his beer on the table. Gaius began to think about how long he would have to be with this regiment in this forlorn frontier.

"I'd like to get started immediately finishing the Claudius Temple. Let's meet in the morning at the Temple and see where this statue is to be placed and what walls and mosaics need to be finished. The road crew will just continue with our supervision. The arched walkway surrounding the Temple needs to be finished, too. Does anyone have a preference for what they would like to supervise?" asked Gaius. He thought it would be best to organize these men now and finish the project so everyone could get home or get on to their next assignment as soon as possible. Gaius took the most important job of erecting the huge bronze statue of Claudius, transported to this new settlement.

"How is the Empire paying for all this development in Britannia?" he asked.

"That's the beauty of conquering," smirked Dracus. "We tax the locals. They end up paying for the Temple and statue of Claudius. They pay for the Baths, streets, barracks! We pay nothing for the land where Camulodunum sits. We just move the tribe out and take it."

"Some of that has gone on in the towns near Herculaneum. Taking land from people without payment can create anger and resentment," reflected Gaius. He thought about the riots between Nuceria and Pompeii. Part of the cause of the fight was the Empire taking land from Nucerians and giving it to retiring soldiers.

"It's all about who is more powerful, my friend," reminded Dracus.

The more time Gaius spent with these architects and engineers, the more he wanted to finish this project and return home. At night they only looked forward to visiting the brothels, challenging each other, and gambling. They were not married and the brothel was a service available to the army. In fact, marriage was discouraged but not forbidden. Empire leaders realized family matters always distracted infantry. Still, some soldiers had relationships and brought them to the settlement.

Gaius preferred family life to soldier life, but not all men felt the same. He remained stone-faced and distant, his way to cope. He just needed to endure this last assignment. The army thankfully put money away for his retirement, twenty per cent of his pay waited for him. It would not be long before he could reap the benefits of a soldier's life. Soon he would be headed home to the life of peace he coveted, with money to prosper.

"Gaius, we are going to worship Mithras, the god of war, tonight. New converts are being inducted and rituals will be performed. You need to come," suggested Pontius.

"I'm not installed," replied Gaius.

Pontius was surprised. Not only was it nearly demanded of officers to join the religious cult, but prestige and promised advancement in the regiment came with the higher stages of rank in Mithras.

"Oh? I can help you to be installed. I will see what I can do for you."

Gaius nodded. He didn't feel the need to join or tell Pontius that he was not interested. He considered himself an engineer for the Empire, not infantry.

My life is not in danger. Mithras is for those that fight and can lose their life. Mithras takes those that fight to an afterlife for bravery. I am not in danger, he thought. He dismissed the invitation and went to work that night on his drawings for erecting the immense statue of the deity, Emperor Claudius.

The next day, Gaius climbed the marble steps and checked construction as he walked around the unfinished majestic Temple designed in a traditional octastyle, poured with a strong and deep foundation of mortar in stone trenches. Ten columns lined each side with eight in the front. He walked to the interior. It seemed to be a popular place for local children to play and explore. Several giggled and ran, hiding from each other behind the pillars. That would need to change to show respect for Emperor Claudius. He would suggest an area for exercise and games to the commander so the children would have a different place to play. Perhaps, he could create one before he left.

"Out of here!" He chastised the children, scattering them.

In back of the cella, a chamber close to where the statue would be placed, young people sat on the floor talking with each other. They were not misbehaving. It was a place of shelter from the cold and rain, windowless with grandiose bronze doors. Without the statue, it was understandable that the children would not realize this as a place to worship Emperor Claudius.

Gaius calculated how many men it would take to raise the towering bronze and copper statue. He would requisition the largest wagon and animals to deliver it. Scribbling measurements, recording materials for ropes and pulleys, he labored over details until confident his task could be done, unaware of ominous forces of vengeance awaiting.

Later, he found relaxation in the tavern sitting alone, appreciating a comforting beer. Other soldiers interrupted him, eager to discuss the unrest in the colony.

"Governor Suetonius Paulinus blames current and past adversity on the local religion. The Druid priests use magic and myth to control the Celts. Some say they practice human sacrifice, studying the entrails to intimidate. I think they put a curse on my entrails; I haven't been able to hold a good meal in me for weeks!" They all laughed.

"Paulinus thinks the unrest will continue until he subdues the Druids," another soldier commented. "In truth, they occupy the most lush and fertile land and rule the copper mines. We need to take control of that area for the Empire. In fact, my barrack mates heard that we may be moving north very soon to subdue and conquer them."

"Good!" shouted another. "I've had enough of this boring life, cleaning latrines and practicing fighting with sticks. I am ready to use my freshly polished dagger to slay the beastly barbarians!" He patted his beautiful side arm with its handle of inlaid silver and bone.

AFTER MANY DELAYS of supplies and weather, and training soldiers to raise the treasured statue, the day of Gaius's crowning achievement in Britannia came, the reason he'd come all this way and left his family behind. A wagon delivered the statue after prepared wooden ramps covered the steps to the Temple. A rail and pulley system erected on high frames stood ready to hoist Claudius to his feet on the marble pedestal. When the process began, the soldiers struggled against the swaying Emperor to position him perfectly on the stone slab. Children of the neighborhood gathered, watching the final act completing the Temple, cheering as the statue of the Emperor Tiberius Claudius Caesar Augustus Germanicus settled without injury. Their innocent eyes traveled up the giant muscular body of Claudius and rested on the polished head with its unforgiving likeness, portraying his weak chin, low forehead, and protruding ears.

"Yes, that is him," remarked Pontius as he stood back and passed judgment. "I saw him once in Rome near the Senate building. Not a handsome man, but remarkably intelligent and learned, a talented orator. The body is laughable. He was actually quite twisted, and had a bad leg."

Gaius finished directing the operation removing the frame and ramps. It took longer than planned but the project commanded respect from the subservient soldiers. He displayed unflappable comportment without arrogance. Watchful eyes of young boys examined and studied his behavior memorizing his attributes to nurture in their own lives. Soon they would be old enough to join the ranks of Roman Soldier of the most powerful Empire in the world. For now, they played at being soldiers, sparring with weapons, marching, wearing pretend uniforms, and watching the commanders. It would be a proud future for them and their families to defend or conquer lands for the superpower.

Gaius turned his thoughts toward home after a letter arrived from Calitoria. It was tucked in a package containing more woolen socks knitted by his mother and a figurine of Jupiter that had been blessed to carry protection against harm or evil.

The letter began with greetings from his wife and news of her pregnancy. He smiled while reading the letter. He knew how desperately she wanted a child, and it thrilled him to know that he was going to be a father. The letter continued with alarming news that the young slave girl whom he adored was missing. Calitoria outlined her attempts to find her without success. She clearly was frustrated by the authorities lack of concern and that Telesphorus had also been unable to locate her. Immediately, Gaius remembered the phantom Vitalia at Puteoli. *Minerva again?*

Chapter Twenty-One

Later that week, Gaius sensed the camp activity alter from its typical routine. Wagons pulled into the main street loaded with crossbows, javelins, and other weaponry. Soldiers counted and packed food. Cavalry groomed their mounts and dressed them with leather and metal gear. The Legion was moving out, preparing for battle, led by Governor Suetonius Paulinus, marching north and west to the Isle of Mona, the holy area for the Celts, where escaped rebels found protection and where the Druids sent out commands. Gaius would stay in Camulodunum as part of a small group of engineers to continue construction and activities separate from the movement of troops securing the region.

Hushed rumors of Celts gathering in revolt reached the town, of Iceni and Trinovantes tribes united in the East and as many as one hundred and twenty thousand rebels gathered under the command of a woman. Suetonius Paulinus asked his advisor, Decianus, if it was possible this woman, Boudicca, Queen of the Iceni, was capable of planning a rebellion. "Impossible!" Decianus bragged. "The widow queen is weak and submissive. My soldiers tied her to a stake, stripped her and beat her, then made her watch as we raped her young daughters. She is defeated. She knows that Rome conquered Britannia. The Iceni are a powerless, bankrupt tribe without weaponry."

Thus reassured, Paulinus pulled his Legion away as planned, but the townspeople panicked. The remaining families and officers sent messages to him pleading for protection. No fort wall surrounded the garrison. They felt unsafe. To placate them, Paulinus sent back a force of two hundred men to remain in their barracks.

It was hard to adjust to the uneventful town with most of the populace missing. Weeks went by with very little distraction from the cold and dismal weather. During the shortened days of winter, Gaius and his group of engineers busied themselves with the archway construction. At nightfall, which came quite early in winter, they lounged in the bars drinking and gambling with the rest of the spiritless soldiers.

"Fire!" came a shout from the street. "Fire!" Tavern chairs and tables tumbled as patrons jumped to run outside and help.

Every available adult ran to the east edge of town where flames turned the nighttime sky red. Gaius ran with the others toward the orange hue. A burning shack with flames licking the sky, threatening to spread its torch through the town, pulled everyone together to set up a chain to transport buckets of water from the river to extinguish the threat.

"Stay back!" Gaius yelled pulling curious youngsters out of the way pushing them to the edge of the forest. The fire refused to surrender and spread devastation from one shack to the next, part of a sinister plan.

As if they had disturbed a hornet's nest, hundreds of two-wheeled chariots ambushed out of the dark. Swords flashed from invaders who stabbed and chopped at bodies from every direction. The barbarians screamed threats in a foreign tongue as they chased and hacked. Chariots whirled down the street, torches were thrown into homes and barracks. Gaius gathered the children yelling for others to follow him as he headed away from the enemy, up the street toward the center of town. Rebels leaped from chariots slashing and stabbing face to face. Women and children were not spared. Those hiding were dragged from their homes and slaughtered. Gaius shouted to his group to head to the safest structure in Camulodunum, the Temple of Claudius. The residents understood and pushed past him toward the temple.

A young lad fell hard in front of him. Gaius scooped him under his left arm running with the mob of civilians and soldiers. He grabbed the hand of another child pulling her faster than she could run dragging her to the Temple. They ran up the steps surrounded by an arc of soldiers forming a perimeter of protection.

The tribes could not be stopped. They hacked and fought, screaming, while the charioteers continued torching the town. Residents that did not make it to the Temple could be heard pleading for their lives. Gaius turned to join the fight near the outer columns, assessing the melee, searching for safety. He stabbed and fought gripping his sword with both hands meeting jabs left, right, diagonally, dodging to keep from being hit. The swift counter attack left a deep wound to his arm. He fell back to the floor searching for escape.

"Everyone to the cella!" yelled a soldier. That would be the best protection. They retreated deep into the Temple running for the cella. Gaius grasped the young children, and picked up a fallen boy, guiding them to the cella. Time stopped when one young, slim girl called out to him, "No, not that way! You will all die there. Come, follow me."

Gaius pulled his young friends with him to follow her. They ran out the back of the Temple to the woods. The young girl stood at the edge dressed in a simple white tunic, barefoot, warm and dry in the drizzle and cold. She pointed to the ground and disappeared. It looked like there was nothing there but dirt and debris, but the children understood what to do. They dove into trenches, dug in the past, where they daily played. The children had been imitating the soldiers by digging safe holes in the ground for weeks! They pulled branches and turf over their heads, blending into their surroundings. Gaius hushed the children and settled into the moist hole.

"No one make a sound. No matter what you hear or see, do not move or make a sound." He put his arm around the unconscious boy and mopped the wound on his forehead. His own arm ached and bled but must be ignored.

Screams of women and children could be heard echoing from the town. The smell of burning human flesh seeped into their burrow. Chariots rumbled up and down the streets killing everything in sight. Gaius crawled up, finding a small hole in the debris, to watch what was happening. Hundreds of barbarians surrounded the Temple as soldier against Celt slashed and stabbed. Shouts and growls of warriors, and the clang of iron swords, resounded a chaotic rhythm. Then he saw her. The queen named Boudicca.

She rode her horse with skill unlike any woman he knew. The slim, athletic body of warrior queen and steed appeared as one. Her gauche gown of red and gold would never be worn by any Roman woman. A brightly woven cape held in place by a golden Celtic brooch flowed behind her, covering her shoulders and the horse. The gallant queen's long red hair followed the wind, mimicking the tongues of flames that burned the homes around her. She turned her mount sharply to face a two-wheeled cart driven by two young girls, her daughters, who joined in the slaughter. Boudicca raised her sword and shouted deadly commands in her harsh voice. This was the woman the Romans mistakenly thought was a stupid barbarian incapable of leading a rebellion.

Celts rode their horses up the majestic Temple steps, tied ropes around the statue of Claudius, pulled it off its pedestal, and dragged it into the street. The bronze head broke free, leaving the huge body behind. The horse and rider joyfully heaved the head behind and through the town toward the river. Screams and cheers rang out when the tribes saw the severed head, the symbol of their oppression, as if they'd killed the Emperor himself. Gaius looked back at the Temple of Claudius. Bloodied bodies littered the marble steps as the fighting continued. Near the archway, the barbarians raised wooden staffs with skewered residents aloft. Maniacs even hacked at dead bodies waving dismembered parts above their heads.

Gaius eased back down into the trench to see who hid with him. No other soldier had made it to the edge of the forest. He was alone with this crew. His eyes fell on each member of his small group one by one. Two young boys of around ten years old, a four-year-old little girl and this lad that he cradled in his arms. There was no sign of the slim girl dressed in white that had directed them to this spot.

The siege went on for hours. By daybreak, smoke and flames had withered to small fires and embers, the whole town and camp incinerated. Greedy Celts feverishly worked like roaches to sort through valuables, looting in the street, and loading goods into chariots. Fighting had stopped at the Temple. There were no more Romans to fight. Anyone left alive cloistered inside the cella. Gaius could tell that the Celts did not know how to get into the cella to finish killing the rest of the civilians and soldiers. The Iceni and Trinovantes circled their chariots in frustration.

Hours passed.

"I need to find my mother."

"I saw my mother and little sister go in the Temple."

The little girl complained of thirst and hunger, not understanding how perilous their situation. Gaius worked to quiet the children, resting a hand on a shoulder, patting an arm, with constant worry they might be heard. The small lad with the head wound never moved, sleeping or unconscious. How could he make them realize they could be killed? He decided to allow the older boys to peer through the turf and watch what was happening. Their faces reflected understanding. The four-year-old little girl curled next to him as if attached to his side. Whenever she began to speak or complain, he covered her mouth with his good hand and held it there until she quit. His wound festered. He stuffed it with dirt to control the bleeding and wrapped it. Like birds in a cage they nested all day resting quietly until the second night fell upon them. The barbarians became quiet, too.

On the second day, the Celts decided to take no prisoners. Wagons and debris were pushed up against the door of the cella, preventing anyone from leaving, as torches set the debris on fire. Then they watched. The children put their hands over their ears to muffle the cries of the people burning inside. Gaius held them all in his arms wrapping them in comfort. Soon, it was over. The rebels left, celebrating their massacre of the Romans.

When it was safe, Gaius and the children crawled from the trenches to find food and water. The hum of death surrounded them. Gaius carried the young boy over his shoulder, now dead. He held the hand of the sweet girl and coaxed the boys to follow. Nothing moved that had been alive. Eyes searched for life. Smoldering embers gave the air a scent of the end of their world. They stepped over bodies and friends. Pontius had perished; his eyes stared up to the sky, vacant. He was gone. Gaius scanned the area around the Temple to find the girl in the white tunic hoping she survived.

They walked to the east end of the street in shock, void of emotions. Gaius picked through the rubble of a home to find warm garments, wrapping them around the children, and jugs to fill with water from the river. Gaius laid the young boy down next to a cluster of bodies, ceremoniously scattered three handfuls of dirt on him, and tucked a blanket over him covering his face. What should he do with his set of characters? These innocent ones followed as if led by the shepherd. He set out for the next closest settlement to find help. It would take several days for them to walk the road to Londinium.

~

"I sAW my mother and little sister go into the Temple." The lad paused, not saying the obvious. "My father is with the soldiers fighting the Druids up north with the governor."

"Mine, too. I know my mother is gone. It might be a long time before papa comes back."

Gaius led the innocents, not telling them anything about tribes or Druids. The children asked very little, perhaps not wanting to hear the truth or already knowing the truth having witnessed the warriors at work. He searched their young faces for understanding of the tragedy, wondering how this experience of the world would measure their future by cutting it short, altering it for good or bad, or writing hate deep on their hearts. *They are too young to know they must cling to their childhood now lost. It all appears as a game as they play at hiking, camping under the sky, gazing at stars. After all, they have a joyful plan. They are taking eager steps to find their fathers, planning a celebration at the end of this adventure.*

Gaius called the boys Romulus and Remus in an affectionate way to distract them from the gravity of their circumstance. He gave them orders to make a camp each night, building fires, imitating their soldier fathers. The little girl played with twigs and stones, building houses in the dirt with pretend animals, chatting cheerfully to herself in a delightful fantasy.

Gaius hoped to run into the returning Legion and turn over his charges. As they walked daily toward Londinium, Gaius realized he failed to anticipate one danger. What if the travelers that they were sure to encounter were not Romans but rebels instead? He pushed the children to keep moving quickly to get off Watling Street and find safety.

~

MESSENGERS REACHED Suetonius Paulinus on the Isle of Mona and delivered the news of the Camulodunum massacre. The governor gathered a mounted group of soldiers, leaving desperate forces succumbing to the Druids behind, and headed straight to Londinium, a sister settlement of commerce east of the Walbrook Stream, full of traders and travelers. There was no need to go to Camulodunum. There was nothing left to save. Upon his arrival in Londinium, he determined that the city could not be protected. Abandoning the settlement, he turned away with his men to Watling Street to plan some sort of attack of his own crafting.

That night, they watched the sky turn orange as Londinium fell to the Celts in the same way as Camulodunum.

BOADICEA the BRITISH QUEEN
Animating the Britons to defend their Country against the Romans

An engraving by William Sharp after Thomas Stothard line engraving (1812)

Map of Britannia and Boudicca Revolt

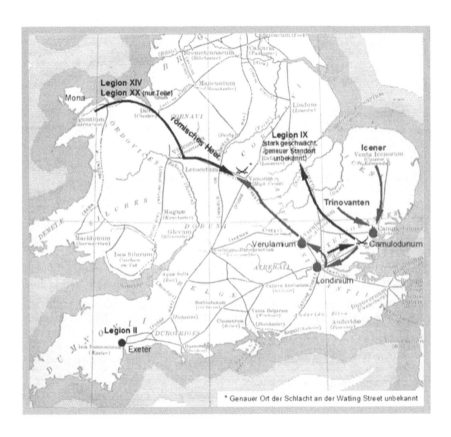

* Genauer Ort der Schlacht an der Watling Street unbekannt

Chapter Twenty-Two

HERCULANEUM

Calitoria prepared to visit Severus's barrack. Talistia structured her hair, applied soft soot to her eyes, and slight beetle juice to her lips. Burnt cork mixed with oil lengthened her lashes. Everyone knew excessive sex made your lashes fall out, so Calitoria insisted that her lashes be thick and long. Appearances prevailed. They left to walk to Severus's door.

"Wait here," she said to Talistia, pointing to the front step of the entrance.

Why do we make this trip several times a week? I should not think about it. I can only guess what is going on inside, Talistia thought. She once heard Calitoria speaking with her friend Lasennia as they gossiped about Caesar's nymphomaniac daughter, Julia. "I never take on a passenger unless the ship is full," they quoted Julia and both giggled. *Could that be what is going on?*

Upon their return, the tranquil villa continued to adjust to Gaius's absence. Never full of the soldier's deep, soothing voice as before but empty and lonely. Telesphorus pulled the tablinum curtain across the entrance to the office area announcing to the household to stay away. Thana stood at her loom, calmly weaving, keeping distant from others. There was always weaving to be done, and being a virtuous woman and talented *matrona,* she counted and threaded the weft in and out, calming her erratic emotions. Lavinia and her fellow slaves resided in the kitchen most of the day at the far end of the villa.

There was a heavy knock on the door. Talistia used a hurried skip to the atrium, opened the door, and escorted their neighbor, Lucius Venidius Ennychus, to the tablinum to find Telesphorus.

"I am here to see Gaius Petronius Stephanus's mother, Thana Petronius," he said with performed arrogance, "and I would like for the wife of Gaius to be present."

"Why would you need to see the women?" answered Telesphorus. "I am handling all business affairs for Gaius in his absence."

"Then you should be present also, although my business is with Thana Petronius. I am a citizen of the Roman Empire and will deal only with the owner."

"Ask Thana and Calitoria to come to the tablinum," Telesphorus ordered Talistia.

Lucius Venidius Ennychus waited in silence until the two bewildered women arrived. Calitoria's face reflected her contempt for the social outcast. There was nothing to like about him. An unattractive human being with his greasy hair pasted down, unkempt beard covering his jowls like a bear, his hands and clothing soiled with filth caused all to step back to avoid his odor. "The Roman way is to visit the Baths and be clean, Lucius," she muttered.

Thana came slowly, passing by the impluvium, holding on to Talistia's arm to walk. Her stiffness and joint pain had worsened until she was severely crippled. Gray hair untethered, she lifted a hip to sit on the corner stool. Her eyes darted to the left.

"Did you see that?" she asked. "That dark demon just rushed to the corner to hide from me. Hello, Lucius. I heard you have a new little girl."

"Why, yes, I do. She is nearly a year now which vested me a Roman citizen. I have applied for all the legal documents and the Proconsul is processing them. I will have my name engraved at the Basilica on the list of Roman citizens allowed to vote in all elections now," he informed, or better, he performed.

"Why are you here?" asked Calitoria. The skinny man with his gnarled face and hands was eager to answer.

"I am here to make Thana Petronius an offer of money for her farm property next to my vineyard on the mountain."

Telesphorus stared at him and shook his head, "Well, it is not for sale."

"I'm sure it will be. Since the death of Gaius Petronius Stephanus, the property passes back to his mother, and since she has not the mental or physical wellness to run a farm, I will generously buy it from her. The wife, Calitoria, who is present, cannot inherit the farm because she is a female and has no child from her marriage to Gaius."

"What are you talking about? Gaius is serving in Britannia, not dead, just absent," answered Telesphorus.

"I apologize." He bowed. "You have not heard. Well, I must be the first to tell you. I know he was serving in Camulodunum, and it has come through reliable political channels that all residents and anyone in service outside of infantry in Camulodunum was murdered by the rebel tribesmen." He paused. "Everyone. And Londinium, and Verulamium were destroyed, as well. Burned to the ground. Nothing left. No one."

Calitoria grabbed her throat with both hands. Thana moaned and cried out.

"Get out!" cried Telesphorus, as he shoved him toward the door.

"Don't touch me! You are nothing but a slave to them! And also a Jew. Don't you realize? Why do you care about them? I maintain my offer to Thana. In addition, I will make a cash offer to keep you! Perhaps, you can persuade her that it would be in her best interest."

Telesphorus moved in face to face. He towered over the stunted man. Slowly, he backed him toward the door, leaving no choice but for Lucius to open the door and leave.

"Think it over. I am not offended. I will be back!" Lucius yelled over his shoulder as the door slammed behind him.

"It can't be true," said Calitoria. "I just had a letter from him."

Finally, Telesphorus spoke. "I think we should go see Balbus. If anyone knows of Nero's troops in Britannia or the movement of the infantry and the latest news, it would be Balbus. Calitoria, will you accompany me? Talistia, find Lavinia and ask her to come and take care of Thana. Thana, wouldn't you like to have some warm mulsum and bread with Lavinia?" He helped her to her feet and began walking her to the kitchen.

Calitoria stared up at the sun's rays descending from the opening above the impluvium. *Lucius is correct. A wife without offspring can't inherit. I'm sure Gaius did not create a will in case of his death. If he had, he would have adopted a respected man to inherit as a son. If that happened I could stay, but he didn't. I'm going to be turned out. But this child that could inherit is inside me. Still, it will be many months before I give birth. If the child lives, I can remain in this household as the mistress. If the child dies, I have nothing. Thana won't take me. Our relationship is one of tolerance only because Gaius married me. Thana would be glad to have me leave.*

Any other woman would be thinking first of her grief over losing her husband, but Calitoria was practical if not surreptitious. She wasn't even sure she cared that deeply for Gaius when she married him. *How quickly life changes. How quickly home, security, money can be lost.*

THE MOMENT CALITORIA and Telesphorus arrived, Balbus knew why. He was aware of the disaster in Britannia, and he knew Gaius was there. Of course, it was expected that soldiers put their lives in danger and die, but Gaius was not in infantry and it was not expected that he should have been in peril. Balbus knew they had come with questions and he would have to give the bad news.

"I am afraid it is true. The dispatch from Rome came last night. All have perished. The only possible survivors were the soldiers in combat with the Druids in Mona. They were absent from Camulodunum at the time. The residents and soldiers left behind in the town were slaughtered. No one survived. All buildings were burned to the ground in Camulodunum, Londinium, and Verulamium. They were caught without defenses, surprise attacks. The rebels stayed until they had slaughtered everyone."

"Have you had specific word that Gaius was killed?" asked Calitoria.

"Dear one, the dispatch says all were slaughtered, seventy thousand Romans killed in total. They found no one alive in the settlement of Camulodunum. Gaius would not have been away in Mona fighting. He would have been guiding construction in Camulodunum and remained in the town. He is gone. You are confused and suffering. I will send for Lasennia. She will come and sit with you."

When Calitoria saw Lasennia, she renewed her smile and nodded to her as if it was any other day. Lasennia put her arm around her friend's waist and walked toward the garden. They passed workmen and construction and chaos along the way.

"What are you creating?" asked Calitoria.

"We are solving a problem for my mother-in-law with a new wall enclosing part of the house. We have divided our home in two. She will have her home, and we will have ours. The only way she can come here is through the front door." Lasennia smiled. "It will make me very happy to be the mistress of my own home and family. She will be happy ordering around her slaves. I will no longer feel like one of them."

"Of course, you will be much happier now," Calitoria said, pleased to be confided in. "Your mother-in-law is quite powerful in your family. It is time for you to run your household. It is wonderful that your husband, Marcus Nonius Balbus, realizes your need."

"You are so kind, but Marcus has also suffered his mother's absence of charm and will be happy with the separation," answered Lasennia.

"I am in a terrible situation," confessed Calitoria as they seated themselves on a bench in the peristyle. Her eyes wandered over the beauty of the foliage in the Balbus garden. Fragrant oleander bushes surrounded them, and the flowing fountain's tranquil music calmed her spirit. Bronze statues gave comfort, as if the ancients were present to listen without judgment. "I have lost my husband, my home, my slaves, my identity, everything. What will I do? Thana owns everything now."

Lasennia took her hand and held it while she spoke.

"You carry Thana's grandchild. She will want to keep you for that reason. The child you carry is your future and Thana's. You have only one choice. You must endear yourself to Thana. Care for her. Be kind. Then she will keep you with her and you will have a home."

"I don't know if I can. She is crazy and hates me. How can I overcome that? Besides, I hate her."

"You must no longer hate her. I know this is the best plan for you. Truly, you can do this," Lasennia said. "Look at what happened for me. I worked hard to get along with my mother-in-law though she is a beast. Impossible woman! Finally, it is all working in my favor. My husband sees the truth. Very kindly, he offered his mother her own dwelling separate from our family. I can feel the resistance leaving me now. I no longer have to wear a suit of armor to protect myself from her horrible jabs. Ah, the relief from that irritating voice! She will be behind the wall! Construction is almost finished. Now, *you* must wear your suit of armor. You must not allow Thana to destroy you. The only way to win is to bear up under her jabs until the baby comes and you become the mistress of the house. Besides, it is the law. Make it work for you.

"Now, go and take care of yourself and get ready for the birth of this child, and stay away from Severus." Calitoria gasped. Lasennia knew she had been visiting the retired Gladiator. "People talk. People wonder. They rarely say kind things about even the nicest people."

Lasennia walked Calitoria back to the atrium where Telesphorus was speaking with Marcus Balbus. The men were concerned that the farm would be lost without Gaius and there would be no profits.

"You need to go up to the farm and secure your boundaries. Reassure your foreman and slaves that nothing will change," said Balbus. "Your neighbor, Lucius Venidius Ennychus, should be watched. He has filed numerous boundary complaints in the courts. He will try to steal your property. He moves the stakes of property when you are absent, and then goes to court claiming the land is his. He may try to do the same with your farm."

"Ennychus has already paid us a visit to try and buy the farm," Telesphorus confirmed. "You are right. I need to check on things. The construction of improvements is underway and we were hoping Gaius's pension from his service would pay for the them. Plus, we have a loan with Jucundus in Pompeii. I need to work on the numbers and may have to abandon some projects. Be assured, I will secure the boundary stakes."

They left the Balbus villa with a focus on life without Gaius. Telesphorus would leave immediately for the farm. Not only to check on the boundaries, but he had some personal concerns to check. Calitoria walked, deep in thought, planning to change her whole personality to survive.

Chapter Twenty-Three

Vita sat alone among flowering grasses dreamily watching bright clouds move against the cerulean sky. They joined together like lovers, then pulled apart separating forever. Some were whisper white on the outside, but their gray bosom seemed to harbor something ominous. The sun hid, then burst forth only to retreat again, mimicking illusive divine love.

"Vitalia, come quickly!" Amedius's urgent call broke her moment of heavenly peace, and she sighed as she rose.

I wish I could not be found. What emergency is important enough to interrupt me on my lovely mountain, so lush and beautiful with the azure sea sparkling in the distance?

Amedius always knew where to find her. Her fellow slave watched over her and protected her.

In answer to her thoughts, he shouted, "It is Telesphorus! He is here, now!"

Vita's heart swelled with joy.

It had been months since that strange morning when Telesphorus sent her to the farm to save her life after discovering Calitoria planned to have her killed by Severus as soon as Gaius left for Britannia. Was it luck that saved her, or was it the gods, or was it Telesphorus's Jewish God? Vita didn't know but she was thankful.

Telesphorus found out the plan by accident from Talistia. He asked her one day, "Where do you and Calitoria go so often?" He was preoccupied with Gaius's upcoming mission and didn't really expect much of an answer, but Talistia naively responded, "To see the gladiator, Severus. I think it strange for the wife of Gaius to be interested in him. What could they have to build a friendship?"

Telesphorus's interest piqued. He'd expected Calitoria and Talistia to be visiting Lasennia or the Baths. But, Severus?

"I have to wait outside, no matter the weather," she confided. "But I do hear things." Her quick, furtive glance around was telling.

"Severus often guards the family," Telesphorus said carefully. "Perhaps she is hiring him?"

At that, Talistia's eyes welled with tears. She shuddered and shook her head. "Not to guard," then added, "They have a secret together," but refused to say more.

Telesphorus's suspicions aroused, he boldly visited Severus, who very happily shared his important menu of services to the community, which included beating rebellious slaves and even disposing of them, allowable because a slave was property. The clairvoyant slave realized Calitoria's plan, but he could not tell Gaius. He would never believe him, and Calitoria would deny it. Instead, Telesphorus risked his life to save his favorite friend, Vita, by sending her to the farm without permission. There was no greater sacrifice for one you cared about.

With Vita safe at the farm, he frustrated Calitoria, who was unable to carry out her plan. Now, Gaius no longer existed to judge his actions. Gaius had cared deeply for Vita even in a divine way.

Gaius would have approved, thought Telesphorus.

VITA RAN with Amedius back to the farm villa. Amedius and the other three slaves had become friends remembering Vita from her first visit. They sheltered her from Reticulus, protecting the young girl that had brought them her own food and drink when they were in chains.

Reticulus, still difficult, wondered why he should do anything that Telesphorus said since he was a slave and Reticulus a freeman, but he feared Gaius's wrath and knew his job could be easily lost. Telesphorus did not tell him Gaius was dead.

Telesphorus first checked the boundary stakes and immediately noticed their altered positions, small increments and hardly noticeable unless you were a man of numbers and measurements. The four slaves helped him return them to their previous positions and were told to keep watch over them. Red ties were applied to the metal stakes as a warning in case Ennychus tried to move them again.

Vita ran up to Telesphorus and threw her arms around his neck. "I am so happy to see you!" she said. "I have no one to read to me here. I miss you."

"I brought you more parchment for drawing," he said as he pulled the rolls from his bag.

"Wonderful. I have been sketching faces and completed a few. Do you want to see them? I am working on one of Amedius right now. He is very good to me. I also take care of the bees and harvest their honey. You can take that back to sell. Reticulus has me cleaning the wool from the sheep. We have several bales that can be sold for weaving. The lambs will be coming soon, so the flock will be doubling itself. It is so beautiful here. You should come more often!" she said as she ambled delightfully up the path to the barn.

Telesphorus could not help but notice the changes in the girl. She was slightly taller, or was it that she held herself in a more confident way? Her hair was growing out so she no longer looked boyish. She previewed a womanly beauty coming to maturity.

He found himself constantly watching her. She ran ahead on the path and walked backwards in front of him tossing her hair away from her face. She looked deeply into his eyes to make sure he was listening.

"We need a dog! The five of us take turns laying out under the sky at night watching for lions or wolves that might attack our sheep, but I tend to fall asleep and so do the others! If we had a dog, it would bark and wake us up if bad animals start creeping around the flock."

He thought she was delightful, the way her voice would rise and fall and then she would come close to his ear to whisper how Reticulus was so annoyed that he couldn't chain all of them up at night. Then she danced ahead as they neared the barn to run in and get her sketches.

She laid them out on a rock in the sun and placed small stones on the corners to anchor them. "I only have charcoal from the fire to draw with, so I have to be careful and roll them up without touching them too much. Sometimes, I drag my arm across them undoing all the careful lines I have drawn. I have learned to put in shadows and make them look like they could pop off the parchment!"

He found himself admiring her instead of the drawings. She acted so happy. Could it be that she did not know her life was still in danger?

"Vitalia, we need to talk somewhere. Seriously, we have some things to work out."

"I know where we can go," she said sitting up straight as if new life had just begun. "We can walk over to a beautiful villa not far from here. It might take up a few hours of the day if you have time. I would like to show you some of the paintings on the walls. They are old but I want to show you the workmanship."

She rolled up her drawings and carried them under one arm to the barn. He could only follow, enchanted by her excitement.

"The first time I saw the frescoes, I was stirred inside with so much eagerness to paint that way. Of course they aren't perfect. I would change some things, but some of it I could never be so skilled to achieve. I found them when Reticulus sent me to the villa, Synistor, to trade some honey for cheese. It is an amazing farm and villa."

He listened to her excitement wishing he could stay and be a part of her world, away from the tense problems with Calitoria. Freedom would be the only way they could ever be together. Walking ahead of him unaware of his concern, she chatted about her bees and honey. He reached out and took her shoulders to stop her and turned her towards him. She questioned with her eyes waiting for him to speak.

"Vitalia, no Vitalis." He laughed. The name was beginning to fit her determined spirit. "We must plan a way for us to buy our manumission. Our freedom will save our lives. We are in peril as long as we are slaves."

"I know," she said seriously.

"But we need to work harder to get it. I have an idea for myself, but I don't have one for you. We both need to earn a wage higher than we are now. We will still have to share it with the Petronius family as long as we are slaves. So we need to have a higher wage that will allow us to save. I have your money that you earned at the docks, but you are not earning anything now. And you can't come back to Herculaneum.

Calitoria does not know you are alive or where you are. It is too dangerous."

"And Gaius, the master?" she asked.

He waited wondering if he should tell her that Gaius was dead. He decided it would only make her afraid. She might even run away if she knew Gaius was gone.

"Gaius will go along with whatever we plan," he answered.

"I was hoping to go back for a visit to see my friends and Thana," she said.

"And Quintus?" he asked. Why did he ask that? He was surprised at his fear of having her see Quintus.

"Yes, of course. I long to see him again. I didn't even get to tell him goodbye. Could you take a message to him for me?"

She took one of the scraps of parchment and paused. What could she say? She put the scrap down and looked up at Telesphorus. "He thinks I am gone forever, doesn't he? It would be better if you would tell him that I am alive in person. Then you can tell him where I am, and he can come see me."

Instead of writing on the parchment, she ran into the barn and came out with her cap. Every morning, when she and Quintus walked to the docks, this was the cap that held her hair up. This cap transformed her from the little slave girl Vitalia into a young boy. The boy named Vitalis.

"Here," she said as she handed Telesphorus the gray cap with the band of colored embroidery. "He will know that I am sending him the message that I am alive if you give this to him."

He knew he wouldn't, but he told her he would.

They walked on the path to the Synistor Villa which sprawled across the mountain. Vita knew the slaves and used the side entrance. She cheerfully greeted the hard-working kitchen staff and asked if the owner was home. Since he was in Rome, she entered the villa to show Telesphorus the frescoes.

"Look how they make you feel that there is a window here! It is just a wall but is so well formed with shadow and perfect hues that you believe you are looking out a window! The painted columns look so round that you want to walk around them to the other side. So perfect!" She walked to the wall and laid her hand on the cold stucco and surveyed the design. "The artists are no longer living. These were done many years ago," she said with admiration. She stood in awe memorizing the line and shapes, colors and composition. He was not so moved but enjoyed watching the excitement in her face.

They walked from room to room. She pointed out the glass bowl with fruit in it. "How did the artist paint a glass bowl! You can see the fruit resting inside the bowl. Look at the painted ivy draping in front of the dark red and gold." In the next room, the colors were vibrant. "Where did the artist get the pigment to create this bright red? And why is this beautiful craftsmanship here on a farm where so few eyes can admire it? What could be more wonderful than being able to take a flat wall and make it look like the view from a window or to paint characters from a story and make them look real?"

She could have stayed longer, but Telesphorus was ready to leave. She would try to practice drawing all that she had seen.

As they walked back to their own farm, she could tell Telesphorus had many concerns. Something was bothering him.

"We have to buy our freedom," he said again. He could only think about their future now that Thana was the owner of the villa and farm. Her mind was ill and could easily be manipulated to sell them all or have them destroyed. He hoped to have some influence over her, but with Calitoria trying to inherit everything through her child in a few months, he feared it could be worse if she made the decisions. She already felt she was entitled to everything. If Calitoria did not get her way, she easily would take revenge on all of them even to the point of calculating how she could make them suffer in some way, justifying whatever she decided to do by blaming her situation on Thana or even the departed Gaius.

Fresco from P. Fannius Synistor Villa 50-40 B.C.E. Boscoreale
Public Domain

Chapter Twenty-Four

~∞~

Telesphorus left. He stared vacantly while the horse pulled the wagon rocking him into a trance. The calm rhythm and confident gait allowed heavy thought.

I couldn't let Vitalia be harmed. I had to hide her. "Thou shalt not kill". As a child of Israel, if nothing else, I saved Calitoria from becoming a murderer and that is what it would have been, a murder. The Rabbi Paul said Jesus taught to love others as yourself. He wouldn't turn his back to such evil and let Vitalia be killed. The horse startled, surprised by a bird taking flight. Telesphorus spoke in his gentle, reassuring voice, "Nothing there boy, good job."

It would be so much easier not to be Jewish. If I believed in the gods, I could sacrifice something and be done with it. There would be no mark on my soul. I could just let it happen and not care. After all, Vitalia is just a slave. Slaves can be killed. Others, who believe in the gods, don't think about harming their soul in this life.

He straightened his posture, knowing he spoke the truth.

My visit to Puteoli changed me. I heard the Apostle Paul explain the prophecies and how Jesus fulfilled them. I chose. I have to do what is right... but I could lose... everything.

~

VITA RETURNED to the farm kitchen to help with the cooking. The workers would all be hungry, and the female slave that Reticulus kept for himself did most of the kitchen work. After the cooking was done, Vita decided to make her salve from the sheep oils. She shared it with the slaves, including Amedius, who was the most encouraging friend. It still smelled like sheep, with an offensive odor, but she thought sweaty men smelled bad anyway.

She had her pot near the fireplace and decided to let it heat until warm by the fire. She took a lemon and squeezed the juice into the sheep salve. A lovely clean fragrance arose, but now the salve was too runny. *Maybe add some beeswax to make it a soft solid?* The warmth from the fire melted the beeswax full of honey. She let it sit to harden and went to help the slave woman, Fradia, with chores. When she came back, it had hardened so solid it was impossible to use. She heated it back up and decided to add more olive oil. *Next time, I will add only a little beeswax,* she thought.

The salve was now soft, slightly yellow in color, smelled like lemons, and was soothing. As she rubbed it on her skin, it seemed to remove the dry areas and make her skin glow. She offered some to Fradia.

"Oh, this is nice," she said as she rubbed it on her hands and arms.

"I think I can feel the gritty beeswax," Vita observed, knowing it was her best yet, but still not satisfied. "I'll make some more but leave out the beeswax. I wonder what will happen?"

She made a new batch with just the sheep salve, olive oil, and lemon juice. At first, she rubbed it on the backs of her hands.

"This is so soft, I think I would like it on my face." Vita took some on her finger and applied it to her cheeks. Fradia tried it, too.

"Well, you have made something very special. I like this! It might make me beautiful again," she giggled.

Vita realized she had made something nicer than her mother made back in Ephesus. That salve was used to prepare brides for their wedding day, bathing them, massaging them with oils, and styling their hair and applying their makeup. The memory murmured the love of her mother.

"This salve is amazing! I hope you don't mind if I use it all," Fradia said as she massaged the fragrant lotion on her legs and even her feet and let the salve make them soft and glowing.

"It smells lovely," said Vita. "I wonder if I could sell this?"

They massaged the softer cream on their faces and used the gritty beeswax lotion to soften their tired feet. Vita took the rest of the sheep lotion with the new fresh scent for the other slaves to use on their injured hands. It lessened the pain of cuts and hurried the healing.

"Thank you, Vitalia," said Amedius. "You are such a sweet girl."

Old for a slave, bony, and ragged, he was a very kind man in spite of his difficult life and situation. That never mattered to him. Vita never shared the salve with Reticulus. He was such a mean man that she never wanted to be near him. His eyes followed her too often with lust. She knew he would harm her if he could.

TELESPHORUS PAUSED, his courage suddenly waning on the Petronius threshold. He could not make himself grasp the handle to enter. Maybe he could use the servant entrance and avoid seeing Calitoria. Her complaints since Gaius died could not be stopped, but he knew she needed his comfort. He shut his eyes and took a deep breath to prepare himself for the tirade behind the door. He turned the handle but found quiet. *She must be asleep.*

He strode back to the cooking area to find someone to help unload the wagon. No wagons were allowed in the pedestrian street across from the Forum, and he had a lot to carry up the road to the villa. Lavinia was absent, probably in the garden, but Thana was perched on her stool. She hopped down to greet him. "Did you bring me anything?" she asked, as if a child.

"Of course! I brought you honey from the farm." He handed her the jar and watched as she pulled out the wax honeycomb and sucked the sticky, golden syrup. Escaping liquid ran down her chin. Telesphorus laughed, "You have it all over you, dear one!"

No one had bothered to control Thana's gray hair which added to her crazed look. Her eyes were wide with the excitement of sweets, and she hummed as she swallowed and sucked the honey. Her spiral into insanity had increased rapidly since Gaius's departure. She often talked of her son and fantasized that he was returning.

"I know he is alive. I see him. He comes to me in my mind. I would know if he was gone," she said repeatedly. She still entered the sacred room to pray to the ancestors and household gods and saved some honey to sacrifice later in the day.

Aquilina and the silent Certa followed Telesphorus down the street past the public fountain to the edge of town. Certa hoisted heavy bags of vegetables and left while Aquilina gathered baskets of wool. She picked up the first basket and stopped.

"Telesphorus! This is Vitalia's cap! The one she wore when she masqueraded as Vitalis at the docks. I have found Vitalia's cap!" She looked at his face and saw no surprise at all. He looked guilty! "You know! You know something! You know her cap is here. What have you done with her?"

How could he be so careless, to leave it in a place where someone could find it? He shut his eyes. "Aquilina, please, you must be quiet! Yes, it is Vitalia's cap." His mind raced for a lie to cover for himself and a plan to protect Vitalia, but nothing came to him. "Please, you must be quiet. It is dangerous for Vitalia."

"Then it is her cap. She must be alive! You knew all along she was alive!"

"Yes, she is alive."

"How could you not tell us? When did you find her? We have suffered so much. You watched us cry and hurt for so long, you heartless excuse for a man, and a Jew! You caused this! You are supposed to have mercy and compassion, and you teach us to treat each other with love. Have you no empathy for others?"

"Of course I do. I have empathy for Vitalia," he hissed. "I saved her. I didn't harm her. Calitoria, with her cruel nature, was plotting to kill her!" There it was out, he had said it. Now, he wanted to take it back. Could he trust Aquilina to hide the secret with him?

"How do you know such a thing?" Aquilina accused. "I know Calitoria's ways but to kill Vitalia? Yes, she was jealous of her because Gaius and Thana thought she was a goddess, and she tried to cause her to fail in every way, but to kill her? No."

"She was hiring the gladiator, Severus, to kill her! Ask Talistia how many times she visited him. I spoke with him about his practice of punishing and disposing of slaves. Plus, you saw how distressed she was when Vitalia disappeared. It wasn't that she cared for Vitalia, she was out of her mind because her plan to kill her failed! She only hopes she is dead somewhere. She doesn't know for sure. She only wants to find her so she can kill her!"

Aquilina sat down in the wagon, overwhelmed with the truth that her friend was not dead but hiding somewhere.

"You must not go back to the villa until you can hide this face you are wearing," warned Telesphorus. "No one can know. Don't you see that if you tell one of them, they won't be able to hide it from the others? Vitalia will be discovered."

"And so will you! Where is she?" Aquilina asked.

"I can't tell you."

"Well, she is obviously somewhere you have been today. Is she at the farm? She is. She must be at the farm. I want to see her. You have to take me. Arrange for me to help at the farm so that I can go see her. If you do that, I will tell no one, and I will erase this unpleasant face that hates you right now."

"I can't take you. To let anyone find out would be harming your friend and would cause us both to be punished or killed. That includes Quintus. You can't tell Quintus! You must pretend at all times that you know nothing."

"Telesphorus! Who are you? What kind of man would do this? You allowed us to hurt all these months and search everywhere for her while you knew all along that she was safe. I can't even feel the joy that Vitalia is alive because of you."

"You will get over it, and you will love me instead because I saved her," he said without emotion. He grabbed a bag of vegetables for Lavinia, threw them over his shoulder and headed toward the villa. "Don't come until you fix that face of yours!" he yelled.

If Aquilina reacted this way, what wrath would come from the others when they find out. Telesphorus felt his guts bind. *Was it the right thing to do, to save Vitalia from Calitoria's plan? We are under the master's rule. The God of Israel freed the Jews in ancient Egypt, but I am still a slave.*

"I must buy my freedom," he said aloud.

Chapter Twenty-Five

The letter finally came. A courier from Rome delivered it, addressed to Calitoria and dated from several weeks earlier. Aquilina carried the letter in her hand turning it back and forth, studying the rolled parchment, disappointed that it would not reveal its contents. Calitoria rose from her bed weary with the weight of the babe, pushing her unbound hair from her eyes. Her daily disheveled appearance was purposeful to ensure a gentle birth. No knots were in her sash, she never crossed her legs or fingers, her hair was loose, and she prayed daily to the gods for the child to deliver itself gently. All her thoughts centered around her pregnancy. She never noticed the slaves or the routine of the villa anymore, until this letter was handed to her. She recognized the seal. It was from Gaius.

"He is alive," she whispered as her eyes deciphered the words.

Aquilina backed out of the bedchamber, while Calitoria continued to read the letter. As soon as she reached the atrium, she turned to sprint to tell Telesphorus.

"Gaius is alive! A letter has just come!" The scholar interrupted his thoughts long enough to listen and stare at her. She paused to catch her breath and ran on to tell the others in the kitchen.

"Gaius is not dead! A letter has just come from Rome!" announced Aquilina. Lavinia screamed with delight. Thana heard what was said, but poor Thana, she could not understand the good news. Maybe she never comprehended that her son was dead. She only watched the joy of everyone hugging and crying in disbelief.

Aquilina ran back to Telesphorus. "All will be well again for us! Gaius will make things right!"

Calitoria waddled out to the tablinum.

"Is he really alive?" he asked.

"It seems so. I don't know how to think. I wanted him to be alive but convinced myself that I would be as disturbed as Thana to expect it. Now, it is true." She looked down toward her enormous abdomen. "All this before the baby comes. Now, the baby is not important or necessary. The villa is going to be mine anyway. If Gaius was dead, a baby boy would have confirmed it. This never would have happened if Thana had not made it clear that I would lose everything if her son was dead."

Aquilina watched Telesphorus cringe. "I think you should go back to your room and rest. The news is confusing you."

"I will. I need to think how this is going to work out. Would you call on the midwives to visit and bring the birthing chair? I feel that my time will be soon," she answered. Her eyes were dull and her face expressionless as she shuffled back to her bed. They studied her as she walked.

"Not a lot of joy that her husband is now alive and not dead. It must be because the child will be coming soon."

"Lavinia says women become more extreme in their emotions when they are pregnant, crying easily," said Aquilina.

"She should be more worried about her own chance of death from birthing a child," said Telesphorus.

"I've been counting on my fingers, and this baby should have come already. It sure takes Calitoria a long time to make a baby!" said Aquilina.

A birthing chair was deposited in the atrium, a reminder of the terror of childbirth for Calitoria, and sat unused for weeks. The midwives visited every few days to check on her pregnancy. They delivered small statues of Juno Lucina, the goddess of childbirth, placed them near her bedside, and gave her ointment of goose fat to apply in the birth canal to ease the child from her body. However, they would soon leave since there were still no signs that the delivery of the child was imminent.

~

"I WANT TO GO SEE VITALIA," demanded Aquilina in a whispered voice.

"You can't. Someone will become suspicious," said Telesphorus.

"Yes, they will be more than suspicious, because I will tell if you don't let me see her."

"You would put her life in danger just because you want to see her?"

"Why is she in danger? You just hid her from us."

Telesphorus knew he had to honor her persistent request or Aquilina would give away his secret. How could his plan for saving Vita's life be the right thing to do in God's eyes, but be so painful and difficult for him to carry out? Now that Gaius was alive, Telesphorus realized he was trapped. *Vitalia is at the farm, soon to be discovered when Gaius returns. Aquilina knows where she is and has been and she threatens to tell if she does not get to visit her. Worse than that is my fear, Calitoria will find out. I will pray for God to intervene.*

Aquilina still stood in front of him.

"Oh, for this damned lie to be over and put right!" he swore to her. "Stop with this demand! I love this missing slave more than you could ever care about her! I can't bear the thought of her being harmed or killed. She doesn't know how close she was to death! I must have your promise to never tell where she is." He held his forehead in his hands, then looked up. "Yes, I will take you to see her. I have no choice. By God's love, I will take you. It will make her happy and that is what I want for her."

~

THE NEXT DAY Telesphorus used the excuse of needing supplies from the farm and said he needed Aquilina to go with him. She packed food for the trip, collected sweet wine and dates from Lavinia, and climbed in the wagon at dawn. They would arrive before midday, a time which seemed to never come as they traveled the uneven road that wound up the mountain. They passed vineyards and grazing sheep on the hillside of Mount Vesuvius, while the scent of freshly cut and stacked hay made Aquilina breathe deep and gather in the lovely fragrance.

"I have been in the town of Herculaneum too long and have forgotten the hillside filled with natural beauty," she exclaimed.

"Yes, it is God's artistic landscape. Here we see the golden light and lush greenery, but we will pass the entrances to the evil fires. It is a breathing mountain that spews stench in barren patches," said Telesphorus.

"What are you talking about? There is nothing evil here." She waved her hand across the scenery, then pivoted to look down the mountain. "If you look behind us, you can see the sea far below sparkling with sunlight on this clear day. It is pure joy."

"You just wait. We will pass the entrance to Hades up here. You will smell the stench first, and then you will see steam clouds vent from below. You must always be careful when walking up here so you don't slip down into a crevasse. Many people and animals have disappeared in a vent, just wandering. There are also stories of the mountain belching deadly air, and herdsman have found whole flocks lifeless."

"I thought Hercules lived in the mountain. Why would he do that? Is he an evil god?"

"Your questions have no answers that I can give you. I don't know about Hercules, but my God is a vengeful God to the wicked. I heard a man called Paul speak at Puteoli some time ago, and he said my God loves those who worship Him and forgives us our mistakes and errors. That we should repent. I wonder if the God of my Jewish brethren will forgive me my lies to Calitoria and all of you about Vitalia."

"If that is true about your God, that he loves us, he would surely forgive your choice to save Vitalia's life. Anyway, was it truly a lie? Or was it that you just didn't tell where she was because you knew it would save her from harm?"

Telesphorus laughed and looked down at Aquilina's innocent face. "I guess you could look at it that way if you wanted forgiveness. Can I negotiate with God? I'm not sure it was the right thing to do now. It seems it can never be right or go away. I can't sleep at night for worrying about how this can ever end. Deceit can never be good, but I did keep Calitoria from committing a worse evil and that would be jealousy, revenge, and murder if she finished her plan. Perhaps God will help me find a way to fix this tangled web of secrets. I am sure that my God says "Thou shalt not kill," and I know that is right. I know I heard Him in all this, but now I fear the judgment of Gaius and Calitoria. I am still a slave to them. Calitoria was wrong in planning murder. I will be punished for her choices. How can this be of God? What can I do to fix this?" He knew he had said too much to Aquilina.

"I am confused. The gods don't love us. I think they love themselves. They love themselves so much they need our sacrifices and worship," said Aquilina.

"I'm talking about the God Jehovah. Not the ones that Thana and Gaius worship."

THEY ARRIVED at midday as planned. Aquilina hopped from the wagon, forgetting her duty to help unload the tools and supplies, and ran to the farmhouse to find Vita. She stood in the doorway of the simple building waiting for her eyes to adjust but only found Fradia, the farm servant girl, standing by a table preparing food.

"You startled me," said Fradia. "Who are you? What do you want?"

"I'm Vitalia's friend. Where is she?"

"She is out caring for the bees this morning. You can find her if you follow the path around the building and down toward the grape vines."

Aquilina spun around, gathered up her tunic to free her legs, and danced down the path. She could see Vita in the distance. The young girl standing on the hill had changed into a lovely woman, taller, with long chestnut colored hair. She stood erect as the sun chose to highlight her even features, with ice blue eyes shadowed by heavy lashes. The girl had transformed into a beauty.

"Vitalia!" she called as she ran up to her. "You look so good! What has happened to you? This farm life has changed you. I hardly see the cute impish girl I knew."

"Oh, Aquilina!" She wrapped her arms around her friend. "I wish I knew you were coming. I would have loved anticipating the fun of seeing you again. What a surprise!

I love it here. It is so peaceful. No one really tells me what to do! I just have to work and do what is needed each day."

Vita gave her a tight hug, then took her hand, pulling her down the path. "I will show you my bees. I have been selling the honey. Best of all, Fradia and I have been making lovely lotions with the wax. I'll send some home with you. Come on, let me introduce you to my bees."

They walked to where there were large dirt tubes stacked horizontally. Vita reached in one of the tubes with a long stick that had a paddle shape at the end. She pulled out a piece of yellow wax. Aquilina stood back in fear.

"Aren't you afraid of being stung?"

"I have been stung, but the bees know me now. I don't upset them, so they allow me to take some of their wax and honey. I help them keep their hives tidy, and they work hard for me," Vita explained.

"For my lotions, I take the wax and crush it in water. Fradia and I heat it and the wax melts and rises to the top. Then, we skim it off. I squeeze it through loosely woven cloth two or three times to clean it up. Then we stir in olive oil, fragrances, and water. We had to try several times to get it right. We still add sheep sweat like I made for you, but we add lemon or something that makes it smell better."

"Maybe I can sell some to the ladies in Herculaneum for you," replied Aquilina.

"I have plenty of wax left over. Maybe I could sell it to the artists who are painting wall scenes for landowners up here. Most of the beautiful villas are owned by generals or politicians, and they are magnificent. Wall paintings tell the story of the gods, but some just have scenes of nature.

"I want the artists to teach me how to paint. However, they don't allow women. I might have to become the boy, Vitalis, again!" she laughed. "I could show them my drawings. I'm sure I could be a specialist because I am so good! I can do faces really well. Telesphorus will be so pleased. I'm sure they would pay me, and it would be more than working at the docks!"

Aquilina stepped back and looked at Vita with concern. She scanned the perfectly symmetrical face, thick black lashes, feminine shoulders, and clear skin. "Do you really think you can make them believe you are a young boy?"

"What do you mean? I did it before, and I can do it again."

"Well, you look very different now. Maybe if you cover up and hide that hair. Maybe if you change your voice and walk like this." Aquilina demonstrated by hunching her shoulders and planting her feet wide with a swaying motion back and forth.

Vita laughed. "You mean like this?" she asked as she dropped down to swing her arms and stuck out her jaw.

"Yes, now you look like a boy!"

They both laughed uncontrollably as they ridiculed the men of the world.

"Have you actually been making money yet?" asked Aquilina after she composed herself and began to think of Vita's future.

"It is hard up here. I make lotions and clean wool but have not been able to get them to a market. Perhaps, you and Telesphorus can do that part, since I am not able to leave the farm. Telesphorus says my life is in danger in Herculaneum. However, I am so happy here.

"Aquilina, I'm in the middle of making more homes for the bees," she continued. "I need to finish before I can go back to the farm villa with you. They might dry out without being formed properly if I stop now. You can help me. I am increasing the number of hives, so I can have more honey and beeswax."

Vita showed Aquilina mats of straw and mud laid out on the grass. She placed bundles of twigs on the edge of each one, then showed Aquilina how to roll the wet mud flats around the twigs. When they were finished, Vita said they would leave them to dry in the sun for several days before she could remove the twig bundles, revealing the tunnels, and stack the new hives.

"Where did you learn how to do all this? How do you know how to care for bees?"

"From my father when we were in Ephesus. My father was a ship-builder and worked on warships for the Romans. The ships needed to be painted and sealed with beeswax, so he began to sell wax to the builders. We harvested the wax from our own hives. The bees do most of the work, we would just help them finish the job and sell the wax. We also sold the honey," replied Vita.

"I think you have found a way to buy your manumission, Vitalia."

THEIR VISIT WAS CUT short by the sun as it journeyed toward the sea. Vita packed jars of lotion and honey to send to the markets in Herculaneum. She would have liked to sell them herself but knew that she still needed to hide. Aquilina helped. They made trips to the wagon until it was all loaded.

"Do you ever see Quintus?"

Aquilina knew the question would come but was surprised that Vita had waited till they were leaving to ask it.

"Not really," she answered looking directly at Vita.

It was a lie. She knew Quintus had moved on with his life and was becoming well-known for his gems and jewelry. Quintus thought Vita was dead and had worked to recover from the worry and grief of wondering what happened to her. He never came around to the villa anymore asking about her. No longer an apprentice, he focused on his work and paid attention to the vacationing patrons from Rome who found him to be a worthy artist. Word spread that his craftsmanship was genius, making the jewels more valuable and the gem shop busy with customers. The Petronius slaves saw him frequently at the markets and docks buying raw Egyptian gemstones. He was too busy to speak to them.

"No, I haven't seen him."

"I'm older now. More grown up, not the young girl he knew. I am ready for him to love me. He is the only one who will ever have my heart."

Vita watched the wagon carrying her best friends disappear down the path to Herculaneum. Standing on the edge of the mountain, the fresh sea air joined with the warmth of the sun. She stood there alone when they left, the breeze caressing her cheeks, folding her hair away from her face. Her eyes closed as she imagined a reunion filled with love for Quintus.

Chapter Twenty-Six

It was dusk when Aquilina and Telesphorus arrived at the Herculaneum villa. Lamps flickered in the atrium. A strange woman scurried past. Startled, they dropped their bags and watched the intruder dash to the kitchen carrying a bowl. Aquilina scanned the room for the birthing chair, an atrium fixture for the past month, absent for the first time.

"I think the baby is coming. The chair is missing, but I don't hear anything," she said to Telesphorus. "Lavinia said there would be screaming and shouting. I want to see. Maybe the screaming will start soon."

"I'll be in the tablinum," said Telesphorus.

Aquilina peered into the master bedchamber and saw Calitoria sitting upright on the birthing throne with its long chair legs and crescent shaped open seat. The experienced midwife knelt, twisting herself beneath the seat to see the birth canal as Calitoria tried to push the babe out. Two women clasped their arms around her shoulders anchoring their bodies to the mother, rocking with her. The midwife lathered her hands with olive oil and rubbed it on the genitalia.

"Hold on and press your breath as you push down. Stay calm. We don't want an insane personality to be planted in this child," said the midwife. Aquilina stood in the doorway watching beads of sweat drip down Calitoria's forehead as she pressed her eyes shut bearing down.

"Focus on the demands your body is making. Let the goddess Juno Lucina inhabit your body to birth this child."

They darkened the room and purred soft hums. Musty herbs burned in the oil lamps. Calitoria's slender fingers wrapped around the amulet charm hanging from her neck. It was the figurine of Juno, the goddess that would bring the babe from the darkness of the womb into the light.

Aquilina turned away.

I am never having a child. I'll wait here by the door and see how long this takes and see if she screams when it hurts.

AFTER A LONG NIGHT, the babe presented itself head first, flushing its way into the waiting arms of the kneeling midwife who deftly tied the cord with binding string. A wail came from his lips as towels dried his head and limbs. Red curly hair appeared as they dried him.

"The hair is bright orange. Have you ever seen that before?" they asked Calitoria.

Her eyes widened with surprise. "No, I have never seen that before!" She pulled back the cloth to assess the hair on the newborn. She pulled it back even further to see the sex. "At least it is a boy." Her head dropped back to the chair and her eyes closed, savoring shallow breaths.

Aquilina peaked around the door frame. *She should be satisfied now. Calitoria has won more than a child. She won a villa.*

She had a child. She had a boy. She had the villa. Gaius would return but even if he was dead, Calitoria knew she owned everything.

Aquilina ran to the kitchen in the back of the villa. "It's a boy! Orange, curly hair! Calitoria is fine and the babe is chubby."

"Good. The child must be fat and healthy in the beginning to have a chance at the first of life. Fiery orange, curly hair, I've never heard of that," said Lavinia.

When Telesphorus heard the news, he was not so surprised. He had seen orange hair before and he knew where.

The group of familia slaves continued working in the kitchen while

Thana sat on her residential perch, as usual. Smitten with insanity, but coherent enough to scoot off her stool to commit the tradition of grandmother to the mother and child, she stood for a moment then walked slowly toward Calitoria's bedchamber.

"Where are you going, Thana?" asked Aquilina. It was difficult to communicate with her distant soul. She seemed to always have part of her spirit in a vacant form.

"Watch her, Aquilina," said Lavinia as she noticed Thana leaving. "Do not let her wander off and leave the villa."

Thana hobbled to the maternal bedchamber with painful steps, limping past the gardens to the darkened bedchamber. Aquilina held her elbow. They entered the cubiculum. The grandmother, Thana, with unkempt fluttering gray hair and widened eyes, walked up to Calitoria and reached out for the child. Calitoria lifted him to her. Thana cradled the infant in her arms and gazed at the small face. Aquilina watched as Thana collected saliva from her mouth with her gnarled finger, then traced wet circular lines on the child's forehead, then on his lips.

"Protect this child from the curse of the evil eye, protect this one from sickness, harm, and hardship. Bless the goddess Juno Lucina for bringing him into the light," she proclaimed. Thana raised the child toward heaven and held him there as she seemed to search for a sign. Satisfied, she delivered the new soul back to his mother. Thana slowly turned, resumed her vacant gaze, and offered an arm to Aquilina for support to leave. Reality left Thana like an extinguished candle as she reentered the comfort of her hallucinations. Aquilina helped her back to the kitchen to her favorite spot.

"What happened?" Lavinia asked as the old matriarch climbed up on her stool to stare at nothing.

"Well, Thana put spit on the baby and spoke to the gods about protecting and keeping the newborn healthy and asking for an easy life. Who is the evil eye? Is there an evil eye? I sure hope somebody spit on my forehead when I was born and asked for an easy life, but I think no one did considering I am forever a slave. But better to be slave to a rich man than to be a poor freed slave."

"It will be so wonderful to have a babe in the villa. A small sweet soul to make us all happy. I can't wait to see him," said Lavinia. "It will be several days before he has a name. I hope he survives long enough for that."

Aquilina grumbled back, "At least Calitoria will be focused on the babe for a while and the rest of us can work without her coming around."

"Hush!" Lavinia looked at Thana to see if she comprehended the conversation and walked closer to Aquilina. "Don't ever say or even think those thoughts. You forget who you are. Don't be a fool," whispered Lavinia. All sweetness left her voice.

"Well, I'm going out while she is busy. Goodbye!" Aquilina did not like being corrected. *It's not her place to tell me what to do,* she thought as she stomped out the side entrance and walked to the market looking for Quintus.

He no longer worked in the booth where oysters were sold. This morning he shopped for uncut gems from Egypt. She watched him hold rocks up to the light to see if the desired colors might exist inside the crusty exterior of each pebble. His instincts coupled with his experience judged the interior, shrouded by dirt and gray outer debris. Many now considered him an expert in his field and he was at the market early to buy the best gems.

"Quintus!"

"Aquilina! Good to see you." He smiled and walked toward her.

"I have news!" she said.

There was only one bit of news that Quintus wanted to hear. Could it be that Vita had been found?

"We have a new baby boy. Calitoria had the babe this morning."

Disappointment cut into his heart and wrote on his face. "I thought it might be something about my Vitalis. No one has heard anything?"

Aquilina wanted to yell that Vita was alive and she knew where she was and she had spent the day with her. Instead she raised her brows with a slight grin and grasped her mouth. Quintus did not miss the clues.

"You know something! What is it? It is happy news that I see in your face." He snatched her shoulders, pulled her to the side of the market, and held her directly in his snare.

"I can't." Aquilina shook her head, and her expression changed to fear.

"You will tell me, now!" he yelled as he held her. "I have thought of nothing else. Is she dead? Is she hurt? Does someone have her and are they harming her? The silence from everyone is killing me. I want to be her protector. I let her down. You know something! Where is she? I can't go to her and save her if I don't know where she is! I saw your smile that she is alive." He looked to the sky and yelled, "Why do the gods torment me so? Return my Vitalis back to me!"

Aquilina was shocked by his angry reaction. Maybe she could get away from him and run but he would only chase her down until she told. Her promise to keep the secret gave way to her fear of Quintus's strength.

She told everything.

Quintus's eyes filled with tears. He listened and heard. Vita was safe.

Impossible to have the dead become alive again. His heart longed for the happiness and faith of the past. If only he could return to those days when he picked her up at the villa, when they walked together in the quiet of the morning filled with promise, the birds calling from the sea, the touch of her hand grabbing his to step together through life. How Vita had transformed him to appreciate life and have hope was the foundation on which he now relied. He would not believe she was alive unless he touched her himself.

"I will go to her."

~

How many beings have lost a loved one and wished for their return? It is a simple fact of life: Taking for granted common daily activities that include your loved one, only to have them snatched from your life by death, or even worse, by their choice. Quintus could not believe that Vita would choose to leave him and cause so much heartache and worry. It was better to believe she was dead. There could be no other explanation. He tormented himself with visions of the harm that could have come to her, hoping she did not suffer. His thoughts crazed him while he was awake and even worse in his sleep. He still loved the sweet waif.

Why didn't I tell her? Why didn't I wait for her? I will go see her.

~

QUINTUS SAW Vita standing in the meadow surrounded by tall grass, sheep grazing in the distance, all nature glittering around her from the tears in his eyes. He dismounted and walked to her. She had become a rare beauty, the kind of beauty that occurs by chance, skipping generations. He reached out and took her face into both hands holding her gaze.

"At last, your soft skin, your kind eyes, your small frame, chaste Vitalis from my term at the docks of Herculaneum, how can you be alive?"

"I knew you would come," she whispered.

"You did not tell me you were alive. I thought you were dead and gone from my life forever." He kissed her and held her. "Finally, the gods have brought us together. Sweet Venus and Apollo, Hercules, and all the others, thank you."

They laid in the meadow holding each other so close, a gentle kiss, in love, becoming one in flesh. Vita always knew they would be together. No one else held her heart and thrilled her like Quintus. Just his touch, his arms around her holding her, a beginning and ending, a forever.

THE DAY GREW long and Quintus returned to Herculaneum. Vita encouraged it so no one would suspect that he had found her. They separated but knew they existed forever in each other's hearts. At last, Quintus belonged to Vita and Vita belonged to him. She started the walk back toward the farmhouse alone, filled with love and longing to be with him every moment of every day.

Her life and future were solid now. She had all she wanted and needed in Quintus. He was her childhood and now he would be her life, they would be together and they would have children. Quintus would love her, and protect her and she no longer would be without a family of her own. These thoughts were so powerful that she did not notice how the wind picked up its force laying the long legs of grass and weeds flat around her. Even trees bowed in submission to the invisible power.

Thick black clouds chased her. She cowered and bent low, clawing her way up the path with eyes half closed. She could control her destiny but not the wind. The unseen power stirred the dust while birds cried, soared, and struggled for safety. The sky darkened and the rain began. At first, it was small droplets but then became large missiles stinging her skin and pelting her with hard smacks. Gusts picked up and mourned through the trees with a deafening dirge. Lightning arced across the sky hesitating its explosions.

I can make it, she thought. *I see the farmhouse. I will not lay down and give up.* Stings and barbs beat her like fists. Finally, her hand reached out through the pelting rain and found the latch. Struggling against the wind, she pulled the door open, shut it behind her, and dropped the latch cutting off the wind.

Smoothing her hair and checking her tunic belt and sandals, there was no harm. She had saved herself.

Chapter Twenty-Seven

T he next morning Vita was up early. Quintus's return to her life and love empowered her to work for her freedom. Her future stood before her but must be bought. She knew a distant neighbor's extravagant villa, used as a vacation resort, was being decorated about six miles away. It belonged to Emperor Nero's new wife, whose family had built their fortune making bricks for the Empire. Ever since Nero married her, the villa had been under construction.

"I'm pretty sure I can get a job drawing and painting at Poppaea's villa. The artisans are there now creating frescoes. If I am a boy, I have a chance at being hired."

She stood in the farmhouse while Fradia wrapped a long white cloth tightly around Vita's breasts. This time she would not cut her hair. She wound her long locks on top of her head and secured them with a thin stick. A round cap covered the bun and most of her hair.

"That should do it. I can pass for a boy again. I am Vitalis the artist now."

"I am not sure. I think I can still tell you are a girl. Your chin is weak for a boy and your arms have no muscle. Your neck looks slim. You have no beard! Well, you look like a lovely boy!" laughed Fradia.

"I will walk like a boy and adjust my crotch frequently. I have done this before. I am Vitalis again." She walked bow-legged across the plank floor and grumbled in a deep voice.

"I don't think changing your name from Vitalia to Vitalis is enough." Fradia judged.

"Well, surely the gods will be with me and cloak me with this disguise."

"Do you have permission to do this? You will have to take the horse. You look like you are trying to be freeborn."

"I was freeborn."

"Well, you are a slave now, and the Empire is searching for runaway slaves. You've heard about it. They want us to wear a certain type of clothing to show we are slaves."

"They won't make us do that. If they did, they would see that half the people are slaves and we could gather like Spartacus rebels did a hundred years ago and defeat them."

Vita left the farmhouse strutting her boy-self and headed to the villa where artisans were working on wall decorations. She entered through open doors into the cavern-like atrium. Everything was white, a mystical mirage absent of all color. The four walls were prepped with sparkling plaster, and artificial columns, inserted shelves, cornices, and ceilings that glittered like the bright sun. She gazed adoringly at sculptures of artificially formed columns and cornices memorizing their shapes and details.

A team of dark earthy artisans interrupted the blaze of white, adding a layer of powdered marble and lime. Their singular sounds were the softened scrapes and claps of plaster. First the men applied the wet slurry, then another team smoothed the surface behind them. Tables were set up with mortars and pestles where pebbles could be crushed to dust. Hands worked feverishly seeming to communicate without voices in automatic movements trained by years of repetition. Suddenly, an irritated correction from a lead artist cut the air, and the rebuke slashed the momentum to a halt. As they turned around to fix the error, they noticed Vita standing in the doorway.

"My name is Vitalis, and I am looking for work as an artist. I am experienced," she stated. They could not have been more disinterested in this intruder. The synchronized skill of the craftsmen refocused and continued.

The lead craftsman turned back around. "Help crush the marble to dust with the pestle." For a moment, he stared at her, then turned back to the wall. There was no talk of pay.

She stood by the table, grabbed the pestle and poured some marble pebbles into the mortar made of granite. She ground and crushed. Randus stuck his hand in the dust and twisted it between his fingers shaking his head. Again and again she dove into the dust with the pestle. She pushed and ground for hours until her wrist ached with each movement. Soon it was dusk and the team ended their work abruptly.

"Tell me your name?" Randus asked as he collected his bag and tools, never actually looking at her.

"Vitalis."

"Be back at dawn," he commanded.

This day would be even longer, as it was her turn to watch the sheep at night. There would be no sleep. Determined to learn the craft of wall decoration and to earn money for her manumission, she would be awake for two full days. "I can sleep later," she told herself. "But someone is going to have to help with my chores. I'll talk to Telesphorus on his next visit about a dog again. A dog would stay awake and watch the sheep, and I could get a little sleep."

QUINTUS CAME BACK three days later. The artisans took a break to make drawings and sketches of the ornamental design that would be applied to the walls. Colors would be chosen and supplies purchased. Vita's help was not requested for the planning. Disappointed, because drawing was everything to her, she desperately wanted to be included. Drawing was all she did when time was hers.

"I can do it," she told herself. "It's my talent, my father's gift to me, I just need a chance."

However, today was a welcomed day of rest. She was exhausted but delighted Quintus had come to see her. They visited the hives to check on her production of honey and pulled some for themselves with sticks. They sucked the sweetness of honey and of their life and love. He laughed and she giggled as the honey dripped down their chins and made them stick together when they kissed. Vita felt so secure and sheltered as Quintus held her and told her of his love and her beauty and caressed her neck with his lips. His hands adored her body arousing her desire.

"I made this for you," he said before he left and handed her a small drawstring bag made of flax. She opened it and stared at a golden ring with a red center stone. On the stone he'd carved a mother hen with her chicks. The carving was no bigger than a lemon seed and beautifully crafted. Only the wives of wealthy men would own such a ring.

"It is so beautiful." She slipped it on her finger and wrapped her arms around his neck. "I love you."

TELESPHORUS ARRIVED with Aquilina on their weekly visit to see Vita and to gather supplies and give instructions. Telesphorus had been diligent about tending to the farm while Gaius was in Britannia. Reticulus, the overseer, had decided to cooperate rather than be exiled. The expansion was successful, the buildings were completed, the slaves were healthier, and the business was pulling a nice profit. It also gave a chance for Telesphorus to see Vita.

The two visitors from Herculaneum lumbered into the farm villa knocking over chairs with their packages from the markets and set them down by the hearth. There were seedling vines to plant for the vineyard, grain from Egypt, fabrics for Fradia, and jars.

"We brought lots of jars. Some for the lotion and some for the honey," said Aquilina happily. "Everything is selling so fast! We are making lots of money. Telesphorus can barely keep up with the finances."

"Yes, but I need to buy more slaves soon. Where is Vitalia?" asked Telesphorus.

"She is working today with the artisans at the magnificent seaside villa," said Fradia proudly. "It is two weeks now that they pay her."

"When will she return?"

"Not long now. They don't work when it is getting dark."

There was much to do. Telesphorus went out with sacks to collect the olive produce. Vita arrived and began helping Aquilina and Fradia fill jars with the prepared lotion.

"You know many of the ladies who are buying this lotion want it to lighten their skin. Would there be a way to add something white?" said Aquilina. "You know how women like to look as if they never work out in the sun and only have a life of leisure. Something with white could create another lotion for me to sell."

"In Ephesus, my mother scraped the sweet white crystal from the side of the lead cooking pot to make a light lotion. That would certainly be possible," Vita said. "Or maybe the artisans would let me borrow a mortar and pestle at night to crush white marble into powder. I have had a lot of practice making dust! I wonder if white marble dust could be added to lighten the lotion. We can try it. We will practice on Fradia!"

They all laughed for she had the darkest suntanned skin of all three.

VITA WALKED with Telesphorus out to the bee hives to check on them. She knew he wanted time alone with her but she just wanted him to pack up and leave. Being so full of dreams and fantasies about Quintus made it hard to carry on a long conversation about the gods or his God which they always talked about.

"What are all these small sticks piled up?" He'd noticed the ones she and Quintus had been using to rob some of the honey. "Are you eating a lot of honey?"

"Yes, I am," she answered.

"I think it is best to sell the honey and not eat so much of it," said Telesphorus. He paused waiting for her to laugh or answer, but she was strangely quiet. "Does your work with the artisans make you tired?"

"Oh no, I love it and soon I will have an opportunity to show them how I can draw. I'm just waiting for a chance." Vita moved away from him toward the hives.

"I'm coming back next week. Will you be glad to see me?"

"Of course. I am always glad to see you. You saved my life and gave me this perfect place to live. The mountain is covered with olive trees, grape vineyards, the sheep are like children to me, and I have the most wonderful friends here. I wake up to birds singing and a view of the sea below. Sometimes the mountain shakes to remind me to look and see the colors of life everywhere, then it belches an ugly sulphur smell to remind me to savor the fresh scent of grapes and grass and flowers." She hesitated, then asked, "How are things with Calitoria? When will I be able to come back to Herculaneum?"

"She had the baby." He watched her twist a lock of her hair.

"Oh." She tried to seem interested.

"Why do you want to leave? You are happy here and safe, you are working." He waited to see if she would say more.

Her eyes sought the security of the farmhouse, yearning to avoid any more conversation. She started walking back.

Telesphorus's body ached watching her walk away, wondering what he had done to cause her rejection.

VITA AND AQUILINA packed the many jars of lotion and made several trips loading them in the wagon.

"Do you think you can sell all of this?" asked Vita.

"Oh yes, I could sell more. The ladies talk to each other about the lotion and how it smooths their skin and heals their scars and blemishes. They are using it on their faces and hands, all over their bodies! We have people from Pompeii asking for it. We could probably sell it there in the market or at least deliver it to someone to sell. Quintus goes to Pompeii to sell his jewelry sometimes. He could take it for us."

"He is so perfect," Vita sighed. "Thank you for telling Quintus where I am. I am so in love with him."

Aquilina paled and turned to look at Vita. "I thought it was a friendship...I thought he worried about you because he felt responsible. Didn't he tell you he is married with a child on the way?"

"No. No. No!" Vita's hand covered her mouth. "But he loves me! He comes here to be with me! We are one, together, it's forever!"

"He didn't tell you? He comes here to be with you and he didn't tell you! What kind of man would do that?" Aquilina cried. "He has a wife and soon a child! He has a different life now. If he would hurt you this way, he only thinks of himself. A man like that will only bring you unhappiness and you will end up alone. He doesn't love you. He wants only one thing. Why would you want to be with a man like that? Forget him! How dare he hurt you this way. You are my dear friend. Forget him!"

"I can't. I love him. He says he loves me. It is only because he thought I was dead that he must have married."

"But you can't change what has happened. He will leave you. You will be alone!"

Vita looked down and put her hand on her stomach. "You don't know, Aquilina. You have never been in love. We are one, I am his. It is a strong love. You know nothing about this!"

"Yes, I know nothing about this. And you are making a mistake. It is easy for women in this time and place to be used by men. That is what I know. He is not being honest with you! Find someone else. What happened to the girl that was going to be free and buy her freedom? What happened to Vitalis the girl who pretended to be a boy and was strong enough to go to the docks, the girl who battled in Pompeii and risked her life so bravely, only to crumble when this boy says he loves her! Be smart, Vitalia!"

"I hate you, Aquilina!" She ran to the barn, away from the truth, and hid. "This can't be," she sobbed. "He loves me. I am his. We planned a future together. He chose me. He would have told me if it was true. Aquilina is wrong. She only told me this because she has nobody."

Vita's next days were horrible. Trapped by her love for Quintus and still a slave, she couldn't leave and run away, she couldn't go back to Ephesus. It no longer existed for her without her parents alive and waiting to comfort her. Quintus was not a savior for her. He'd used her love. Using someone was not real love.

Her daily chores and work with the artisans sustained her. She would not allow herself to think or feel. One emotion would not leave her, and that was the anger. It was like hot stew bubbling inside her. The love she had for Quintus was now cancelled out by her outrage at being used. And it wasn't just Quintus. Calitoria controlled her, too. Her attempt to get rid of Vita had forced her to the farm and caused all this to happen.

At first, she wasn't hungry so she didn't eat. Maybe she just would not eat and show everybody that they could not force her to do anything, just some water and a bite of bread if she had to have something. Five days with no food. Fury sustained her. She could feel it rush through her body. It felt good.

I feel strong. It all makes sense to me now. This trap has a way out. I am no fool.

Would she be able to tell Quintus to never come see her again?

Chapter Twenty-Eight

It wasn't even two days before Quintus came strolling up the path where Vita tended her bees. She understood bees. They were predictable. The bees saved their sting for the dangers in life, but because they trusted Vita they gave her passage into their world of work and honey. Each one did its job, some caring for the newborns, some adventuring out into the world to search, some cleaning the hive, some fluttering their wings to cool the air for the others' comfort. Not one better than the other, no one owning anyone else.

Pretending not to see Quintus approaching, she pulled a honeycomb out and scraped the sweet substance into an iron pot. Quintus did not deserve the sweetness of her adoring gaze. She knew the truth now. However, she saved the sting of her anger. Should she give him an opportunity to confess?

"Vitalis!" he called.

She turned. His chiseled jaw held the smile he saved for her. His dark eyes reflected the love in his heart. At first, she began to soften. Such a handsome man. Her soul reached out to him but her intellect cringed. This was the man she was going to give her life to? Now, to give herself to him would be the same as destroying the spirit of herself. She faced him, cocked her head to one side, and glared at him.

"So your wife is with child and you come here to me during her time of heavy burden!" Her preoccupation with his deceit unleashed her tongue to truthfulness.

He was unable to plot a response. "No! I assure you, it is not that way."

"Oh, it is not? How can you say that when it is so? You think me stupid. Just because I am female and trapped in this slavery, you think I can be used?" she said.

"You misunderstand. I love you. I thought you were dead, gone forever. So I married. Not for love, but for trying to have what we had, a friendship, a companion, someone to be with to enjoy life."

"But you did not tell me you were married. Why not? Because you are trying to convince me to accept half a friendship, half of someone to love. This would be a convenience for you, to have all you want. Not all I want. I just want to love you completely, but loving you would have to include respecting you. And I can't respect someone who hides the truth so they can have everything they want."

"Please, we can still be together. I am making a fortune selling my jewelry. I have enough to share with you. Let's enjoy our time together. Don't make this the end." He stepped closer and clasped her hand to pull her towards him. "You don't want that."

Vita snapped her hand away and wrapped her arms around herself.

"Even now you try to use me. Stay away. I won't settle for half a life. You want to share your fortune with me like you will buy me?" She stared into his perfectly shaped eyes, steeling herself to not give in. "I will make my own fortune."

How could the only girl he wanted reject him? Quintus stepped back and tried to hurt her with his own sharp tongue. "You will be sorry. You can't make your own fortune, stupid girl. You should take my offer. I would take care of you. No one else will."

Vita watched him turn and walk away not looking back. He thought she would come after him.

Arrogant, she thought.

THE NEXT MORNING the sun lightened the shadows with yellow warmth. Vita wandered like death through daily chores, tending the bees, drafting the lanolin from the sheep's wool, adding the white dust to her lotions. *What happens to us that makes us this way?* she thought. So unhappy, the hardest part was reliving the love she once felt. Still angry, she glued it to her righteous soul, and it became a part of her. So changed. So hardened. She lost herself.

She went to check on the sheep. One of the slaves had stayed up to watch through the night, but she found him sleeping. He jumped at the sound of her feet crunching on the gravel and pretended that he was just pulling a blanket over his shoulders.

"How was everything last night?" she asked.

"Didn't hear anything last night but we can walk around and check on everybody. Sheep are like children. Need to check on them," he laughed.

She saw the bloody body of a lamb and she wept. "That makes three this week. They don't even eat the whole thing! They kill just to kill for pleasure, not hunger or fear! Sheep harm no one and yet they are prey for the more powerful." More anger. It was her constant companion. " We have to do something. Why can't you stay awake for one night!"

Chapter Twenty-Nine

Aquilina gently touched the handle of the servants' door to the Herculaneum villa pulling the lever down. Hopefully, Lavinia was not in the kitchen. She used her elbow to hold the door open as she balanced the box of containers filled with Vita's lotion. She walked softly across the stone floor to the usual hiding place far under the bottom shelf. Bending low, she shoved the crate as far as she could and hid it with a carefully tucked towel. She stood up and saw Lavinia in the doorway watching her with hands on her hips.

"What is that you are hiding?" she asked.

"Just some supplies from the farm. I'm not hiding it, just moving it," Aquilina answered.

Lavinia walked over and pulled the crate out and removed the covering. She picked up one of the jars and poured the lotion in her hand.

"This is Vitalia's lotion. You brought it from the farm." She watched Aquilina's face. "No one else knows how to make this."

"I can make it," Aquilina lied. "I have been selling it at the market."

"So, how do you make it?"

"Well, I take sheep wool and boil it, then scrape the residue from the top and put it in little pots." Her mind raced as she tried to remember the procedure Vita had used the only time she'd watched. She looked toward the door.

Lavinia took off the stopper of one of the containers and sniffed the lovely fragrance.

"This is different. It smells lovely. How did you change the scent to make it more pleasing?"

"I add something." Aquilina panicked as she planned her next lie.

"What thing?"

Lavinia glared, watching Aquilina struggle. She waited for a convincing answer, but Aquilina pressed her lips together and stared down at her hands.

"Vitalia is at the farm, isn't she!"

Lavinia grabbed Aquilina's arm and pulled her to the tablinum where Telesphorus sat secluded, knowing that he also had been to the farm. She faced him squeezing Aquilina's arm.

"How long have you known Vitalia is at the farm?" she asked Telesphorus.

"I did not tell! She guessed!" said Aquilina.

Telesphorus leaned out from his chair searching for anyone who might hear. He held his head in his hands studying the geometric marble pattern of the mosaic terra, as if noticing it for the first time, and shook his head slowly. His wall of protection for Vita was crashing one stone at a time.

First Aquilina knew, now Lavinia knew. Gaius would be home soon, and he would know. Fear for Vita's life and his own reminded him of beatings and the killing of deceptive slaves. Never had his plan for Vita included Gaius's return. Why hadn't he thought of that? Now, Calitoria would find out. He shook his head knowing the end was near.

"I cry aloud to God, aloud to God, that He may hear me. In the day of my trouble I seek the Lord... my hand is stretched out in the night, and does not rest; my soul refuses to be comforted. I remember God, and I moan; I meditate and my spirit faints."

Lavinia and Aquilina watched as the young scholar seemed to enter a trance reciting his scripture. He sat with eyes closed not speaking, not responding, breathing slowly and deliberately, calming himself. Finally, he spoke.

"Don't you know that Calitoria will react with anger and retaliation?" He shook his head. The sound of his voice was low and grave. "No one can keep a secret here. That is why I didn't tell you even when I saw you suffering. Now, I will be discovered, and I fear what she will do to Vitalia."

"Then, it is true," Lavinia whispered.

"Leave me," he said.

CALITORIA STEPPED out of her bedchamber with the baby and noticed Telesphorus pacing in the tablinum, bent over, frantically running his fingers through his hair over and over again. She could tell something was very wrong.

"Telesphorus, what are you so worried about? Is the farm failing? Have you heard bad news about Gaius? What is so wrong that you are unable to sit still? You are always so calm studying your documents. What has happened?"

He halted and realized Calitoria had caught him in his frenzied state and wondered how to distract her. The baby wriggled in her arms, so he walked over to him. A cap covered the infant's head hiding his orange hair, the damning characteristic.

"How is the young one today? Have you chosen a name yet?"

"He will have one on the ninth day. No, I haven't decided yet. I was hoping Gaius might arrive home before that time comes. Have you heard anything?"

"No, but I will go to the Baths today and see if there is any news about Britannia. They will try to regain peace, and Gaius will be working very hard, I am sure. Perhaps a letter will come again. Have you recovered from your confinement and giving birth?"

"Yes," she giggled. "I can walk upright again. Hopefully, the next babe will arrive with less work."

"Already planning another?"

"Oh yes. The Empire encourages more children, and there will be some forgiveness of taxes. I know that it will be financially rewarding to our family if I can produce at least three children, preferably boys."

"I thought you were only producing an heir for Gaius and yourself so that you would become the mistress and inherit everything when he dies."

"I don't like you saying such a carping comment to me. Perhaps, I like having children. It is not that difficult for me. Did you not consider that I might be a good mother?"

"That is not what I am talking about. I know you very well, Calitoria. Being a good mother was not your goal. Securing your situation as a woman was your goal. Just remember that I have known you longer than anyone in this villa."

"Because of your friendship and faithfulness to me, and as your mistress, I will forget your acid tongue. Your corrupt thoughts, however, shall remain unspoken forever, as you remember you are a slave in this family."

"As your slave, I will keep my knowledge and understanding of you and your situation to myself." He bowed to her.

He reached over and pulled the babe's cap back and fondled his orange hair. He stared directly into Calitoria's eyes with a slight tilt and nod of his head. Calitoria gasped. There was only one other human in this small village who had orange hair and the power of this unspoken truth screamed between them. Telesphorus knew the real father. At that moment, her childhood tutor and friend became her enemy. He now held power over her. She knew he could tell Gaius at any time.

"I will leave you to your figures and plans," she said.

Telesphorus watched her leave and wondered if he made a mistake revealing that he knew her secret. His own secret, if Calitoria found out, might give her reason to discard him. Roman law would allow it. Disobedient slaves could be put to death. For now, she only knew that he held her secret.

THE NEXT AFTERNOON Telesphorus distracted himself with work from the farm and the comfort of his numbers. Clients sat on a bench outside, along the wall of the villa, waiting their turn to ask for work or to sell supplies. He called them in one by one hardly looking up when the next solicitor approached.

"My brother in The Way, peace be with you."

"I recognize that voice! Marci Helvii Erotis! My friend!" He jumped up with an embrace.

"Telesphorus, you have been on my mind. I think about you so often, but now I make an effort to come see you. What have you been doing?"

"Running the farm, managing the finances, all the usual responsibilities."

"No, really, what have you been doing?" Marci studied his friend. "Something is on your face that I see but can't understand. You look like you have a heavy burden. Not the relaxed Jew that left me after hearing Paul speak in Puteoli."

"It is strange that you happen to come now." Telesphorus paused and turned away. "I do need someone to talk to about something, a problem I have made for myself. I am trapped; there is no way I can get myself out of this. We have to talk somewhere else, though. Do you have time?"

They walked down to the coast and found a point where they could sit and watch men moving heavy crates and boxes from unsteady boats to the secure docks. Telesphorus debated in his mind whether to speak about his secret. He studied his friend's face. *Such a compassionate man that lives his faith.* They watched another crate being removed from a bobbing vessel, releasing its burden to another. Marci waited. Clouds moved slowly suspending time. Finally, Telesphorus confessed that Gaius would be home soon and a deception might destroy the trust of his master and require punishment.

Telesphorus paused. "You are not commenting. Why?"

"I am waiting for you to finish unloading the burden you are carrying."

Telesphorus stood up and paced a few steps. Marci sat with his hands on his knees watching his friend's face. "You seem so troubled."

Telesphorus continued to pace.

"Vitalia was so smart she could converse with me on any subject. I confided in her about my Jewish faith and my visit to hear Paul speak. I shared all my thoughts. I found myself admiring her as a friend. Others in the home thought she was a goddess because of the aura that she carried. She has a countenance that is beautiful and endearing. If you saw her, you would know what I mean."

He gazed afar, his profile etched with suffering.

"I have now fallen in love with her. Her kindness and purity is what I want to be with always. Her talent for anything she has attempted is inspiring, and she has become a great beauty. While Gaius was home, Calitoria hid her contempt for her, but when Gaius left for Britannia, it became dangerous. Calitoria planned to have Vitalia killed by a local gladiator, who earns money in various ways, one being as a punisher of slaves."

"But why did your mistress want to have her killed?"

"She could see that everyone, including Gaius, loved her. It is harder to feel the same about Calitoria. The more she despised Vitalia, the more dislikable she became. It consumed her. I saved Vitalia by hiding her at the farm and lying. I told everyone that I did not know where she was. Now, I am set to be caught in my deceptions. I have not only created a problem for myself but also for Vitalia. I don't know what to do. I felt I was doing the right thing when I was saving her from harm." He rubbed his forehead, trying to wipe away the pain. "I can't see any way out of this."

"You love this girl."

"With all my heart."

"Does she love you?"

"It is torture. I believe she loves another, a young man here in the village. Perhaps, she cares for me, but her love is for another. I see it in her and it is destroying me." His dark eyes were moist. "My secret has already been discovered by two of the house slaves. The master will return and want answers. I'm sure the two slaves will tell when forced. What can I do." He said as a statement not as a question for there was no answer.

Marci discerned spiritual need. They were both Jews, one a Craestus Jew, the other a faltering Jew. Finally, he spoke.

"A group that believes the Messiah has already come for us, and are some of the friends you met when we listened to Paul in Puteoli, are having meetings in Pompeii. The meetings are in a large inn where the owner allows us to meet for a fee. I will tell you how to find it. Maybe the answer to your pain will be found there."

"I must try something."

"We are under severe criticism, so we are forced to hide. They call us Christians and we are not popular. We are considered at the least, troublesome, at the most, cannibals. The meetings are not announced. You must find it on your own without asking questions of the locals. It is a large inn near the Stabian Baths and east of the Forum. Drusus is the owner. Ask for Maria."

~

TELESPHORUS HATED TRAVELING. He would rather be with his numbers and studies. He hated the anxiety of new people to meet and talk to, coins to be carried that could be stolen, and finding his way where he was unfamiliar. Pompeii was not as bad a city as others he had tried, but other ventures secured the thought that he did not take joy in travel. Never had he gone to Pompeii alone, and finding the Inn without asking for directions seemed impossible.

He arrived at the city of Pompeii, packed with sailors, gamblers, and aggressive souls, under the guise of needing to speak personally with Jucundus regarding business matters. Calitoria had barely listened to his well-crafted excuse. Now, he needed to find a sect of believers that were trying to be invisible in Pompeii, of all places, where only a few people knew God's commandments and only a few chose to follow them.

The sun climbed to its peak, heating the stone walkways. Awnings provided shade, so he crossed over, ducking under each refuge. He passed the Forum where visions of the awful night of riots blurred his goal. So many people, loud with voices, the odor of fish and over-ripe vegetables—he needed to avoid the chaos and turned away toward the Baths. Standing on the corner, lost in the city with its many inns, he searched the roadway for help. An old man, obviously a slave who labored sweeping the walk, looked friendly. Perhaps, he could ask the old man if he knew where an unpopular Christian group—harassed by the Emperor, gathered in secret because of hatred, afraid for their lives— might be found. He laughed to himself. It was impossible to know how to find these friends of Marci Helvii Erotis.

Glancing down he caught sight of graffiti on the wall next to him with the name 'Maria'. He looked closer and under her name it said "Bovios is listening to the Christians, cruel haters." Could this be the Maria whom Marci mentioned? He guessed that someone must have been waiting on their friend at this same corner and passed the time by writing on the wall. Perhaps they were annoyed that Bovios, whoever he was, attended a meeting of righteous people delaying their evening of gambling and drinking.

Created by T.Griffith from Pompeii Graffiti

This could be the Inn where the followers of Jesus meet, he thought and walked around the corner to the entrance. He faced an inn that lacked elegance, displaying only practical function for travelers. The red walls with black rectangle accents were common decor with small vignette murals of birds and foliage. He walked up to the manager to inquire about a room.

"I was told to ask for Maria at your inn."

"Oh, you are one of those," the innkeeper answered, turning to look and judge the new guest. "Meetings are in the room over there. How will you pay for your lodging and will you need services from our prostitute?"

"No, just a room, please."

He followed the innkeeper upstairs. A welcome sight was in front of him, a bed, and a pillow. He rested.

Chapter Thirty

H unger pulled at Telesphorus's resolve to hide in his room. As the sun set to take its seat over the sea, he ventured out to find a meal. Passing several thermopolia, he judged their offerings by sight and smell, settling on one that had decorated frescoes indicating it must be a popular stop for travelers. The counter was long with four built-in holes harboring food choices. Some salty fish, baked cheese, bread, and spicy wine would numb the moan of his stomach. An outdoor stone bench provided a brief seat to balance his meal on his lap. Other patrons were socializing, so he kept his eyes on his meal and rushed to eat.

Returning to the Inn, he found a quiet gathering of men and women in the corner of the atrium greeting one another. His eyes searched for Marci, but he had made no promise of attending when he suggested the meeting might help Telesphorus. *No need to speak to the others*, he thought.

As they settled into their worship, he heard familiar chants of Jewish psalms. Some he had memorized himself as a personal challenge, competing with others who memorized whole books of the holy story of his people. They spoke from the popular scriptures of Isaiah:

He was despised and rejected by men,
a man of sorrows, and familiar with suffering.

Like one from whom men hide their faces
he was despised and we esteemed him not.
Surely he took up our infirmities
and carried our sorrows.

The words recited in unison hummed through the air and touched
his heart. Telesphorus knew of his own infirmities and sorrows, though
his sorrows seemed more about the snare he had created for himself. He
only felt guilt as he listened again.

We all, like sheep, have gone astray,
each of us has turned to his own way;
and the Lord has laid on him
the iniquity of us all.

He knew they were reciting the prophecies of Jesus from the Holy
Book. Those verses were familiar to him from his childhood when his
parents took him to the Temple for teaching and worship. It seemed so
long ago.

"We are blessed that an eyewitness is with us that saw our Messiah
and heard Him speak." With that announcement, an elderly man stood
up dressed like any other Jew in homespun cloth with belt and pouch.

"Our Jesus, a teacher, so wise, won over many Jews and Greeks to
accept the new life, but He was despised and rejected by those who
loved Yahweh. Even though the Holy One told us in prophecy over and
over again, our Messiah was with us and we did not recognize Him. So
many prophecies foretold His coming. Isaiah:

Then the eyes of the blind will be opened,
And the ears of the deaf will be unstopped.
Then the lame will leap like a deer,
And the tongue of the dumb will shout for joy.

"I saw all these things happen. We even knew He would be born in
Bethlehem from the branch of David, from Micah:

But as for you, Bethlehem Ephrathah,
Too little to be among the clans of Judah,
From you One will go forth for Me to be ruler in Israel.
His goings forth are from long ago,
From the days of eternity.

"and Jeremiah:

I shall raise up from David a righteous Branch;

And He will reign as king and act
wisely
And do justice and righteousness
in the land.

"Then came the horrible day He was arrested. It says:

Even my close friend in whom I
trusted,
Who ate my bread,
Has lifted up his heel against me.

"He was betrayed by one of His own for 30 pieces of silver just like the prophecy in Zechariah:

and I said to them, 'If it is good in your sight,
give me my wages; but if not, never mind!'
So they weighed out thirty shekels of silver as my wages."

His throat caught and he paused with head bowed until he could speak again.

"I saw it; I was there. They crucified Him. I knew He could do miracles. He could have gotten down from that cross, but He chose to be the payment for all the wrongs of the people the Holy One loves. When He hung on the cross, more prophecies were fulfilled. He said, 'Into thy hand I commit my spirit,' as in 31. The soldiers came to break His legs to speed His death along, but they didn't because He was already dead, as predicted in 34. Just to make sure, they stabbed Him in the heart as in Zechariah.

"We thought it was over, but at the sixth hour when the sun was overhead, a darkness as dark as night covered the land until the ninth hour, just as forecasted in Amos.

And it will come about in that day, declares the Lord God,
That I shall make the sun go down at noon
And make the earth dark in broad day light.

"We should have known He was the Messiah. Someone said Jesus could have fulfilled all those prophecies on purpose. Can a man choose his place of birth, can a man design his manner of death and people's reactions, can a man control being stabbed after death? After He died, we asked to take Him down and find a place for burial. A wealthy man from Arimathea named Joseph asked Pilate for the body and wrapped it in a clean linen cloth and put Him in his own tomb. I will quote the scripture from Isaiah. 'His grave was assigned to be with wicked men, yet with a rich man in His death.'"

Telesphorus stood in the back of the group and listened. The eyewitness was passionate. There was nothing false about him. This group had something so different from anyone in Herculaneum. *There are Jews here. They seem to believe this.* Then the eyewitness continued with more testimony.

"Jesus said He would be raised on the third day. We did not understand. He said He would rise again from the dead. I must admit, I did not understand. When He said that, I fell away. I didn't believe it. But the Rabbis did and were so afraid of His teaching, they put guards at the tomb with a sealed stone at the entrance. It is a mystery and a fact that Jesus was gone when the stone was rolled away. They said the grave cloths were left behind. No one disputes that Jesus was gone from the tomb, not the soldiers, not the Jews, not Pilate, not the followers.

"I went to Galilee. Jesus said He would go before us after he rose from the dead and be in Galilee. I had to be there. We waited on the mountain in Galilee and He came to us. We all saw him. I am an old man, still here to tell you, but many of the others have already passed."

Telesphorus turned to leave. *I don't see how any of this is helping me with my trap. I did not get an answer. I will still lose everything—my home, my job, my life, and I will lose Vitalia,* he thought.

THE NEXT MORNING he collected his belongings, paid his bill, and left, heading toward the sea to find his boat back to Herculaneum. He waited by the city gate as the usual vendors approached offering him food, perfume, or leather goods, just like he was any other visitor. His gesture of waving them off showed his irritation, but his eyes fell upon a young man who had a litter of puppies.

Before he came to his senses, he purchased the downy white one. The dog gazed up with sleepy black eyes, sniffed with his pudgy nose, and licked the hand that cradled him. "I'll call you Pax." He tucked him in his bag. *What is the matter with me? I bought a dog,* he thought and boarded his boat determined to nurture his dark mood.

His arrival in Herculaneum with the puppy would cause hysterical screams and laughter from the women and a disapproving soliloquy from Calitoria. He wished Gaius would come back and restore order to the family. The only male other than himself was Certa, who mostly stayed in the garden and had never spoken a word since his purchase. Aquilina said she heard him humming to himself, but no one else could testify to ever hearing him make a sound.

Facing the villa full of women and a baby brought about his crusty nature. *I'm going directly to the farm.* He disembarked from the boat in Herculaneum, hired a horse, and rode up the mountain to see the only other personality he could tolerate, Vita.

Chapter Thirty-One

Tall grass with feathery tops surrounded Vita, snatching sequenced billows of wind. A secluded patch of shade in the mountain olive grove gave her quiet time to be alone. Thoughts of Quintus's betrayal crowded her thinking. She still loved him or at least wanted to be in love with him, like the flower that wants to grow and bloom and produce seed amidst the beauty of color and freshness. Memories of their happiest moments came rushing, then waves of grief and loss of the future. Emotions rolled, repeating a constant ride of love followed by despair, all life and hope smothered. Even the joy she felt in the hypocritical sunshine gave her reason for her dark mood: fickle light of day, first the sun then the clouds to take the light away.

She sketched on parchment under the trees. Her fingers gripped the charcoal, memorizing the movement needed to make her drawings life-like. She practiced her drawing because it broke the cycle of despair, but today it consumed her. The pleasure of black contrasting with white gave the flat blank parchment shape, as if it could be picked up off the page. Simple lines came together to create a familiar form so accurate that she detached from this world with pride. She never heard him call to her or saw him standing there watching her tenderly. Finally, he spoke.

"Vitalia," he smiled, amused that she was not aware of anything around her. "What are you working on?"

"Telesphorus, you surprised me. I didn't expect to see you today." She needed a friend, especially this one that cared for her. They could talk for hours or simply sit quietly together in silence

"I'm practicing drawing hands. Hands that hold something precious, hands that gesture with a sign, hands that reach out or hang at the side. The artisans are allowing me to help with the sketching on wet crushed marble before the pigment is added. We work quickly as a team. Everyone has a job and this is mine. I just do the hands. I must be fast and confident with no mistakes. The slurry dries quickly, then one of my artist friends adds the pigment colors following my form and shadows. It is so much fun, and they pay me very well."

"I am so proud of you. You deserve it. Your lotions are doing well at the market. Aquilina sells them there but other ladies are asking for them and send their handmaidens to pick them up at the villa." He decided not to tell her that the lotions had exposed the secret of her hiding at the farm to Lavinia. "The honey sells well, too. Both are some of the most expensive items at the market."

He sat down beside her. The tall grass protected them. Vita hid her scorched heart, and Telesphorus harbored his own approaching shipwreck that was sure to crash with Gaius's return from Britannia.

"You look well," he said. "You are very beautiful, you know." There was more he wanted to say, that she carried a glow, an illusion of saintly beauty that was beyond rare, eyes the color of the sea, dark hair that gently framed her perfect face.

"That is nice to hear." She looked up at him, reluctant to accept a compliment when she felt so miserable, but to settle into his arms and feel protected seemed natural.

"I'll always take care of you," he said.

She nestled closer. He said exactly what she needed to hear. She felt alone and her heart cried out for someone to love her.

"Where have you been?" she asked.

"I went to Pompeii to hear the followers of Jesus speak. I hoped for more than I got. Part of me wanted to believe what they said, but to accept that belief requires so much. I can't just say I believe. It must show in your life transforming your thinking about everything. If I give in to the belief, it must be my whole truth not just a ritual. The gods and goddesses we worship in our home and city do not require a change; they just require attention and sacrifice. This is different. It must be an inner change to become better as a person. No hypocrisy."

"You sound conflicted. What would you change about yourself? You are a good person."

"A lot of self-sacrifice, thinking and helping others and they say to love my enemies. I need to think all that through, about what it means, before I give my life to follow the teachings. I can't just pretend. So, for now I am not worrying about it. I came to see you because you make me feel good, and I enjoy you more than anyone else. I couldn't go back to the villa yet. It is chaos with a baby and all the women chattering. The tradesmen constantly call and interrupt." He curled his arm around her.

She gave in to his touch. The physical need for love aroused by Quintus made her turn to look in his eyes to see a softness that she could trust, a trust that glowed without deceit. She wrapped her arms around his neck. He moved close, and they relaxed in the delight of the taste of their first kiss. The afternoon was theirs to give in to each other and become one.

~

THEY WALKED BACK to the farm villa without touching should anyone suspect their affection.

"I have something for you," he said. "I brought a gift from Pompeii."

Entering the farm villa, Vita saw Fradia standing guard over a woven basket next to the hearth, filled with a puff of white fur. At first, she thought it resembled the fluff of wool that came at shearing time until a little face with a black nose and two round eyes woke up and looked at her shaking its tail. Vita melted at the sight and immediately picked him up.

"His name is Pax. He's very young, and he will need some training to watch the sheep. You mustn't get too attached," he said, already worrying about her reaction. "You can only keep him with you until he is half-grown, and then he must sleep and eat and live with the sheep so that he thinks he is one of them. Bred to protect and defend, he will fight to the death for his adopted kin. You will never have to worry about predators attacking the sheep without warning anymore, and should you fall asleep on your watch, he will never forget to be alert."

Those words were ignored as she showed her love for this darling dog, cradling him like a baby. Pax licked her face, nibbled her ears, and pulled at her hair making her giggle. Vita gazed at Telesphorus knowing that she wasn't in love with him, but this was a man she could trust to love her. He had saved her life, put her above all else, watched over her safety, fulfilled her needs rather than his own. Compared to finding love with Quintus, which started because he was handsome in the beginning, this man rested in her heart in a different way. His too-lean body was not attractive but his love soothed her. *He is such a good man. Maybe there is wisdom in this second choice and I could be safe allowing him in my heart,* she thought.

Vita had no way of knowing that Telesphorus was thinking about his own fate. He had to return to Herculaneum and hope Lavinia and Aquilina would not reveal the secret that Vita was alive and at the farm.

"Could you stay the night?" Vita asked him to stay and he agreed. They took Pax with them to the barn to make a comfortable refuge for the three of them. The puppy fell asleep, leaving them alone to hold each other close and talk.

"You know the artisans still think I am Vitalis, the boy who can draw," she giggled. "I swagger and talk tough with them. I know all the bad words. Lately, they seem to be a bit kinder around me. Maybe, because I can draw. I have so much to do here at the farm, and now I sell the beeswax to the manager which they use to melt and mix in with their pigments. I have to filter it several times to make it clean and a very light color." She dug into her pocket and pulled out the bag of coins she'd earned and delivered them to Telesphorus.

"You always amaze me," he said. "We already have a large sum to pay for your freedom. I am hopeful that I can negotiate with Gaius a fair cost that will release you, if that is still what you want."

"I want my freedom back more than anything."

"You know Calitoria doesn't know you are here. I am wondering how I am going to tell her."

"Well, don't. I'll stay here until Gaius comes home."

"It might get difficult for me now, because not only does Aquilina know you are here but now Lavinia knows."

"And so does Quintus," she added.

"Why does he know?" Telesphorus felt a wave of jealousy. Could she hear the irritation in his voice?

"I asked Aquilina to tell him so he wouldn't keep worrying." Vita hid her relationship and break with Quintus holding the secret for now.

"If everyone tells one person then it will no longer be safe for you. Calitoria will still want you killed. At first, her reason was jealousy, now you are a runaway slave. It's a trap for both of us. Even if I could calm her down, she would have you flogged. A flogged slave can never be freed."

"Did you feel that?" Vita put her hand on the ground. It shook again. "It does that all the time. Thana says Hercules lives in the mountain, and he is angry. Do you think he is angry at us for what we have done?"

"There is one God, and it is not Hercules. When the ground shakes, it shakes everywhere, not just where we are."

They held each other with the sleeping puppy nearby until morning when Telesphorus returned to the villa in Herculaneum.

Chapter Thirty-Two

Telesphorus could hear the commotion before he opened the door: the baby crying, Calitoria laughing, female voices filled with excitement, and a man's voice. He opened the door that separated him and saw Gaius.

"Home at last!" he shouted as he dashed forward and threw an arm around the soldier's neck. The friends united, shutting their eyes, both thankful to be together again. "O wandering man, we have been filled with anxiety for you. Are you home for good? When did you get here?"

"Yes, for good, no more distant assignments for me. We arrived by military ship and traveled from Puteoli this morning, only arriving some time before you came through our door."

"We?" Telesphorus looked past Gaius and saw three disheveled small figures in a line behind him.

"And I have returned with three young comrades that united with me while the battle raged. Two young boys and a younger girl who are now orphans and will be part of our family."

Telesphorus looked at the children then searched to study Calitoria's reaction. She stood behind Gaius cradling the baby boy that fussed in her arms. A forced grin sat uncomfortably on her face, while her eyes stared vacantly at the back of Gaius as if she was carving him into little pieces. *At least she knows not to say anything just now,* he thought.

Maybe she is so happy to have Gaius home that the extra urchins will be accepted. She is controlling her emotions and sharp tongue. Perhaps, I have not been able to see that she has matured.

"Oh, Gaius. It is to be expected with your heart for children," said Telesphorus as he turned to inspect the three. Older now after following Gaius for more than a year in Britannia while he completed buildings and streets for the legions, they stood together in layered garments as if they wore everything they owned. It might be that the harsh weather they escaped required heavy fabrics, but in the mild climate of Herculaneum it looked peculiar at this time of year. They each wore a cap covering unruly hair and carried a small sack of possessions.

Thana sat in the corner weeping and fanning herself, her face flushed red with emotion. Even in her dementia, she realized her sacrifices to the gods had been answered. Her son was home from a war.

The atrium echoed, full of family, slaves, and newcomers all talking at once, a suitable welcome home for a hero of the Empire. Lavinia wiped flour from her hands on her tunic as she laughed and smiled. She hugged Aquilina and Talistia as if to say their trials had ended. Every eye gazed on the towering figure of Gaius standing proudly. His deep voice filled the air with security and sanity, which the villa had lacked for so long. Lavinia walked over to the three orphans and looked directly into their eyes.

"You are safe now." It was as if she saw the fear in their souls and knew exactly how to lovingly console them. "Let's go get you something to eat. You must be starved."

Talistia and Aquilina followed, chattering to the children about the long journey they'd endured, pointing out the roses in the garden, the oleander, and fig trees, showing them the kitchen and helping them find stools to sit on.

Lavinia caught Aquilina's eye with a glance of worry. Their secret lingered over the celebration like a menacing cloud before a mighty storm. Aquilina shook her head signaling that no one should speak of it now. The fresh bruise on Aquilina's cheek was visible where Calitoria had stuck her, suspicious, demanding an answer from Aquilina, when friends came to her with compliments on the cosmetics asking for more. Aquilina took the abuse but confessed when Calitoria flew into a rage, shoving her against the wall, threatening her with all the power a slave-owner could deliver. She finally told.

"Telesphorus needs to know that the secret has been discovered before Calitoria has a chance to confront him," whispered Aquilina to Lavinia.

The moment came when Telesphorus walked back to check on the children.

"Telesphorus," Lavinia said, pulling him to the corner by his sleeve. "She knows. Calitoria knows. Aquilina had to tell." He saw the bruise and darkened eye. "What can we do?"

"Don't say anything. Just let it be common knowledge. If anyone asks, tell them that we thought everyone knew she had been found and is fine." He covered his eyes for a moment to help him think and left to find Calitoria.

She was in her cubiculum settling the baby down for a nap. He watched how carefully she tended the babe she called Regulus, meaning 'little king'. She bent and bestowed a soft kiss on his brow, tucked the covers tenderly around him and stood, startled, noticing Telesphorus at the door. She looked directly at him with shoulders square and a scowl of contempt.

"I know everything. Soon I will be rid of the one you call Vitalia. I will tell everyone what you have done, and you both will be gone." Calitoria hissed. "Hiding her at the farm as if she is entitled to have your privileged attention! People think you are good. I will tell the truth of what you have done, and the deceit you have imparted on me and Gaius."

"Ha, you say people think I am good. What about your deceit? If that happens, I will quickly tell Gaius who the real father is, and if that is not enough to scal your scheming lips, I will tell everyone."

After a sustained pause, she knew she was ensnared. This brazen response upset the owner and slave relationship. She spoke again. "Fine. Are you the only one that knows Regulus's real father?"

"Yes."

"Then we have our secrets. You cover for me, and I will cover for you." She turned her back to him and bent low to kiss the sleeping babe.

The deal was done and seemed secure. He felt some vengeance of a sort, a powerful victory. He was the winner. His private soul knew her evil, and the saga seemed finished.

～

OWNER AND SLAVE, more equal than unequal, the two men depended on each other. Telesphorus had always been content in his position as legalist and accountant for the family. His talents were needed and appreciated here. Gaius pulled the curtain dividing the tablinum from the atrium to relax and discuss the past year with his friend.

"So what was it like to be in Britannia during the rebellion of the nasty Celts?" asked Telesphorus.

"Those barbarians are wild and unpredictable subhumans, totally ungovernable. They live on milk and flesh and wear animal skins, a terrifying appearance. They weave garments of dyed wool in gauche colors one against another. They shave their bodies except for the upper lip and head which they allow to grow uncut, then paint their bodies with a blue dye for battle, the evil Picts. The women allow their hair to be untied and wild streaming down their backs! They even have commanding roles in their rebellion. Celts live in tiny round huts with thatched roofs, never making roads or temples.

"We offer them such an opportunity to become like us, I can't imagine why they want to stay the way they are, stupid barbarians. I'm not really satisfied that we have them conquered, small battles are continuing. We lived in perpetual terror waiting for the next attack. Finally, Roman brilliance defeated the ugly Picts on Watling Street. Paulinus planned an attack where they were trapped and could not retreat, formed the traditional fighting wedge, marched forward, and slaughtered everything, just as the Iceni did in Camulodunum, Londinum, and Verulanium. Killed every one of them, even women, children, and their animals. They won't rise again."

"And why did you bring back the three orphans?"

"I'm very protective of them. We went through a lot together. They watched their family and friends die in Camulodunum, and I found out that their fathers died in the battle on Watling Street." Gaius didn't want to say any more. The visual memories of the slaughter and burning of the Temple with all the residents inside haunted him. Somehow, he felt he should have saved them. He stared at the mosaic floor, owner of sorrowful memories along with his three orphans.

"You know, during the worst attack a lady in white led me to safety with the children to a place we could hide. Remember your friend Marci prayed for my safety?" Joy spread across his face. He paused to weigh whether he should share more and decided he said too much.

He asked instead, "Where is that young slave Vitalia? I don't see her in the villa."

"I took her up to the farm. She is there." He nodded slowly with brows knit together.

"Why did you do that? You puzzle me. I wanted her here. She was so helpful with Mother and she seemed so bright. What happened in my absence? You seem so troubled. Tell me."

Now Telesphorus needed to invent a good reason for having Vita at the farm. Some form of half truth might be the easiest way to appear believable without disclosing Calitoria's plot to have her killed.

"It seemed...I decided...of course the little orphan was quite unhappy due to her circumstance, as you know. She seemed to relive her loss daily. I care for her, too. So I felt she might be happier at the farm, which turned out to be true. You would hardly recognize her now. Since you left, she has, shall we say, changed." He wanted to say she had grown into a remarkable beauty, but considered it might reveal his deep feelings of love for her. "In fact, she has several talents that have been financially good for our family."

He wanted to change the subject but didn't need to because at that moment Aquilina interrupted, eyes wide with panic.

"Something is wrong with Thana! She can't breathe!"

Both men jumped to follow her to Thana's bedchamber where they found Thana lying on her back, holding her jaw, in a sweat, trying to take deep breaths.

"Mother, what is wrong?"

"I hurt."

"Get some wet cloths to cool her. I think she has contracted the swamp vapors."

"But we are in a drought," said Telesphorus.

Gaius knew this but his role as paterfamilias compelled him to give medical attention to his family, and he had no other diagnosis. "I think the invisible flying creatures have made her humors out of balance. She is hot so we must make her cold."

Thana struggled to breath. Calitoria appeared at the door. "What is the matter with our beloved Thana?" It was a show of compassion that was not genuine. Her heart bore no emotion, but she forced an amount of concern for Thana. There was no sympathy for the pain of another creature. She felt only jealousy from battling the mother-son relationship that interfered with her possession of Gaius's love. Always strategic in positioning herself closer, she'd push Thana away from Gaius, making sure his time belonged to his wife, not his mother. Now, with Gaius home again the system of barriers would return to control every conversation, every affection, every opinion.

Thana's eyes flickered with recognition as she hallucinated seeing the dead ones. She began to speak in her Etruscan tongue.

"What is she saying?" asked Telesphorus.

"I don't know. I only understand a word or two. I don't understand her family language. It was considered uncultured when I was a child so I refused to learn it." Thana raised her hand to the heavens and continued to call out to the unseen, to Minerva, to the gods.

"She told me before that Vitalia is Minerva. Mother thinks the goddess is masquerading as our orphan slave. Let's bring her here. Vitalia knows the Etruscan language and can tell us what mother is saying." He paused evaluating his decision. "Vitalia can comfort my dear mother." His face darkened with panic.

The sun was beginning to set, and the mountain would be impassible in the dark. Telesphorus would leave to bring Vita to Herculaneum in the morning.

Chapter Thirty-Three

"Don't make me go down there. I am happy here. You told me it was dangerous for me to be around Calitoria and now you are taking me there?" It wasn't really a question. She confronted Telesphorus with the treachery he was performing. He said he loved her so why was he making her go.

"I am not making you go. You have been told to go by Gaius. There is no choice for you. I can't give you that choice. Remember who I am. I am a slave, too."

"You have influence with them. You could have come up with an idea to keep me here. You are the brilliant one with all the plans. The way you move the finances, the way you tell Gaius and Calitoria what to do in a way that they think it is their idea and they are in charge. You let them think that. You could have thought of something to keep me away from her. You said yourself that she wants to kill me, and she can because I am a slave."

"She can't do that now that Gaius is here."

Vita paced around the farmhouse glancing left and right at vacant corners searching her mind for a way to escape. *Nothing has changed, still a slave, still trapped. Another man who says he loves me only to look out for himself when his choice benefits his needs. Again, a man disappoints.*

"You are giving me up to her. I am the sacrifice you use to keep favor with them."

"They are my masters. They give me my place, my job, my home. Gaius is my friend."

"And what is Calitoria to you?" Vita asked.

"She's part of the rules! She goes with Gaius. I have to be careful with her, or I will lose my place."

Vita looked at him reading his soul, finding less and less to respect. Her friend and now lover couldn't find a way to protect her. Vita picked up a basket and dropped in her art supplies and some clothes.

"I need to say goodbye to Fradia and the others. I don't know when I will see them again. Fradia can take a message to the artisans that I will not be able to work with them for now." She walked over to the corner and lifted a plank of flooring to pull out a leather pouch of money.

"Here, my most recent wages. I still believe you are honest and will keep your promise to protect my share. My freedom depends on you. Will you still help me?" She didn't wait for the answer. Her eyes pierced through him. Telesphorus saw the look and set of her jaw as her teeth clenched. She was asking him to choose, to stand up to his slave owner if he loved her.

She walked over to a pile of rags in the corner and picked up the white puppy and tucked him under her arm.

"You aren't taking the dog," he stated.

"Yes, I am."

"The dog is to be trained as a protector of sheep and needs to stay here."

"He is my protector now." And she marched out the door.

TELESPHORUS AND VITA rode together down the mountain on horseback. Both horses seemed skittish, tossing their heads with tightened muscles. Vita turned to look behind her. She heard the mountain rumbling. *Hercules knows I am cursed by this family*, she thought. *He is telling me to run away.*

A startled flock of birds took flight maneuvering in concert, changing shape like a puff of smoke as they read her thoughts, each bird choosing to flee to be safe. Vita wondered what they knew.

The horses balked, stepping off the trail, and refused to go. They dismounted and walked for a while leading the horses to a small brook. Vita sadly stared at the water stumbling over stones hurrying down the mountain toward Herculaneum. "It doesn't know it is rushing down only to be swallowed up by the sea and disappear," she said making the point to Telesphorus of her doom in the analogy.

"You would think the horses would be used to the shaking mountain. It happens all the time," Vita stated.

"They seem more aware today." *Am I taking her into danger?* he worried. "When they see their food in Herculaneum they will forget. I think we can ride again. They have relaxed."

THEY LEFT the horses at the town stable and walked the rest of the way to the Petronius villa. Vita watched Telesphorus push open the thick atrium door. A gust of wind pushed Vita from behind forcing her to step over the threshold. No one came to meet them. Vita directed her steps to Thana's bedchamber obeying the commanded task. She found the old woman barely alive and gray as the mourning dove. Aquilina sat at the bedside dipping a cloth in a bowl of cool water and dabbing at Thana's brow. Vita bent low hugging Aquilina around her shoulders.

"Aquilina, I am here," Vita whispered.

"Oh Vitalia, at last. Thana thinks I am you. She calls for the goddess Vitalia and tells me things I don't understand in her language. I don't know what to do to help her."

"Let me see if I can help." Vita sat down beside the bed and caressed Thana's hand. Compassion for the matriarch that had befriended her returned.

"Minerva. Goddess."

"She is just a confused old woman," said Telesphorus lurking in the corner, watching.

Vita dismissed the comment coming from behind her. She softly touched Thana's arm and spoke in Etruscan. "I have come to help you, Thana. What is it you need?"

"There is evil here. I need to warn you. There isn't much time. The ancients have come for me." Thana motioned to invisible spirits standing in the bedchamber. "You are in danger. There is nothing good for you here. One will take from you your most precious loved one." She tried to take a breath. "It will be soon. Be on your guard. I will ask my son to protect you. I will demand it. You are the good one. My ancient ones are telling me that this is so. Don't leave me."

"I won't. I'm here now. You must rest," said Vita.

Telesphorus and Aquilina studied Vita's pale face desperate to know what had been said. She hid behind a blank expression, sequestering the alarm she felt. *I will not share this prophecy. These things could be said to anyone. Life projects dangers from time to time. Loved ones die from time to time. It is part of life.*

"Thana will need a drink of chamomile and parsley. There is nothing else we can do. I am afraid she knows she is dying. The master should be told. She has something she wants to tell him."

Vita left to take her bags and the dog to her room and settle back into this distressing villa. The next days would be spent comforting Thana as she passed on to join her spirits. Nagging her thoughts, dragging her down, Vita wondered what loved one would be taken away and by whom.

NIGHTTIME FELL. It was late. All the slaves and family were asleep except for Vita. Selfless and forgetting about resentments, she traversed alone through the peristyle to the atrium to collect water for Lavinia's basins. Having the water prepared for the morning extended a small thoughtful kindness to one she loved, the friend who was the first to welcome her to this unfortunate life. Somewhat of a mother substitute for the one that was lost, she taught the behaviors of grace and acceptance, hard work, and a calm spirit. Through her, this villa gave a comfort of home again that was lacking at the farm. Through her amity, a heart that was broken by acrimony could now be healed by affection. Lavinia would be the first one up. Vita wore a grin of private joy as she headed toward the impluvium picturing the surprise on her friend's face when she stumbled into the kitchen rubbing sleep from her eyes and discovered the basins already filled and the kitchen set for a new day.

Only a few oil lamps lit her way as her bare feet padded on the cool mosaic floor. One lamp sat burning on a three legged stand by the impluvium. It had rained that day, ending the drought, so the water was cool and fresh. She dipped the urn, filling it to the brim, then shivered knowing eyes watched her. Glancing behind her she noticed his large figure sitting there in the dark. Gaius relaxed in a chair along the frescoed wall still wearing his soldier tunic and belt, watching her as she rose up holding the urn, delighting in the grace of her subtle body. *Easy to be attracted to such a divine creature,* he thought. Her dark curls framed her glistening face as she nodded to his presence. *Why is he always watching me?* Vita wondered.

It had been years since he left for Britannia, and now they were alone. She had forgotten the power he exuded, this massive man slouching in his chair confident in his domain, a soldier, a master, an owner of property, rich, and now, with a son. He watched her alluring movements with a stare of impatience.

"Come closer," he said aloud, but to himself he said, *This slave glows in the lamplight. This quiet villa becomes a Temple respecting her grace and deity. Minerva exists.*

"Come closer. Are you afraid of me?"

"No sir. I am not afraid."

"I believe you. I can tell you are not but your smile is weak. Did you miss me?"

"I was aware that you were gone."

He stood up towering over her and brushed the hair from her brow with a gentle stroke. He backed her against the wall, caging her with his arms. His eyes searched her body. His hand caught her waist pulling her to him. Vita froze from the intimate touch wanting to run, but with no freedom to do so.

Chapter Thirty-Four

Months passed and the days slipped by one after another. Thana's death removed the ghouls and spirits from the villa allowing the family to relax with no more fear of unseen demons. Gaius mourned his mother, but she had been lost to him for some time. Her altered mind removed the loving companionship they enjoyed. He replaced the memories of insanity with past memories of the joy of his boyhood.

A new skill developed for Vita, avoiding Gaius. Sometimes she hid, sometimes she scurried away at the sound of his distinctive bass voice. He sought her unceasingly, his eyes following her everywhere. This inferior position, without the privilege of choice, made Vita's yearning for freedom an obsession. To be used as a possession, without love from the keeper, made her feel sullied.

He invented a trap to keep her near.

"I want a fresco in the tablinum. It needs to be the story of the goddess Venus and the irresistible Mars falling in love. I saw this popular painting in Pompeii in some of the villas. Venus in all her beauty and Mars filled with passion desperately caressing each other before they fulfill their desire in Vulcan's bed. A happy time for them. I hear you are a talented artisan. Let me see your work."

"I know this painting and similar ones of this story. I remember the winged cupids play with Mars's helmet and shield. Venus is relaxing in his arms. I don't think I am good enough to do this painting. My experience is with a team of artists. I can find other artisans to do it for you."

"Why would I pay others to do what you can do without pay? No questions. You will start."

∿

GAIUS SAT WATCHING Vita prepare the wall with slurry, stretching her body across the surface, reaching her arm to the furthest point then bending to load the flat applicator. Working from top to bottom, she sketched the lovers rapidly, Venus leaning against Mars's athletic body, clutching her chair, agonizing over her thoughts of adultery yet overcome with lust. Several baby cupids were outlined in the background.

Oh dear, my babies look like old men. How many were there? What did the helmet look like? It needs to look like metal. I don't know how to do clouds. I'll dapple these white puffs on the bold blue. I wish I could see the original in Pompeii again. I know Venus had a crown, and her face needs to be faded because she avoids the sun.

Gaius enjoyed the twists and turns of Vita's feminine body standing on a stool then bending low to reach her paint pots. The pigments were mixed with her filtered beeswax sitting in miniature bowls over warmers, red oxide, black charcoal, golden ochre, and blue. She felt his eyes following her like a wolf stalking. Telesphorus came in, drawing the curtain for privacy. Both sat captivated by her curved body and talented hands, watching and staring. She worked quickly against drying time. Beads of sweat across her upper lip glistened, moisture from her brow only made her more beautiful creating ringlets around her face and neck.

Annoyed by the audience, an idea of jest and disrespect for her master grew. The most handsome man she knew was Quintus. Even though he disappointed her he would be the image of Mars. She knew his face so well, and he certainly knew the ways of adultery. She painted his likeness in the fresco. Neither man recognized the resemblance.

She finished. "It's not very good. I'm used to working with a team instead of doing everything myself. At least it is rather small and not the whole wall. The black and yellow frame gives it elegance. That is pleasing."

"I think it is very good," said Telesphorus. "I'll call for Lavinia and Aquilina. They will assure you that you are very talented."

Aquilina and Lavinia halted their baking and hurried to see Vita's finished masterpiece. Stumbling into the tablinum still carrying their kitchen towels, they stood before the fresco. Aquilina gasped. Lavinia raised her eyebrows in stunned silence.

"I love it. And it is so lifelike," said Aquilina.

"Fine work. Seems like they are people I could see on the street, they are so well formed," said Lavinia.

They dashed back to the kitchen.

"She is a frightfully clever girl," said Lavinia.

"And she does lovely portraits!" said Aquilina sending them into such fits of laughter, they had to hide in the latrine with the curtain closed until they could control themselves.

"She has Quintus as Mars the adulterer!" said Aquilina.

"Bite your tongue! Stop laughing. You are making me laugh. No one must know."

"Well, Vitalia knows!" which only bent them over trying to control their snorts and chortles.

Repaired image by T. Griffith of Fresco in the House of the Bicentenary

"REMOVE THIS AGONY WITH WORK," Vita told herself. "Make money toward manumission."

Her lotions and perfumes were popular wherever ladies met. Vita could be found spending time at the public baths giving massages, explaining the medicinal qualities of her creams along with the lanolin glow of moist skin. Rashes, acne, scars disappeared, causing a frenzy among nobles, amazed at how quickly skin could improve. They easily could afford such luxuries, buying extra for friends. Tourists spread the word of the softening of skin by one lotion, and healing by a different lotion for blemishes, and perfumes that comforted the senses. As the business expanded, travelers stopped in Herculaneum and now Pompeii and Stabiae to buy the salves.

Aquilina and Vita worked day and night. Finally Gaius purchased more slaves to help with the labor and found a larger space for manufacture. Vita created, Aquilina managed, Telesphorus calculated the finances. He soon realized that Vita had more than enough money to buy her freedom.

What will I do if she leaves? he thought.

"AHHHHHHHH! MMBBBBBAHH! CAAAAC!" Certa dropped to his knees and stared at his rose bushes in the peristyle garden.

Vita and Aquilina ran with the other slaves toward the yelling. They froze when they saw Certa pulling at his hair. Certa paced the garden groaning, shaking his fists.

"Well, he is so loud. I've only heard him hum before," Aquilina whispered.

"I guess he's not happy that we cut off all those rose blossoms," said Vita.

"Maybe we should have told him we were going to do it."

"I am surprised to see him so angry. He never makes a scene."

Certa tossed his head back and searched the group for the girls. He knew who had destroyed his garden. Thana was gone. It was his garden now. He growled again. Both Vita and Aquilina jumped back out of his sight and leaned against the plastered wall.

"Certa! Certa!" Calitoria grabbed Regulas and came running to the garden. "What has happened? Are you hurt?"

"I didn't think she knew his name. She never seemed to notice him," whispered Aquilina.

The two best friends peered around the corner to see Calitoria patting Certa on his shoulder with compassion. The infant, Regulas, was sitting on her hip, as always, clinging to his mother.

"Does she ever put that child down? He is never going to learn to crawl or walk if she holds on to him all the time," said Vita.

"I'm surprised she is so maternal with the babe. I would not have predicted it," said Aquilina as she held her breath and glanced around the corner, aware that the other slaves had fled. "What are we going to do?"

"We are going to confess and remind everyone that our perfume and lotion business brings in more money than the farm, and the harvested rose buds make the rose oil. Now, straighten your back, chin up, walk with confidence, and let's get back to the kitchen and finish crushing the petals."

"Aren't you afraid of Calitoria?" asked Aquilina.

"No. Telesphorus and Gaius will defend us. Money speaks louder than emotions. Calitoria will not win this one."

The two dark haired girls strolled, side by side, with flowing hair and belted homespun tunics past the scene like twin blossoms from the same tree. Beauty and grace doubled and caught the eye of Calitoria. She charged toward them.

"You think you can do whatever you want. The only thing holding me back from destroying you right now is the Minerva spell you cast over Gaius. I know who you are. You are only slaves, disposable slaves. And I will dispose of you."

"The master instructed us to make the rose scented perfume using the blossoms from the garden. We are only obeying. We will go to the kitchen now to render the oil from the freshly picked petals," answered Vita as they continued their walk to the kitchen.

Aquilina shivered. "This cannot end well," she whispered to Vita as they passed through the peristyle leaving Calitoria glaring at them while Regulas howled in fright on her hip.

"Back to work, quickly," said Vita.

They crushed the blossoms in batches with the mortar and pestle, then Vita drenched the mush with olive oil to soak. The next day the scented oil would be strained. The process needed to be repeated several times using the blossoms.

"This will give us an abundance of rose scented oil for our lotions," said Vita. She stood over the bowl and rubbed her back.

"Why don't you sit down," suggested Aquilina as they worked alone at the wooden table.

"I'm fine."

"When will you tell me who the father is?"

Vita thought back to Quintus and the way he touched her with reverence and care. The soft way he kissed her and said he loved her. She loved him in a way that only first time love could bring—excitement, longing, and joy. Then she thought of the one that truly loved her. Only wanting to please her at the expense of his own needs, he caressed her and held her so dearly. The same one where sex was physically unfulfilling at times but the touch brought comfort. She cared for him. Love developed over time joined with respect and friendship. *Maybe this is true love,* she thought. Then the one that seemed to treat her as an object of worship, seeking to fulfill a physical need mechanically performing an act of possession leaving her detached. She never wanted to be touched by him again.

"Maybe tomorrow."

"You always say that. Quintus? Someone else?"

Aquilina knew that Vita would tell her when she was ready. They shared everything, but this one secret would have to wait. The girls were so close now, working together on their lotions, sharing their secret resentment of the Petronius family, fearing the bumps in the night that continued to tease them. In tandem, they focused on expanding their business sanctioned by Gaius and Telesphorus.

Calitoria eyed them suspiciously and quietly tortured them in secret ways. One day their oils would be hidden. Another day their meal was forbidden. If someone intervened in their behalf, an excuse would be fabricated that they were needed elsewhere as slaves always subservient to their masters.

"You are starting to show," Aquilina said.

"Maybe."

"I see Calitoria studying you. I think she knows."

"Maybe."

"That is why Pax growls at night. I hear the footsteps outside our bedroom door. I know you do, too. Could it be Calitoria?"

"You are way too suspicious of her," said Vita.

"It's my turn to say, 'Maybe.' She finds every chance she can to hurt you when the master is not looking."

"I am protected by all of them as long as I continue to make money for the family. Between our cosmetics and the pay from all the painting I do with the artisans, they can't treat me unkindly. Telesphorus keeps reminding Gaius how much money I am bringing in, and you are rewarded, too. You are excused from answering every call from Calitoria because you work with me."

"I am aware of that." Aquilina realized she had pushed too far with her questions. She stepped around the table and forced a hug. "You know I appreciate all of that but most of all I love being your friend and will always help you as much as I am allowed."

"Soon, I will have my freedom, and I will buy you away from this family," whispered Vita as she held her friend.

"Oh, if that could be possible."

Lavinia entered the cooking area. She noticed the girls whispering.

"Quite a morning to wake up with Certa yelling in the peristyle. I understand you girls had something to do with that." Lavinia came closer and stood in front of them. She reached out and took each of their hands and held them softly. She studied their faces with a mixed look of love and concern.

"You must be careful," she whispered. "You are treading danger-ously. Remember your place here. Calitoria is not happy with you, and she has the power and authority to harm you. I can see it coming. This will not end in your favor," she warned. The pup uttered a low growl as he sat in the corner warning that someone was coming. The conversa-tion ended there as slaves returned to their work.

CALITORIA FOUND MORE retaliation by moving the girls to the upper third floor, a smaller room with hard slatted beds and no comforters. The pup, Pax, lay sentry at the door as protector. Deep in the night, footsteps came again to their door and stopped. The pup hummed. Vita's heart raced. Even though she played the part of the brave, reassured girl, a doomed feeling enveloped her like a storm cloud. She felt the spirit of death visit her. The same spirit prophesied by Thana. The same familiar unwanted adversary in her mother and father's death. It was coming, and she knew it would enjoy a teasing torture of not knowing when or where. Death would drive the deepest hurt with glee.

She watched the metal door lever move. Vita froze waiting to see if the door would open. She wanted a weapon. There was nothing. The hinges creaked waking Aquilina. "Vitalia?" The door shut quickly.

"It's nothing. Go back to sleep, Aquilina," Vita answered. Her heart lost its rhythm, racing and fluttering. The earth trembled, shaking their beds, as if it knew the danger.

~

THE NEXT DAY Aquilina and Vita repeated the steps of filtering the rose oil. After laying it to rest, Vita went to the tablinum to help Telesphorus with his calculations. She continued to show her usefulness to the family. So valued was she in helping with the finances that a rough textured curtain, hung on loops over a pole, was drawn to give them privacy. A suspicious movement of the curtain caught her attention, and upon bending low she could see Calitoria's feet. Vita motioned to Telesphorus and pointed to the spying extremities and put a finger to her lips. At that instant the babe who was always adhered to her hip cooed a happy note exposing her, forcing her to slip away.

Of course, the slaps and beatings had ceased since Gaius returned from Britannia as it became difficult for Calitoria to explain the assaults. Still, an arsenal of insults were tossed, calling Vita dirty, stupid, lazy, disobedient and whatever she could slightly justify.

"Why don't you defend me when the mistress abuses me?"

"It is not my place. I can't." He was wondering why he should, although he knew he loved this angel. "I suggest to you that you respond with kindness."

"Really? I prefer silence. I can't believe you would suggest kindness."

"The teacher, Jesus, said to return kindness for evil. For how can you be better if you become like her? If you are only good to those who are good to you, are you better than the evil ones? Even evil people are good to those who are kind. Jesus taught us to love our enemies, do good, and expect nothing in return. That will make you a child of the most high God."

She turned to judge him. "Did Jesus ever say to fight back? Don't you see there's a time when the truth of evil ways should be confronted? Does Jesus expect us to accept evil ways from others? What does He teach about that? Besides, I am kind to her. I provide money for her to spend on every whim and want she desires."

"I do believe there is a time for truth to expose evil. Jesus did confront evil with truth but the time and context must be right. Remember, you are a slave."

"For now, but when is the time right? When she is striking me? Hummph."

Telesphorus looked down at Vita where she sat on the floor holding the tablet of numbers. "Don't fill yourself with hate, Vitalia. You are too pure and gentle to do that to yourself. Don't let her change you. Hate will do that. Try to understand her instead. It will help."

"Next you will say to forgive her. I am not ready to do that. Anyway, I would have to forgive her many times every day." She reached over to pet Pax sleeping beside her.

"Jesus said to forgive an infinite number of times, seventy times seven."

"You say that easily from your seat, from your pleasant, controlled life. You quote Him, but I see that you have not committed to that choice of following Him either." She seethed with irritation. "Then, I am going to start counting. When I get to four hundred and ninety, I will confront her myself. Now, let me forget about her."

Telesphorus felt safe repeating the words from the one they called Christ. He didn't have the need to forgive anyone. He watched Vita's treasured soul that had more wisdom than anyone in the household. *She struggles with her subservient place. It is just the way things are,* he thought to himself. *She must learn to accept it.*

Chapter Thirty-Five

A quilina and Vita sat in their new room near the rafters, listening to the rain patter the roof. The fresh coolness of the morning wafted through the window as birds chirped their joy at the new day. Vita stroked Pax's fur and giggled as the dog sneezed and shook his head.

"The Saturnalia Festival starts today. We should get down early to help Lavinia with the food," said Vita.

"I'll beat you down," said Aquilina jumping up, sliding into her sandals and out the door, slamming it behind her.

"Stinker!" shouted Vita as she tied her sash and smoothed her hair. Pax followed her to the door just as the lock was thrown from the outside. She pulled the handle then pulled again. Her fists pounded the heavy wooden slats. Putting hands on her waist, she stared at the door. Vita had noticed the new slide lock yesterday, and puzzled why it was on the outside of the door until this moment.

"Hey!" she shouted thinking Aquilina had thrown it as a tease. It took a moment until her senses told her someone else had thrown the lock. *How stupid of me to see the lock and not guess this scheme. Aquilina will come back for me when she realizes I'm not there.* She waited.

Calitoria stood in the kitchen yelling orders, directing the slaves to load up the snacks to take to the games at the Herculaneum Palaestra.

The orphans, kitchen slaves, Lavinia, and Talistia all crowded in the small area packing brown bags with thick bread and figs, meat and boiled eggs. Gaius's booming voice could be heard throughout the villa as he paced a course from atrium to kitchen and back again trying to herd everyone out the door. Giving up, he and Telesphorus headed off to the games without them.

"Aquilina, go up and see why Vita is not here yet," said Lavinia noticing that Vita was absent.

"No! You will not," said Calitoria. "No one is allowed out of here until we leave for the Festival." Her eyes dilated with anger as she glared at each of them. "It is her duty to be down here helping. That ugly girl! Now, out all of you!" *No one will hear her yell if I get everyone off to the Festival.*

YOUNG MEN and women from the local village met at the *palaestra* to compete in running, boxing, and any sport using a ball for the Saturnalia. Local athletes carried their reputations to defend, however, neighboring towns, Stabile, Pompeii, and Puteoli, sent competitors to try to steal the titles. Since the arena at Pompeii sustained a ten year punishment for the riot at the Gladiatorial Games, local competitions had became more intense. All in all, these games were much more enjoyable and convivial to families, being absent of the bloody voyeurism. A large field, outlined with columns, separated the crowd from the athletes as they warmed up, stretching and jogging. Aquilina watched as the young athletes stripped down to their linen undergarments. Girls wrapped their chests in gauze to secure their breasts for the running competitions and long jumps. Young men rubbed oil on their skin, displaying developed muscles, preparing for the competitions.

A group of friends sat on the soft earth. Calitoria sat with little Regulas in her lap holding him close, not allowing him to examine rocks or pick at the weeds. His red fluffy hair fluttered in the friendly wind. Shade trees surrounded them, cooling this late autumn day. Calitoria gingerly picked up a fig, chewed it slowly, then took a finger to her mouth and shared the fig juice with Regulas. He eagerly sucked it into his rosebud mouth drooling delightfully. Telesphorus stood nearby leaning against a pillar with arms crossed, curious about the games but not enough to participate. Even though he was young and strong, he displayed only mild interest.

Lasennia was nearby with her children watching and commenting about the athletes to a circle of elite ladies. Conversation centered on the games until Lasennia's mother-in-law brought up Emperor Nero's recent news.

"Empress Octavia was maligned. The rumor that she was an adulteress—a young woman barely out of her teens, married to Nero and of such Imperial pedigree—speaks of something heinous. She is the daughter of our own Emperor Claudius! A virtuous wife! Nero's own stepsister!

"They made up stories that she was having an affair with a slave who is a flute player," she added. "They tortured her maids to try to make a case against her. And you know who was the chief investigator? A lowly born fisherman and breeder of racehorses named Tigellinus who has replaced the Emperor's consult, Burrus. A man who is cruel and greedy and very simply got the job because he likes chariot racing like our Emperor. Appalling that a high-born Empress was interrogated by a low born-oaf."

"Oh mother Volasennia, you must be careful what you say about Nero," said Lasennia.

"Perhaps, but who here will spread this gossip? And is it gossip if it comes from knowledge?"

"I do feel sorry for the girl. Simply because of her birth, she is married to her stepbrother who hates her. No wonder there is no heir that he produced," contributed another.

"You know, Nero is in love with Poppaea, so to have unlimited time with her, he sent her husband, Otho of Pompeii, as far away as possible to be Governor of Lusitannia," said Volasennia.

"I know this Poppaea. Her mother was the most beautiful woman known," said another.

"Ah, yes, very aristocratic, virtuous lady," said Volasennia. "I knew her well. Too bad her daughter did not inherit those characteristics. She did inherit beauty, cleverness and wealth. She wears a veil to half cover her face. 'Oh yes, I am so beautiful I must cover my face,'" she mocked.

"Calitoria, doesn't your slave make the face cream that Poppaea uses? Everyone wants it. Where is she?" asked Lasennia. "No wonder the products are so popular. The most beautiful woman uses them."

"She was unable to come."

Aquilina stood nearby, wishing to compete in the races, when she noticed Quintus stretching his arms and legs, ready to race. His eyes met hers, recognizing her as Vita's friend.

Oh dear here he comes, she thought.

"Is Vitalia here? Where is she? I want to talk to her."

"No. I don't know when she will come."

"Please, tell her I need to see her. I want to warn her about something."

"I don't think she wants to see you."

"I'll come to the villa tonight after dark. Tell her to listen for the call that I used to make when we worked on the docks."

Quintus turned to see his wife stalk up behind him.

"So this is her? This is the one? She isn't even pretty!"

He took her arm and walked back to the starting lines. Aquilina critiqued him. *He is so handsome, dark piercing eyes, splendid body,* she thought. *Tough to resist, but I think Vitalia can do it. Arrogant gem cutter with a wife and child, what could he want? Nothing but torment.*

PAX PACED the bare bedroom cubical, corner to corner and back again. At first Vita sat on the floor and tried to soothe him with petting and kisses, but he could not seem to rest. She watched him finally squat to relieve himself. "Such a good dog," she said to herself. "You tried to wait." At last, he came over plopping down beside her, pushing his white head and black, soulful eyes into her lap. They would be prisoners together today.

A murmuring wind carried cheers from the palaestra over to the villa. Vita imagined the running games, wondering who would be racing, who was winning, probably some of her artisan friends, maybe some of the neighbors, both men and women, maybe Gaius. Of course, Quintus was competing. Longing to be there just to show him that she carried on without him would have been satisfying. She would not cheer for him. That was certain.

Later there would be a parade through town to honor the Magistrates and those that paid for the Festival ending at the markets to celebrate the harvest with sacrifices to the gods. Gaius would be honored for the financial support he gave. Calitoria would love that honor. Tonight there would be a play at the theater, and Gaius and Calitoria would attend. It was sad to miss out on this bit of recreation.

~

THE ROOM GREW dark from the absence of the sun, only to leave a glimmer of moonlight sneaking under the door. The day was passed. She napped and slept quite soundly. Once again a dream from her real family who cared for her on this earthly terrain appeared to her. It was her mother. Sound asleep, Vita was awakened by the gentle caress of her forehead. Not jolted awake, instead lovingly awakened by a loving parent, her mother's voice called her name. No other words were heard, rather a knowing of dialogue entered her consciousness from within. "It will get worse and there is nothing I can do." This same message her mother gave her before.

Her mother was trying but other forces were stronger. *How could it possibly get worse. Slander, beatings, and now imprisonment and surely a horrible punishment ahead.* So lost in her aberration, she did not even hear the lock surreptitiously lifted.

~

"YOU ARE in so much trouble. Even Gaius wants you beaten for disobedience. Why didn't you come? We were all in the kitchen this morning and you never came down," said Aquilina upon her return.

"It wasn't me. Someone locked me in. I was afraid to yell, that would only have made it worse. So I thought someone would come up to get me. I sat here all day with Pax."

There would be no end to the repercussions of her imprisonment. The appearance of disobedience could not be defended without a witness and her only witness was the perpetrator, since no one had come to investigate her absence. Besides, trying to defend herself as a slave would be futile. Once Calitoria presented a diatribe of disobedience to

Gaius ending with this last offense, there could be no cry of foul play. The bridegroom would believe the bride.

"Quintus is coming here tonight. He wants to see you," Aquilina informed, expecting a retort of anger. She was not disappointed.

"What could he possibly want?"

"He impressed everyone in the races today. Still no right to be so handsome. The little boy and the wife were there, beautiful child. Looks just like him. The wife is pretty, too, but it seemed that she was upset with him."

"I don't want to know. Just stop." Vita was frustrated from her confinement and hated to hear how wonderful Quintus looked. "Pax needs a walk. I will take him."

"He's coming here tonight. He says he wants to warn you about something." Aquilina called after her.

"I won't be here," she replied over her departing shoulder.

Everyone was tired or busy in other parts of the villa, allowing her to slip out the side door. Pax hovered as close as her own shadow following her down the road. A swift seaside wind pushed her toward the center of the city, and having no place to go, she let it be in command for a while. Ahead, the town crier perched on his pedestal and gave the news of the Empire. She stopped to listen for a while. It seemed Burrus, one of Nero's advisors, had cancer and died. The uprising in Britannia had been conquered and harsh punishments imposed. Nero was winning chariot races in Rome and divorced his twenty-year-old wife, Claudia Octavia, daughter of his uncle and stepfather, Emperor Claudius.

Divorce, could one divorce another? She considered the flicker of hope. *Quintus could get a divorce and marry me?* She pulled out her necklace hidden from view to study the gold ring with the carved ruby. Pictures appeared in her mind of how it might happen until, she remembered how Quintus had deceived her. *It's simple. I could never trust the fool.*

Vita meandered the city heading back to the villa in the middle of the night. Fog erased all color from the street. Passing the fountain, she noticed a figure parallel to the villa door. "Quintus!" she whispered and stepped back in the shadows pushing Pax against the wall and holding him there. "Quintus, whistling our secret melody and searching the windows above," she cringed. He whistled again.

"I will hide here and let him whistle until he wheezes," she told Pax.

VITA WAS ORDERED to stay in her room until punishment could be decided. A meal was brought up to her by the slave, Certa, and pushed into her room. Vita gave her customary first bite to Pax who was waiting for his treat. He took it and immediately began throwing up. Vita tried to give him water but he refused. He laid down on his side and seemed paralyzed. His eyes found hers as if to say he was hurting.

"Something is wrong with this food," she told herself. When she pulled the tray up to her nose to smell it, Pax rose up and barked a sharp warning. "I won't eat it, Pax," she said, even though she was hungry.

Aquilina heard the bark and snuck upstairs. Pax never barked. The door was locked from the outside. Aquilina waited, afraid to open it for fear of punishment.

"What is wrong?" she whispered through the door.

"I need mustard seed for Pax and charcoal. He is sick. Please be quick."

Aquilina dashed back to the kitchen where their supplies of herbs and oils were stored. She collected the ground mustard seed, charcoal, and some olive oil in case Vita wanted to mix it to make an elixir. She rushed back. This time she took a chance and opened the door, passed the items to Vita and quickly relocked the door glancing over her shoulder to see if anyone observed her disobedience.

Vita mixed the oil and mustard seed, then pulled Pax's cheek up to dribble the solution into his mouth. Eventually, Pax vomited again emptying his stomach. She wondered if she could make him eat the charcoal, and after a few tries he swallowed it. He raised his head feeling better, but she could tell he was still suffering.

"Something in the food made you sick. I am sorry, Pax, but you saved me. I know it." Pax rested while Vita stroked his fur and massaged his neck. Tears fell freely from Vita's eyes, knowing that she had nearly lost her beloved dog. *I've got to get out of here,* she thought. *Maybe this is the loved one that Thana predicted would be lost. I was warned and we triumphed.* It was true, and she realized she could use her wits to escape her enemy. Her life was not meant to be held prisoner and in fear for her life.

Days passed. The only food she allowed herself or Pax to eat came from Aquilina and Lavinia. She could hear voices from downstairs as life in the villa progressed without her. Clients and friends stopped by to visit or conduct business. Aquilina continued to work the cosmetic preparations. At one point, the artisans came to collect Vita for fresco work. They still referred to her as Vitalis although they suspected she was a female. Her feminine beauty could not be concealed. The artists wanted her to paint hand details and gestures in unison with the men specializing in faces, or help with architectural backgrounds. She painted brilliant flowers and birds, fast and easy. The painters were disappointed and turned away.

One afternoon Lasennia came to inquire about some lotions and asked to see Vita. Calitoria tried to convince her that the lotions were not worth her money, but Lasennia knew otherwise and insisted on speaking with Vita.

"Your girl, Vitalia, has a lotion for breakouts on the skin and face. I need some desperately. I can't wait. Where is the girl today?"

"I'm sure you don't need lotions, your skin is perfect."

"Are you sure you see me? Just look! Ever since I gave birth to my second child I have so many breakouts, and the lotion that I buy from Vitalia is the only thing that works."

Calitoria knew she was trapped. The truth that Vita was locked upstairs for being disobedient would be hard to explain for a slave who was so valued. Perhaps, Lasennia would even try to buy the slave or spread word to other women in the city of mistreatment. Calitoria's tight-gripped advantage battling the Minerva goddess slackened. She knew that discovery of the beautiful slave's embattled life of denunciations, retribution, and abuse would only be seen as spite. The value the neighborhood placed on this creative master of salves and cosmetics guaranteed a defense of sorts. Vita's popularity could not be denied.

The lock was thrown. The door opened. Vita and Pax followed Certa downstairs.

"I am so glad to see you," said Lasennia. "I need the medical lotion you make for my face. I have so many spots, and they just keep coming. I used something you made before that I got from Aquilina and it cleared them and wondered if I could have it again."

"That process demands two steps. I don't have any made today, but I am sure I can make some by tomorrow. The ingredients are in season. I can go to the coast and collect the herbs. Would you like for me to deliver it tomorrow evening?" This cunning comment insured her freedom. She would not be locked up again. In truth, she had most of the ingredients except fresh Myrtal.

"That would be perfect," Lasennia replied. Her eyes dropped to notice Vita's swollen abdomen. She couldn't help but think that this slave was pregnant. She said nothing. It was common for a lovely slave to produce a new slave for the household.

After she left, Vita told Calitoria she would need to go to the beach near the cliff to collect Myrtal for the lotion.

"Fine." Calitoria's pink face exposed her anger.

Chapter Thirty-Six

The next morning, Telesphorus knocked on the girls' door on the third floor. He asked to speak to Vita alone. After Aquilina left, he embraced her, their bond secure, a mixture of love and friendship. No words needed to be said. He knew Vita was in trouble.

"I need to have my manumission now. I'm at the point where I have two choices. One is to surrender my dream of freedom and take on the attitude of being a slave, the other is to ask for my freedom now and try to live life out there. Will you go with me?" She felt his body tense.

"I can't leave, Vitalia, my life is here. My work is with Gaius. You already have enough money to buy your freedom. I wanted to tell you before. I know it is what you have wanted since you arrived. It will be difficult, but I will negotiate it for you with Gaius."

Vita pulled away and sat on the wooden bench that was her bed. She stared at the wall feeling abandoned. Finally, she spoke.

"Someone tried to poison me. When Certa brought up my food, Pax ate some first. He almost have died. It was meant for me. I'm scared. I think I need to ask the one you call the Christ to protect me from the evil that is here. Thana's gods are fantasy and legend, favors to buy with sacrifice. You said He loves me, He was the sacrifice for me. He can lead me to freedom. It is time for me to decide if I will accept this Christ." She looked directly at Telesphorus. "When are you going to decide?"

He backed toward the door wanting to leave. He liked the way things were, comfortable.

"I need my freedom," she pleaded. "I'll make sacrifices to your God and Jesus. Where do I go to do that?"

"It doesn't work that way with Jesus," he said.

"That's what everyone does here. They go to the Temples and make a sacrifice to the special god or gods of the misery they are worried about," she said.

"He made the sacrifice for you; it's not a favor to buy or work for."

"I don't get it. I just want my freedom. I am afraid here."

"Calitoria will never let you have what you want." He sat beside her on the bench. "It is a struggle for power with her now. Her hostility is her happiness. It makes her powerful. She sees you only with jaundiced eyes," warned Telesphorus.

"It's just like Pharaoh when Moses kept asking for the Hebrew slaves to be let go. So many plagues were sent by God until he finally relented. The Hebrews were freed but Pharaoh suffered. It will happen the same: she will suffer just as you have." He paused and searched the face of this slave. "You must start asking for manumission."

"Then we agree." Vita remembered the first prophecy Thana made years before when she first arrived, that she would be responsible for revealing the evil in the villa. *What exactly did she say?* Vita tried to remember.

An earth tremor echoed her alarm. The walls shook. Dust fell from the rafters. They brushed it off their arms.

"And now, even Thana's gods speak of my danger." She laughed and looked at her friend and lover with tears in her eyes. She studied him, thinking, *Telesphorus is a cowardly soul, Quintus is like a cauterized wound, and then there is Gaius, the patriarch of the family, not a trembling soldier but blind to his wife's plans.*

CALITORIA SAT down in her chamber early in the morning, erect, with eyes closed while Talistia set her hair. Blonde curls framed her face. The new style made popular by Poppaea the Younger included a full section of hair pulled high to the back and tied. This left a very stylish cascading tendril. Calitoria's perfectly symmetrical features, alabaster skin, and unusual flaxen hair were captivating.

"Another shaking of the earth!" She rolled her eyes. "I would like to tell Hercules to stop. It keeps happening more and more. Things keep falling and breaking."

Aquilina listened as she stood waiting by the cubicula door. Little Regulas sat in his box at her feet desperate to climb out.

"Aquilina, are you trained to make the lotions that the other troublesome slave knows how to make?" Calitoria asked.

"Yes, Mistress."

"The ones that are sold here and in nearby cities? You know how to make them all?"

"Yes, the recipes come from her mother."

"Never mind, you can go now."

AQUILINA AND VITA started preparing salve and astringents for Lasennia while Pax pivoted round in a circle sniffing for the perfect spot to seize a nap.

"Do not boil the honey. If you do, it won't help heal the blemishes," Vita cautioned. They took the stored Lovage root that had soaked in beer for six weeks and strained it, added a bit of high-quality honey from the farm, and poured it into a miniature glass bottle shipped from German glass blowers. This tonic would cleanse Lasennia's skin after scraping.

Vita did not believe in the legendary myths of cures that circulated among the population: drinking gladiator blood, studying entrails, the use of fasting spittle on a boil or blemish. In fact, drool seemed to be a cure for any pain of the body. Earwax currently was another favorite for stings and bites. Perhaps, some would cure but most were rituals. Vita stuck to the teachings of her mother.

"You know, Aquilina, we are having great success with this business. I have another idea. My mother used to be paid for sessions to prepare brides to be married. We could add that to what we offer: soaking baths of goat's milk, full body moisturizers, paring of nails, makeup products and application. So many ideas! What do you think?"

"Oh, Vitalia, I would love that! It sounds so fun, and being a part of new beginnings and happy events would make a merry heart for me. We could train some of the new slaves that are helping us already. It's not a brand new idea. I think the ancients have already done it, but we could do it with our products."

"Yes, that will be our next project. But I am not starting it until I have my freedom. I don't want to make money for that mistress anymore."

"Still, you think that will happen," groaned Aquilina.

"Yes, and I will buy your freedom, too. We will be together making all this fun."

Aquilina's charitable personality harbored no malignant thoughts but something left her soul unsettled. "I should tell you that the mistress asked me today if I knew all your recipes," said Aquilina.

IT WAS time to forget Autumn and embrace the cool wandering winds. The girls left the villa with its dirge of dreams and displeasing masters. Here, the fresh air and lush trees and plants spoke to their senses saying, "leave it behind today."

Pax, loyal friend and white puffy shadow, zig-zagged along the path to the cliffs unable to sniff every leaf, rock, and clump of dirt while wetting every tall weed to mark the trail. A leaf would rustle, pushed by the wind, and grab his instinct for rodents scampering away. Vita and Aquilina giggled watching the joyful tail-wagger work so hard to smell everything.

Damp grasses gave memory of the recent rains, wetting their feet and hems while making them dodge mud puddles. It slowed their walk. They labored carrying large woven baskets and tools for digging medicinal herbs.

"We will look for bayberries to cook down for their wax and the roots to mix with olive oil. We will add Lovage wax to that. We need Myrtal leaves to make an oil for Lasennia to apply to her spots. I will go down to the sea bogs while you search on the upper cliffs for Myrtal."

"Can we eat first? Lavinia sent figs, eggs, and nuts. She added lentil cakes at the last minute and even a cake for Pax. I have mulsum with honey and cinnamon, too."

"Oh yes, good idea."

Pax relaxed beside them on the edge of the cliff hoping for a snack, while watching seagulls practice their flights far below.

"I'm still wondering, who is the father of your baby? When Quintus wanted to talk to you, I thought it was probably him, but instead he wanted to warn you about something. Maybe, that his wife hates you. She gave me such a scowl at the games. Is the master the father? That would be logical, master and slave. I see how you are with Telesphorus and the way he looks at you. Is he the one? Now, I am wondering. Do you know who it is?"

"Yes, I do. Of course," Vita answered and grew pensive. "I hate carrying a child unmarried. My parents did not raise me this way."

"It's not your fault. It is just the way it is for us. You show now. Calitoria has been watching you."

"I know."

"So will you tell me?"

"Yes. I promise. Tonight I will tell you everything when we are alone. You can help me make a plan for this baby and getting my freedom. Tonight, I will tell you," said Vita. "Now, we must get to work. Keep Pax with you up here at the edge of the cliff. I don't want him getting muddy in the bogs down by the sea."

"I'll watch him. Be careful. The rocks are treacherous and the path is steep," called Aquilina as she watched Vita disappear down the twisting trail. A light rain dampened Aquilina's hair making her shiver. She pulled her mantle up from her shoulders and covered her head.

Pax returned to poking his nose into crevices, bounding back and forth along the edge while Aquilina searched for Myrtal. After a time, he wearied settling next to Aquilina while she bent to pick the leaves.

Vita found it easy descending to the sandy areas at the bottom of the cliff but knew she would have to climb up again after she was exhausted from digging bayberry in the sandy bogs. Her feet sloshed through the sucking mud sinking up to her knees, each step a struggle. Slowly, she worked toward the partial shade of slender trees where she could harvest Lungwort leaves.

Someone screamed. Vita thought it came from children playing in the waves, but looking up, she saw Aquilina tumbling down the cliff pummeled by sharp boulders trying to stop her fall. Vita dropped everything and ran to reach her, clawing at rocks across the side of the cliff, each one a barrier holding her back, until she found Aquilina's damaged body near the waves that tried to pull her into the sea.

"Aquilina, what happened?"

"I was pushed."

"Who?"

"I didn't see. I only felt the push."

"You have no enemies. Why?"

Vita stared, watching life slowly leave her friend's broken body, then, "Pax was there with you. They thought it was me!"

"No, Aquilina. No! You can't go. You have to stay with me. We have plans. We have a future. We are going to have our freedom."

"I think I'm dying now." A slight smile crossed her face. "You said you would tell me. Who is the father?" Aquilina whispered. "I won't tell, I can't tell anyone now." She reached up with one hand as if she watched something in the sky, the smile left her face, her eyes closed.

Vita caressed her hair. She leaned down to kiss her cheek, then pulled her close to her breast. She gazed at the sea with its rhythmic waves grabbing the shore. Her heart ached with hopelessness knowing she would never have her friend again.

Why must Aquilina die? Vita wondered but to keep her promise, she looked at Aquilina's sleeping face and whispered the father's name to her best friend who would keep the secret, forever. Then she sobbed.

The townspeople had run to help when they heard the piercing scream. One picked up Aquilina's lifeless body and carried her up the cliff. Curious people followed behind wondering who had fallen. Finally, they reached the villa and the sweet slave was placed on the rough wooden table where Aquilina had learned to knead bread years before. Vita and Pax entered and walked directly to Lavinia who wrapped her arms around her, holding her close while she sobbed and Lavinia wept. The crowd of near strangers gathered around the table. Voices were raised in anger knowing that the slave had been murdered. Lavinia removed her mantle to cover Aquilina's bloodied body while forcing Vita to move away. Gaius and Telesphorus came quickly from the tablinum.

"What happened?" asked Gaius. His eyes searched for answers from someone until he saw Vita's figure in the darkened corner.

"She was pushed on the cliff and fell."

"Who pushed her?"

"I don't know. Maybe someone saw something. She was picking Myrtal at the top while I worked in the bogs below. I heard her scream as she fell. She was still alive when I got to her. She said she felt someone push her."

Gaius walked to the door and held it open. "Thank you to all who helped bring her home. We will have to ask you to leave to give us time to accept what has happened." The kitchen emptied just as Calitoria came in without Regulas in her arms.

"Where is the baby?" asked Telesphorus.

"Talistia has been watching him for a while. What has happened?" Calitoria saw the body on the table. Vita watched her reaction from the corner. "Did Vitalia fall?"

"The girls were gathering herbs for their lotions today," said Telesphorus.

"Oh, the cliffs can be treacherous. Vitalia's dog is always with her and so unruly. I'm sure he tripped her," Calitoria said.

Vita stepped out of the corner and said, "How did you know the dog was on the cliff? This is Aquilina lying here."

Calitoria's face gave her away. What does guilt look like? How does a lie change the face? What words of blame and excuse come from the lips?

"Where were you today?" asked Telesphorus.

"Did you do this?" shouted Gaius. The love for his wife drained away. "You thought it was Vitalia?"

"She is just a slave!" said Calitoria, reminding him it was a lesser crime.

Vita reacted, she wept. She dropped to the floor. Calitoria had won. She missed her mark but won a victory of hurt so deep Vita wanted to die. Calitoria glared at her enemy. Now the victor became the wicked, the unloved, the exposed. Thana's prophesy thus fulfilled.

Vita walked over to the table weighted with Aquilina's broken body and rested her head on her chest. If only she could bring her back. Aquilina left this shell behind without her laughing smile or dancing eye or warmth of life. That part was gone to the place that housed the good people. Vita raised up, as if standing guard over the body, daring anyone to interfere.

Lavinia's tears rolled down each cheek.

Calitoria spoke. "There will be no grief cypress placed at the door. There will be no ceremony of cremation, no mourning of family and placement in the family tomb as with Thana. She will be shoveled in the pit of the public cemetery."

"To dispose of the evidence against you?" asked Gaius.

"She is a slave. There are no repercussions."

"Yes, there are." He turned and left.

Chapter Thirty-Seven

D ays passed. The rhythm of the villa returned to a numb hum of living. The female slave from Britannia replaced Aquilina. It had to be done, Lavinia needed help. Good natured and thrilled to be in the kitchen working beside Lavinia, she chattered cheerfully, oblivious to everyone's sorrow.

Lavinia stood in her kitchen, calm for the moment, surrounded by raw wooden tables with platters and plates stacked in uneven piles, rubbing her dry hands over and over on a towel. She stared at the floor, missing Aquilina's charm and laughter. Grief did not always come as expected. Sometimes it trotted out in all its brazen splendor happy to surge all in sorrow. Being in the kitchen opened that pit of heartbreak. "Oh, Aquilina. Where are you?" she whispered to no one.

Vita came in falling into Lavinia's arms, tucking her head into her shoulder. "What will become of me, Lavinia? Can a broken heart live on? I can't endure the mockery of pretending that evil woman didn't do this. My friend has been murdered by the one who owns me. I want to scream! And it's my fault. I asked Aquilina to watch Pax so he wouldn't get all muddy. If he came with me working in the bogs, she never would've been mistaken for me. Pax was beside her. I should have died, not her."

"Unbearable. I see you tethered here like a wild horse, yearning for your freedom day and night, stomping through the injustice, trapped without hope. Now, with Aquilina gone, she isn't here to comfort you or ask you to be patient. There is no one to distract you from your suffering. It makes the deepest wounds repeat their pain, constantly inflamed." Lavinia smoothed the falling tears. "You will never be happy until you are free. Like the broken horse, locked in the stable, its destiny destroyed."

Vita's eyes vacant of expression, with a husky voice barely heard, "You understand, don't you. I must leave."

She turned and ran upstairs and stopped at the window. She gazed down at the street below measuring the fall, loyal Pax at her side. Could she jump? That would end it. Or walk away without being missed? She gazed down at Pax's searching eyes and spoke to him as if he knew her thoughts.

"Aquilina said slaves caught masquerading as free are killed. Now, I have this infant growing inside me, Pax. My baby can't be born a slave. I must petition to the master to leave. I will ask when Gaius and Telesphorus are finished with business appointments today, at dusk, after the clients are gone."

VITA ENTERED THE TABLINUM. "I am here to request my freedom. I have the money to buy it, you can ask Telesphorus." Straight and tall and with money for power, she delivered the appeal.

"Never," said Gaius equally forceful. "I can't let you go. I have supported you in your shop of cosmetics. I have allowed you to work with the artisans. I care for you as one I love and you are part of this family." His eyes dropped to notice her pregnancy. "You have freedoms no other slave can boast."

"My life is in danger here. Someone tried to poison me, then Aquilina was pushed to her death in place of me." Her voice raised in defiance. "If I don't leave, your wife will...I deserve my freedom."

"You risk discipline. Be careful."

It was time for Telesphorus to choose. Would he defend her or stay compliant? "She has the money, more than enough, quite rich, but perhaps she could continue to have our support in her business in another location, if she just needs to be away."

"You know what I want, Telesphorus. It is my freedom not a new location. Why won't you fight for me? A rich slave still has no freedom. You know that." Telesphorus's heart raced, his position revealed.

As if she was not standing in front of him, Gaius bellowed, "No, no. I can't let her go, she brings too much money into the family."

Calitoria heard the shouting and appeared holding the babe.

"I'll never agree to giving this slave freedom, even if she is a curse in this villa." Regulas squirmed to get down. Calitoria squeezed tighter. The earth trembled. "It's not like Vitalia is some kind of goddess or savior just because she happened to help us a little in Pompeii. She is a female slave, the lowest of the lowly ones. She is lazy and lies." Calitoria glowed red with blotchy skin as she glared at Vita.

"No more discussion!" shouted Gaius.

VITA WONDERED how Calitoria could spend a whole day doing so little while the slaves managed the home and farm. In the morning, she visited the home lararium to say prayers to clay family gods. Little Regulas, captured in the sacred room, felt ill-treated. He hung on the barred gate and protested the visit with cries, pointing to get out and play in the impluvium water. Next, she summoned Talistia to arrange her hair and makeup, followed by a short hour of weaving. Desperate for conversation, she visited friends in Herculaneum, cementing her climb in social standing with elite ladies. The clique spent time complimenting each other, admiring efforts to dress respectably in the proper fashion, hems of togas not too short or too long, hair well-styled, flattering but not seductive, then gossip of those not in attendance or ostracized from the group. Later, a visit to the Baths for cleanliness and massage.

Whispers about Calitoria and the murdered slave began to circulate. The villagers that helped carry Aquilina to the kitchen could not be hushed and spread the word. Suspicious, the ladies stopped inviting her to their group.

Why did Gaius marry her? Convention in social circles encouraged those with property to marry above their rank. Calitoria came from the

Calitorious family as a former slave. Beautiful and intelligent, class conscious, why would Gaius bend low rather than marry a freeborn woman? Not only contrary to convention, but she was a contrary woman. Beauty only lasts when attached to a beautiful soul. Calitoria's beauty included a trap, a face of innocence with tendencies of deceit. The real advantage to the marriage included the dowry. It was not money but a remarkable slave, Telesphorus, from the Calitorious family. His talent for business, speaking Greek and Latin, and knowledge of the laws carried a value beyond class.

After the death of Aquilina, the slaves wondered whether Gaius and Calitoria even slept together. Heartbreaking for Calitoria, but since she already knew she carried her next child, she felt no need to sleep with her husband. Her only way to elevate social standing in the Empire was through her respectable contribution of delivering more children.

The government found too many women using birth control by purchasing an expensive weed, silphium, to rid their body of pregnancy. Now, the flower was nearly extinct. Another cruel method: simply discard unwanted infants by abandoning them to the elements or selling them to slave traders. An old law passed by Emperor Augustus required parents to wait until the child was three before deciding its fate. By waiting three years, the Emperor hoped the parents would care for the child and keep it. The Empire needed a sustained populace for work and war. Some ignored the law and infants still disappeared. Calitoria intended to keep all her babies. Childbirth seemed easy for her and inexplicably she loved fretting over her baby, clinging, afraid he might be harmed.

One day the slaves noticed blood on the bedclothes revealing a miscarriage for the next babe. A midwife was summoned to stop the bleeding.

THE PINK ROSE bushes recovered and blossomed again. Certa pruned at the proper time, watered just enough, and gently picked off the bugs devouring the leaves. Little Regulas took his first steps down the center path stumbling and catching himself on the statue of Pan. He giggled and flopped all day long with Calitoria following. Bugs crawled on the soft flesh of the toddler. Calitoria nervously picked them away. He itched and scratched a rash for days until it festered into blemishes and boils. Gaius became concerned and ordered Vita to use her lotions and herbs to heal the bites. She washed them with the astringent and applied the ointment delicately while the parents watched.

"Let me have my freedom," she said while she doctored the child. The ointment cured Regulas, and Calitoria and Gaius ignored the plea.

Events crescendoed weeks later when Telesphorus returned from the farm alarmed that a poisonous cloud came at night and swept across their flock of sheep killing all of them, one hundred at least. Trying to save some profit, they sheared the fallen animals recovering as much wool as they could to avoid a total loss. Gaius paced the floor in anguish analyzing the financial setback. Next, the city water fountain smelled of sulphur, so disgusting no one could drink it. They had to use the rain water from the impluvium instead.

"Do you think Vitalia is Minerva and has placed a curse on us?" he asked Telesphorus.

"No, of course not. But do you think my God might be pressuring you to grant her freedom?" he answered with sarcasm.

"I can't lose her now when her income is saving us from ruin."

The family separated to their night rooms. Vita circled the impluvium quietly extinguishing the lamps before climbing the stairs. Gaius and Calitoria were behind their cubiculum door, but their heated conversation bled into the atrium, echoing. Vita froze hearing her name. She stepped closer to not miss a word.

"I told you she is a curse. I heard her giving a mantra over bones in the garden. I watched her bury them. I'm not sure what that means, but every bad thing that has happened came after she arrived. Now it is worse. Probably she pushed Aquilina off the cliff."

"I don't think so. She isn't that way. I've only seen good things from her. I agree that she is a spiritual being, though. I can see it."

"Look, we could sell her off. Anyone would want her. Anyone. Even the brothel could use her. She is young. It is stupid to keep a cursed one in your home. Let's sell her."

"She has brought good fortune to us. We have the business she created that is sustaining us through hard times. Some say the Emperor is debasing coins, copper inside gold and silver. Our money is devalued. I'm worried. Everything costs more. It used to be one coin was a day's wage. Now, it is two. I have a large family here including all our slaves and the farm. I need to take care of them. That includes Vitalia. She is very important to our family. I want her happy and I want to keep her here."

Vita slipped away to her room. She fed Pax a few fish tails for a snack, invited him on her bed, and curled up next to him. Her eyes closed but the conversation repeated over in her mind: part of the family, selling her to a brothel, pushing Aquilina off the cliff, then the lie about chanting and burying bones in the garden. Her mind locked in a circle of insults until she fell asleep.

The creak of the door warned her. Pax sat up in bed struggling to see through the dark. Vita woke with hands clawing her throat, pressing hard. She pushed and struck, dragging her fingernails down the rounded cheek, rolling up skin like dough. The hands let go and reached for the bronze lamp, smashing it against the side of her head. Vita fell back and grabbed her pillow for protection. Kicked, stomped, she rolled back pushing her foot into the pelvis of this intruder, shoving the body into the wall. A soft life of leisure competed with a life of labor, lifting, carrying, working. The evil shape folded and rested on the floor. Vita assessed her wounds in the dark, panting, when the hands came again, covering her mouth and nose. She tried to suck air through the clasped fingers. Pax lunged, clamping down on a wrist, sinking his teeth into bare flesh like soft butter. The hands let go and struck Pax. He barked his high pitched, injured squeal followed by a soft whimper. The intruder stopped. Vita could see the silhouette of hate staring at her in the dark. Heavy breathing, hesitation, then grabbing the door handle she left, satisfied with the hurt she applied.

Vita, injured on the floor, massaged her throat. The blow to her head throbbed, pumping blood that trickled down her neck. Pax touched his nose to her forehead measuring her wounds like a loving parent.

"This Jesus, if you are real, I need you," was all she said.

Pax began a repeated bark summoning help. Telesphorus heard and raced up the stairs finding Vita's crumpled shape. He knelt beside her. Pax padded around their bodies and settled against her back comforting her with his warmth.

"Who did this?"

"Who do you think? The only reason I am alive is because Pax bit her, and I am much stronger."

"This can't be ignored. Gaius must act. I love you too much to watch this anymore. I don't care if I lose my life or place in this family. We will petition again. I will take care of this."

He lifted her up and carried her down to his room and placed her on his bed. He climbed in beside her, cradling her head on his chest folding his arms around her. Pax settled on the floor next to them.

"It's dangerous for us to be here together. I belong to Gaius. I am his slave. If you were found out..." she said.

Chapter 38

The next day Calitoria marched along the peristyle lined with its columns, head down, inspecting the mosaic floor while balancing a squirming Regulas on her hip, aiming for the kitchen.

"That last shake of the earth cracked and raised my beautiful floor popping out the chips of marble. Now, it will have to be repaired. Hercules should come and do it himself; he is so keen to undulate the earth, he should have to fix it."

Lavinia whispered a warning to the kitchen slaves, "A foul mood approaches."

"Where is Talistia? I need her. We are going to a play tonight, and my hair must be braided and sewn. Where is Vitalia? I need makeup."

"I will send them to you," answered Lavinia.

The young slave they called Brit, a sweet name to match her sweet nature, followed the mistress back to the triclinium with a tray of mulsum, olives, bread, and boiled eggs where Gaius waited.

"Calitoria! What happened to your face?" he asked noticing the three parallel scratches on her cheek.

"Oh the baby, his nails are so sharp." She placed Regulas on the floor to play with his chariot pull toy, sometimes pulling it, sometimes gnawing it, his mouth drooling. "He will be getting another tooth soon."

"Would he like an olive?"

"Oh no! I just fed him. He only gets food from me."

"When will you stop nursing him? Isn't he old enough now?"

"Well, it is so special for us." Regulas pulled up on his mother's shift, stood and pawed at her chest.

"I guess he wants more," she giggled.

"The play tonight is a dialogue poem by Seneca."

"Nero's tutor! Oh blah. I would rather see something decadent with music and dancing. Something Greek would be so much better. Someone will stand on the stage and put me to sleep. Will we see Balbus and Lasennia?"

"They will be there but sitting in their booth." He reached down and picked up Regulas bouncing him on his knee. "How's my little soldier? You look so much like your mother but where did you get that red hair? I keep waiting for you to look like me," he laughed and lifted the babe's chin gently, smiling at the adorable face.

"Of course they will be in their seats of honor. Money makes for privilege," she hummed. "I know what I am going to wear."

"Can you cover those scratches?"

"Probably." Calitoria knew she couldn't. Unfortunately, her attack had left a mark. She rubbed her cheek feeling the sting.

"You know, Balbus told me there is flooding in the lower level of their villa. It seems either the sea is higher or the ground is lower. No one seems to know why. Engineers had to brick all the lower windows and the Balbuses must abandon the first floor of their home. No other options," said Gaius.

"There are always repairs to these ancient homes. Our mosaics need repair. Some new cracks appeared this morning."

LAVINIA and the kitchen slaves prepared a small meal that included already prepared sauces marinating on fowl. She stood with towel in hand when a knock came to the slave's door. Thinking it might be a delivery, she opened the door to see Quintus standing there.

"Hello," he said in all politeness. "Is Vitalis, I mean, Vitalia here?"

"I'm sure she is unavailable," she said. Knowing the animosity Vita felt after the breakup. She knew not to call her to the kitchen. *I wonder if Quintus might be the father of the baby.*

"I know she has lost her good friend, Aquilina, and I have brought her something I think will ease the pain." He produced a bird cage with a small, colorful bird hopping inside. "It eats seeds and just some water. Easy to care for. I hope it brings her some happiness." He turned without even crossing the threshold and left.

Lavinia took the cage and raised it high to examine the bird as it began to sing. When Vita entered, the delightful bird whistled a familiar melody.

"Oh, I love it." Like bee to the flower, she knelt down to the cage and poked her finger in to pet it. It hopped across the perch away from her intrusion and sang the whistle that Quintus used to call Vita long ago. Tears came to her eyes. "A reminder of a friend I used to have. Where did it come from?"

"Quintus brought it to you this morning. He knew your sadness at losing Aquilina."

She stood and wiped the tears. "He must have taught it the song. I guess he isn't all bad. I'll take it with me to work. Come on, Pax. We have a new bird friend and lots to do today to make cosmetics and medicinals for so many customers."

She lifted the cage, studied the bird, and smiled. "This makes me cheerful inside. I love it." She left followed by her huge fluffy friend, Pax.

Lavinia watched her leave. The girl kept a powerful secret inside her, never carelessly revealing the father. Lavinia guessed it might be one of three and believed each of those three probably determined the child belonged to him. *With time and patience, I will know,* she thought.

Vita's shop had grown to a bustling business. The help of several new slaves allowed the powders, scents, lotions, and medicines to be made in large amounts and packaged in a choice of gold boxes or cheaper versions made of wood or bone, with matching mirrors. Imported glass containers from Germanic craftsmen were filled with perfumes. One popular bottle curved smoothly in the shape of a wingless bird with an open beak glamorizing an alluring scent sold rapidly. Vita knew the containers increased sales.

She entered the shop and began checking pots and barrels filled with urine, sheep sweat, rose water, frankincense, lead for skin whitening, burnt cork for mascara or darkening eyebrows, and cinnamon, myrrh, and black pepper for fragrant oils and perfumes. She guarded the expensive saffron they crushed to a powder for yellow and brown eye shadow. Being in the shop brought a euphoria to her soul. Everywhere she looked, Aquilina appeared in spirit, her friendship still treasured.

Unfortunately, the statesman, Seneca, wrote that makeup held magic meant to seduce, but most fashionable ladies ignored his opinion. Makeup applied properly radiated class and sophistication. Once, Vita and Aquilina both taught its application, now only Vita performed the instruction. Perhaps, the example of Cleopatra coming to Rome nearly a hundred years before established the darkened eyes and brows that women of the Empire desired. Vita knew how to use her artistic sense. Of course, elderly women were some of her best clients, always looking for a lotion to hold off aging. Lanolin from the sheep oils plumped the skin, so faithful customers returned.

Vita's ideas for a bridal preparation business including heat treatments and cleansing, makeup and hair application remained a future dream. Painting mythological frescoes with the artisans might happen again, too.

As the sun neared the horizon, Calitoria and Gaius strolled hand in hand to the theater in Herculaneum. Talistia followed to serve or assist and confirm the appearance of social standing. As they neared the eight wide steps surrounding the front of the building, Gaius studied the two rows of arches and columns above. The spectacular semicircular theater supported decorative bronze statues of prominent citizens dating back nearly a hundred years, and powerful bronze horses crafted by the most gifted artisans lined the edge. Gaius marveled at the beauty of the theater while holding his wife's hand.

They joined with other acquaintances, clustering together at the entrance to pass through to the open air stage. Inside, the golden night sky cast a radiant glow on two tiers of statues resting in niches behind the ornamental marble stage floor, exaggerating the elegance of a proud Empire. Gaius recognized the statue of Nero Drusus, the great-grandfather of Emperor Nero, then the ancestors of his friend Balbus, the historic benefactor, and Marcus Calatorius, another Herculaneum benefactor.

Calitoria grew up in the Calatorius family and was aware of its patriarch, and that family had given Calitoria her freedom to marry Gaius. Calitoria studied their draped bodies and small heads, judging them to be quite ugly except for Marcus Nonius Balbus, the historic benefactor of Herculaneum and Proconsul of Crete. They celebrated his generosity every year with a parade. His likeness revealed a handsome family resemblance carried to his offspring, their friend Balbus.

To each side of the flat orchestra, gilded balconies, possessing their own private staircases, were reserved for the most important citizens. Gaius and Calitoria both waved to Balbus and Lasennia seated in one of the balconies. More reserved seats for the elite were in the first few rows, closed off by bronze gates, followed by eleven levels directly behind for common audience members. Seven pathways separated the six wedged sections for more than two thousand to attend.

Herculaneum Theatre, Old photograph by G. Sommer showing a model of the theatre

Not a popular speech tonight, the theater held plenty of empty space. Talistia carried colorful cushions to their seats placing them on the hard stone benches, then climbed the steps to stand in the back with other slaves. They sat judging the crowd, enjoying the hum of the elegant audience with the open sky above, creating a perfect night. Calitoria and Gaius glanced toward each other with satisfying smiles, their only wish, to be in the first row.

The orator entered the stage and bowed to applause and began his memorized speech. The earth shook a frequent vibration causing Calitoria to comment.

"Seems this speech is not a favorite of Hercules. He rumbles below us."

"He nudges us to keep us from falling asleep," Gaius laughed.

They heard a rhythmic bang in the distance advancing closer and closer, rousing curiosity as the crowd turned their heads searching the sides of the building. The noise seemed alive running towards them. The angry building responded with shakes strong enough to topple some of the statues placed at the back stage. The innocent wall behind crumbled and fell, injuring several. Gaius turned to search for Talistia. The crowd ran toward the exit like a wave from the sea only to be crushed against each other pushing and shoving to leave.

The earth shook violently knocking them to their knees. Gaius turned around and pulled Calitoria to her feet. Calitoria wrenched her fingers around Gaius's arm as he dragged her to the exit.

"Regulas! He is in his bed! I have to get him!" she cried.

Always before, a dizzying smooth wobble could be ignored but never this strong and savage shaking. They dodged falling walls and timbers, stumbled over debris, their arms stretched out for balance as they ran through the streets to the villa. Fires from overturned lamps lit their way like beacons leading them home. All Calitoria could think about was holding little Regulas in her arms to protect him.

Gaius reached the villa first, running straight to Regulas's bed in time to watch a roof timber drop on the child. Struggling alone, he lifted it off as Calitoria entered. She screamed, dashed over and pulled the child free dropping to her knees, cradling his small body rocking him back and forth, her hand smearing the blood from his forehead, trying to remove the tragedy. The earth calmed its aggression, softened its blows as if it had accomplished its goal. Little Regulas had taken his last breath forever.

Chapter 39

The year A.D. 62

THE GODS WERE reluctant to calm the earth. A subtle trembling continued, frightening citizens to the point that some chose to sleep in the street with their families. Some were driven to madness walking aimlessly through town. Some prepared to move away. Some wept endlessly.

The master cubiculum where the baby was killed had been destroyed. The walls upstairs were unstable. Calitoria moved to Thana's old room and stayed there, never emerging. Talistia tried to get her to eat some broth but the food was abandoned.

"I think it might help Calitoria get well if Vitalia moves out. The curse would be lifted," Gaius said quietly one morning in the tablinum.

"Money is part of the problem. Perhaps, we can find a way to still collect income from her," said Telesphorus knowing the financial needs of the villa.

"I will need to replace what I am losing," Gaius agreed.

"I have a plan. If we collect money for her manumission, and I add mine, it would be a substantial amount. I, of course, would stay on as before as your lawyer and accountant, and serve you in all the same ways, but as a freed slave. Perhaps we can free Vitalia but provide a shop in front with a small apartment. We need to repair the damage anyway. A separate entry could be created adjacent to the atrium. She would pay rent for the shop and apartment and gradually pay you back for your investment in the lotion business."

Gaius studied his hands with a troubled expression. He sat motionless surrounded by fallen walls, crumbled frescoes, and broken spirits in a town devastated by Hercules.

Telesphorus continued his logic. "If we do this, there is no reason she should be seen daily by the mistress and you will continue to draw income. Vitalia gets her freedom, a place to live, and a perfect location to market her cosmetics."

"And I would be able to fulfill my responsibility to give my protection as patriarch." Gaius's sadness came from the loss of Regulas and being forced to expel Vita from his life.

"Yes, call her in. I will tell her now. The curse will be lifted."

TELESPHORUS CONTEMPLATED his achievement as he went to find Vita. He could finally give Vita what she wanted most. Stepping over rubble, he found her sweeping up broken pottery in the kitchen which she scooped up on a tray. He watched her walk over to the latrine emptying the shards in the hole.

"Vitalia."

Angry, hopeless and very pregnant she ignored his call.

"Vitalia! You must come with me to see Gaius."

Impatient, he crossed her path and held her shoulders gently.

"It is good news. I promise."

She followed Telesphorus's quick steps to the tablinum.

Uncomfortable in the presence of Gaius, she tightened her belt and wished for something to hold in front of her as a barrier.

"Vitalia, you have your freedom."

At first, she thought it a cruel joke, having wished for it for so long. She looked at Gaius, then at Telesphorus, and a second time at Gaius. Her face reddened, the only sign that she exhibited of her excitement.

"Telesphorus will use your money to buy your freedom from me, and you will pay the five percent tax to the Empire. You will keep all your property. Since you have no where to go and you have built your business here, I would like to provide an apartment and store front right here next to our vestibule. It will have a room for your business—a perfect location right across from the market, and a door into our villa. You will have a cubiculum directly above. Your baby can stay here and grow up with our family. Brit and Lavinia will help raise your baby. You will pay rent for the perfect shop to grow your business."

Gaius stood up in front of her. He placed his right hand on her head.

"I declare that you have your freedom and are no longer a slave in the Roman Empire. I care for my family and you will always be part of it."

"There is a legal transmission to freedom which includes Gaius's responsibility to support you while you become integrated and independent as a self-purchased free slave. It is not mandated that you or I take on his religious practices, although it is customary," said Telesphorus. "And the five per cent tax and the fee for your freedom must be paid immediately."

Vita, now satisfied to be declared free, seemed baffled that it had finally come, no longer a rich slave with no freedom but a truly free woman. The dilemma of where to live and how to raise a baby solved. Gaius gave the answer, cleverly manipulated by Telesphorus and his logic.

Vita possessed more than she dreamed, her freedom, her friends, and her own money. It seemed the babe inside heard the news and jumped for joy. Vita looked down at her swollen self knowing the little one inside was hers forever.

THEY STARTED repairs on the villa along with everyone in Herculaneum who had suffered extensive damage. A flock of more than six hundred sheep perished on the mountainside from vapors! Rumors circulated that Pompeii had even more substantial damage. The Isis Temple, completely destroyed. The port in Ostia encountered a huge wave on the same day believed to be connected to the shaking. Two hundred ships were destroyed in the port that carried the grain for Imperial Rome. Nearly a million people depended on the imported grain from Africa and Egypt. Nero and the Senate worried food riots and political instability would follow as it had happened during Caesar Augustus's reign.

The philosopher, Seneca, said there was a physical reason for the destruction. He explained that vapors were trapped in the earth, some were poisonous, and when they escaped, the earth would tremble. He tried to dispel the popular belief that the gods were angry.

So many families suffered from the earthquake that differences between slave and master became blurred. Everyone worked to restore Herculaneum. Gaius's friend came by to check on the progress in the villa bringing news of the government's help.

"The Proconsul is visiting to access our damage and needed finances," said M. Vinicius Proculus. "It is rare to be visited by him. We are gathering citizens to plead for help. Would you like to join us?"

"Of course. Anything to help. Perhaps he will ask the Senate for funds to rebuild."

"We are also taking this opportunity to formally manumit slaves by their patrons. Herculaneum is normally a town the Proconsul ignores making it difficult to organize such a legal procedure. Tamudius and I have several slaves we are giving freedom. Do you have anyone?"

"Just the two, the young girl and my friend whom I have manumitted, but I would like to elevate and deepen with formal manumission.

"We will meet tomorrow at the Basilica with the Proconsul and witnesses," said Vinicius.

WEEKS LATER, the baby dropped ready to deliver. Vita waddled to and fro trying to escape from the pain. A flush of water flowed rushing down her legs, followed by a river of red blood.

"You must stop walking," said Lavinia. "Maybe the blood will stop if you lie down. Calitoria refuses to call the midwives. We will have to do this without them."

"I can do this," said Vita. She seemed to enter a trance, leaving her body, watching it work from outside it. The blood never stopped; sometimes it slowed to a slight seeping followed by clots. Lavinia worried. Talistia carried water and cold towels to apply to Vita's head. The babe crested and the natural urge to push sanctioned Vita's body rushing the babe into Lavinia's hands.

"A girl!"

"A sweet beautiful girl!" whispered Talistia.

Tears flowed from the eyes of Vita's friends overcome with love for this little one. Vita withered with weakness barely able to respond but uttered the words, "Justa. She shall be named Justa, my babe born in the freedom I have earned and bought. She is freeborn. Out of oppression comes freedom."

Vita delivered the baby but suffered illness. Bedridden, unable to summon strength to walk or eat, unable to nurse her little girl. Calitoria came in to see the baby, picked it up and adored it, petting its brow. She felt her milk drop filling her breasts.

"I will take care of this one."

She walked away ready to nurse, cradling the child.

"Justa," Vita mouthed the words reaching for her babe with outstretched arms.

Chapter 40

Pax curled beside Vita on her bed knowing life ebbed from her body. Lavinia caressed the new mother's forehead alarmed by her sweating, clammy skin, and weakness. The bleeding would not stop. Vita didn't seem to be able to focus her eyes to see clearly. She stared straight ahead at nothing.

Lavinia ran to tell Telesphorus. "I am constantly mopping up the bleeding. This can't be normal. I think we need help. Could we find the midwives?"

"Calitoria has already prohibited their assistance. Gaius is at the farm. I could call the midwives, but I don't have money to pay them. Vita had money but it all went to pay for her manumission and tax."

"I know who can help," said Lavinia. "Quintus. He has money."

Telesphorus cringed at the thought of asking for his help. *Vita might see him and I will lose her. How can I even think this way? I will lose her if she dies. I must do something to save her.*

"You go to him and ask for the money. I will go find the best midwives in the city."

Lavinia slipped out the servant door to avoid detection by Calitoria. Urgent steps led her to Quintus's shop. Her eyes searched for him. *He's not here. Please be here.* She rang the bell chime and waited hand at her throat. Quintus meandered from the back room, then hastened, alarmed by Lavinia's expression.

"Vitalia is dying. She birthed the baby but is not recovering. Telesphorus has gone to find a midwife, but we have no money. Gaius is at the farm and there is no time to reach him. We need his approval to hire the midwife."

"No, we don't!" Quintus shouted. "Where is she? I have to see her. I can help her." Dropping his tools where he stood, still wearing his apron, he raced out of his shop to the Petronius villa, bursting through the door nearly running into Talistia. "Where is she?" he yelled. Talistia pointed to the new door to Vita's shop in the atrium. He took giant leaps up the stairs to the dark cubiculum where Vita lay. The red-soaked bed clothes shocked him, but he went straight to the side of her bed. "I'm here. Help is coming."

When Telesphorus arrived with the midwife, Quintus stood upright challenging anyone who might touch her. "What qualifies you to touch this loved one?"

"I'm trained as a midwife. I have studied in Ostia in the school of Soranus Gynecology. I know the anatomy of the woman and know the birthing process."

"None of this feeding of rooster testicles or powdered pig feces. I won't have it! You will only make her worse," said Quintus.

"No, none of that. Now, step aside and let me see what has happened." The midwife, named Attica, pulled the bedclothes away. "When did she give birth?"

"Several hours ago," answered Talistia.

Attica felt Vita's abdomen searching for the contracted uterus and found it abnormal. She pushed and pressured it. "You can leave me to work now," she said. "I brought clean soft linens, vinegar and honey, but I will need more rain water from the impluvium. Fetch it quickly." She packed Vita's genitals with the linens, washed the blood away and removed the soiled bedclothes replacing them with clean ones. Talistia watched as Vita lay unconscious, sweating, her heart slowly beating. "I will return tomorrow. Do not remove the packing that I have completed. We will wait now. If she awakens keep her in bed. She may ask for water or broth. Give her nothing else for now. Did the babe survive? Where is it?"

"The mistress has the little girl and is nursing it."

"I will evaluate it to see if it is a viable child and be allowed to survive. Take me there."

Attica studied the baby and determined it to be healthy. "A wet nurse should be called to allow the mother to recover."

"I will care for the baby," said Calitoria. "I know how. My milk let down the moment I heard the baby cry."

ATTICA RETURNED the next day to find that Vita had stopped hemorrhaging. "The packing should remain until tomorrow morning. I will come back to remove it. She may survive."

Vita continued to improve but was bedridden with weakness. She seemed to have some delirium calling for her baby, calling for her mother. She opened her eyes to find Quintus at her bedside along with Telesphorus, Gaius, and Lavinia.

"Quintus, you have come."

"Yes, I am here."

"Have you come to break my heart again?"

He ignored the conviction. "I will always care for you and love you."

"Have you seen the baby? Where is she? Is she all right?"

Lavinia stepped over and held Vita's hand. "Yes, she is healthy and we are taking care of her. Calitoria is nursing Justa for you so you can recover."

"Calitoria? Really? Is the baby safe?"

"Time to rest again. Everyone except Lavinia must leave now," instructed Gaius. They quietly left Lavinia to feed Vita.

Gaius stopped Telesphorus in the atrium. "Don't allow that gem maker here again. It is upsetting to Vitalia. He does not belong here."

"But he paid for her care when you were gone. We owe him the chance to see her well again."

"We don't owe him anything, that's nonsense. I will offer to pay him back. That should take care of him. He needs to stay out of her life."

VITA LAY flat praying for the bleeding to cease. *I want to live for my little girl.* Her thoughts raced scolding herself for being unable to accept the solitude and inactivity her body forced on her. She listened to the murmur of the voices in the villa and the carts moving on the street below. *I know your name God. I am yours. You see evil clearly, and good receives your blessings of safety. Help me. Refresh my soul and rest my spirit, I am weary.* A tear seeped from her eye.

Calitoria brought baby Justa to Vita. She had swaddled the babe in cloths, carefully cradling the child next to her own heart. Pax sat up and hummed a growl.

"Vitalia, Justa is a beautiful child and very healthy. I have been nursing her while you recover. Thank you for bringing this new life to our villa. I have suffered such a loss, losing Regulas, my beloved son. Justa is helping me live on without him."

"I don't remember much after giving birth. Perhaps our war with each other is over, and this babe has brought peace and love with her to create a new life for both of us."

"I would like that also. I will share her with you and bring her to you again tomorrow."

Vita knew she needed to accept the kindness Calitoria extended . *Can I trust this woman? Am I a fool?*

Telesphorus came to sit with Vita helping to care for her with his friendship, bringing honey and dates to give her strength and treats for Pax laying by her side.

"You are better every day," he commented.

"I feel stronger. I need to get over to my business to make sure it is not failing."

"I have checked on the production facility and spent time there. Your workers are concerned about you; I will tell them how much better you are feeling."

"I must get back soon. Have you seen the baby? She is beautiful. I think she is the most beautiful baby I have ever seen."

"Ha, spoken like a true mother. 'My baby is the most beautiful,' " he mocked. "But I do agree, she is the most beautiful. Calitoria is taking care of her. She made sure the baby was fed and survived."

"There is so much that has happened, so much hate from her. I am confused," said Vita.

"Maybe now you can forgive."

"I know what you are saying. I have been forced to lie here and torture myself with those thoughts. Forgive your enemies. Your friends teach this. She has been my enemy! She wanted me gone, dead! So many bad things, what about Aquilina! How can God ask me to forgive?"

"Just accept her kindness today. Your enemy is at rest. You need her help and she is giving it. The law supports your freedom, she must change toward you now. That is enough for today. Tomorrow you may be up and out of bed, and we can talk again. Rest now, my love."

I am not a fool. Calitoria is the same but I am different. God protected me and He will protect my baby. I have dreamt of my mother visiting me and Quintus came in my dreams. She pulled out the secreted necklace hidden under her clothing, studying the ring. Fingering the red stone with the hen, she remembered the day on the mountainside when she and Quintus declared their love. *It seemed like he was here. She tucked her necklace away again.*

Chapter 41

The year A.D. 64

THE BABE GREW MEASURING time with her toddler steps. Vita and Calitoria giggled watching Justa in the garden wandering with curiosity in the shelter of her world. She pulled at flowers, removing petals, putting them straight in her mouth. Both ladies jumped up to remove the debris as Justa chewed.

"Oh my, little girl, you can't eat everything!" said Calitoria.

"She is so curious. We have to watch her all the time. Who knows what she will try next," Vita laughed.

"It is time for her nap." Vita gathered the toddler up in her arms smothering her with kisses taking her to her cradle. She didn't want to let go but she laid the child down knowing it was best and stayed rubbing the babe's back. She sang a melody of calm.

"Lay you down in peace, with Adonai, and raise you up to life renewed." She sang the repetitious melody over and over for every nap and every night, softer and softer, until Justa's eyes closed.

Peace entered the villa. The two rivals became friends raising Justa together, both adoring the little girl. Calitoria even knitted socks and bibs; Vita created powders and gentle lotions for the baby's skin. Gaius enjoyed his home again with the two women as friends rather than enemies. He watched from the tablinum one day with Telesphorus.

"Who would have predicted two years ago that these two women could ever be kind to each other?"

"Yes, it is a miracle," said Telesphorus. "Are you going to Pompeii? I hear that Nero and Poppaea Sabina are nearby using their villa and will be surveying the damage and reconstruction in Pompeii. Some say Nero is asking the Treasury to give funds to help with the rebuilding of the Temple Venus and Baths, even roads. It would be a chance to see the Emperor for the first time."

"He was here and gone, now in Neopolis. I have also heard that he was really in town to practice for his acting and singing performances traveling in the area to different theaters. Maybe in Antium now, I can't follow him. You know he is also awaiting the birth of his firstborn child. Poppaea is very pregnant. Balbus's mother says Poppaea is due any day and annoyed that Emperor Nero is always busy with the chariot races or acting." Gaius rolled up his parchment and put away his wax tablet. "I think I'll go out and play with that baby. So cute and so much joy. I was just like her when I was little. So smart."

When he came to the garden, Vita left to visit Lavinia at work preparing meals. Darling Brit sat on Thana's stool, a contrast in age to the old one who sat there for a lifetime. Talistia and some of the new slaves moved about following Lavinia's orders. Lavinia needed an answer to the question everyone wanted.

"Vitalia, does the father of Justa know he is the father?"

Talistia stopped steadfast, holding a heavy amphora, determined to hear the answer.

"Oh men, such creatures. They can't count backwards nine months and remember where they used their divine phallus," answered Vita.

Talistia chuckled. Lavinia hooted.

Brit stared at the flour on the floor squeezing her brows together, "I don't get it."

∾

TELESPHORUS HEARD a knock on the door and guessed it to be another client. Talistia rushed to the tablinum. "It is your friend. He is here with his wife."

"What friend is this?" He walked to the atrium to find Marci Helvii Erotis and his wife. "Marci! And Korinna! What are you doing here?" The last remark reflected their appearance, covered with ash, both looking like beggars from the street.

"Rome is burning!" He grabbed Telesphorus's sleeve. "It has been for nine days. Every living thing had to flee. It is all too horrible. We barely escaped. We were there to support Apostles Paul and Peter. I don't even know where Peter is being held, but Paul is in the Memertine prison. They both are sentenced to death! The Roman soldiers are searching for the rest of us. I pray to our true God of Israel, help us."

"Come to my apartment upstairs. Hush for now."

Talistia brought up apples, figs, and bread along with mulsum for the guests. When Talistia entered, Telesphorus signaled to Marci that she could not be trusted. He created a conversation while she spread food for them.

"We have finished most of our reconstruction after the earthquake. Some frescoes still need repair. My friend Vitalia will be able to help when she has time. Talistia, would you ask Vitalia to come here? I would like her to meet my friends." They watched her leave.

"She has a young child now. Gaius gives me lodging for the accounting and law work that I do for him. I have started a school for young boys to create a secure income. You are safe now. You can stay in my apartment tonight, then we will ask the Rabbi in Herculaneum for help."

"How can you do this for us. Your master will punish you."

"There is some joy here; I am a freedman now. So is my friend that I love, Vitalia. It is part of God's protection and now part of your protection, too. Here she is. Vitalia, these are my friends who study the sacrifice of Jesus and The Way."

"Vitalia, I have heard much about you for years from Telesphorus. I can see God's joy in you," said Marci as he studied her face.

"I have been told God has blessed you with a child," said Korinna.

"She is an amazing gift. Her name is Justa, a name celebrating my manumission. She is more than two now. Have you come to Herculaneum to visit Telesphorus?" She could see they were humble people in distress, wondering how she could help.

"May we speak freely?" Marci asked Telesphorus who gave his nod of assurance. "It has been difficult." He sat with hands clenched. "We can't go back to Puteoli. Our Way with Christ is not tolerated by some. Our meetings are only in secret. We are blamed for every sickness and calamity. They call us a seditious cult. Now, the fire in Rome is blamed on our sect but we are innocent." Korinna wiped a tear. "The fire started near the Circus Maximus then high winds spread it destroying a third of the city. Some think Emperor Nero did it. He wants to build a palace and needs the grounds."

Telesphorus leaned forward aware of the grandiose ideas Nero pushed at the Senate. "Did he start it?"

"Nero is not even in Rome."

"He could pay someone to do it."

"Maybe. Witnesses said they saw soldiers with torches but they might have been back burning to starve the fire. So many have died and the others homeless. A mob is forming and Nero is naming us, the Christians, as the arsonists."

Fire in Rome, Public Domain by Hubert Robert, 1785

Chapter 42

The year A.D. 72

WELL, reader, we could stop the story here. Calitoria is nice, Vita has her freedom and is safe. Vita and Telesphorus have chosen Christ over the many gods and religions of the Empire adding the gift of Christ's sacrifice to their trust in God. Vita is successful in her production of cosmetics and loves helping artisans making frescoes locally. Telesphorus is also free and starting his Greek school for young men. Quintus is successful and still loves Vita, a happy ending after all.

I wish it were the end. In real life, we give our lives to God, accept Jesus into our life, even work with Him to become the people He planned for us to be. But becoming a Christian does not always have a happy ending. More is required for some.

Justa is now a preteen, a beautiful well-behaved young lady, a child any parent could be proud of with intelligence, manners, a lovely disposition, and she is beautiful like her mother. She reflects a secure childhood of being loved, inheriting her grandfather's and mother's talent for drawing and recording the beauty of the world, learning to read and write and do numbers from devoted Telesphorus.

But Calitoria has plans for Justa's future that may conflict with the path God has for her.

The trouble started when Lucius, Quintus's son, enrolled in Telesphorus's school. Seven young boys paid tuition to learn Greek, study debate strategies, Law, Accounting, and History. They met in the College of the Augustales around the corner from the villa. Permission to use the sanctuary was given by the city to Telesphorus for his school.

The all white building had suffered severe damage in the earthquake of A.D. 62 but now was completely repaired by master craftsmen. Visitors and members of the *curia* entered through an immense portal to encounter the central shrine with its colorful frescoes and towering pillars. The ceiling stretched high with an open skylight, creating an echo even though hushed voices prevailed. Some assistance was provided by a servant, hired by the city, who lived in one of the small rooms guarding the premises, keeping it clean. No mischief was ever allowed in the memorial to Emperor Augustus whose bronze bust sat on a pedestal reminding residents of his deity.

The boys sat on benches in the large hall humbled into submission by the grandeur of this impressive building.

"Today we welcome a new student." He was a bright-eyed lad with a flock of brown curls. "Your father is the artisan who crafts jewelry here in Herculaneum?" Of course, Telesphorus knew whose child sat before him.

"Yes, and I am prepared to endure challenging advanced studies. I am literate in Latin and some Greek and enjoy Mathematics taught by my tutor hired by my father."

"And have you studied History and Debate?"

"Not extensively. I am here to extend my education and am interested in entering politics," said Lucius.

Telesphorus nearly raised an eyebrow.

"Will we be required to learn to play a musical instrument?"

"No, you might be thinking that by studying Greek, it will include Greek theatrics. No, we will study Greek literature, such as Homer but not the study of music, as it is believed that it leads to moral corruption. Greek is the language of thought, science, and learning. It will distinguish you in the masses, enabling you to succeed with prowess in public speaking to enter administrative life," said Telesphorus.

~

THAT EVENING the adults of the Petronius family decided to have
vesperna, a light supper, in the peristyle surrounded by the lovely rose
bushes and the rippling sound of the fountain while Justa ate with
Lavinia and the servants in the kitchen. Vita and Telesphorus joined
them joyfully delivering the events of the day.

"I have a new student, Lucius, the jewelry maker's son," said Telesphorus. He searched Vita's face for her reaction but she simply picked
up a fig, put it in her lovely mouth, and gazed directly at her best friend
with head tilted.

"Oh!" said Calitoria. "Marriage opportunity for Justa! They are so
rich." She raised her hands with delight. "An educated, well placed,
favorable match. A step up the ladder of prestige for the family. We
should consider this."

Vita passed over the comment. "How is Justa doing with her studies? She seems to know how to read and write in Latin and is quick to
help me with accounts in our production of cosmetics."

"She should be focusing on her beauty and becoming an appealing
wife," said Calitoria. "It is good that she has education: it will be an
attractive asset to a suitor."

"She is accomplished," said Telesphorus as he curiously took on the
paternal responsibility of the family.

"It is good you have taught her," said Gaius. "You are the best one in
the family to do that. It only makes sense for us. Much better than if I
did it."

"Well, it is time for Justa to study her religion. I will take her to the
Isis Temple to begin her instruction," added Calitoria as she sipped
some local red wine in a lovely glass goblet ordered and delivered from
the Germanic glass makers.

"No, I don't want her studying that," said Vita.

"In a few years she will be ready to marry. She needs to be ready."

"I don't believe in Isis, and I am her mother. It is my responsibility
to raise her in my faith."

"Why not teach her both and let Justa choose?" said Calitoria.

"Let a ten-year-old child choose? Choose a god who cut up her
husband and then put him back together and had a baby with him? Or

choose God who loves us and prepares a place for us to spend eternity?"

"I'll just take her to the Isis Temple and see if she likes it."

"Oh, she will like it, there will be music and choirs singing, but no teaching of being a person who does good and has love." Vita raised her voice. "No, you will not take her."

Gaius spoke, "I have a say in this." He sensed a family fracture in his household. "I think we should wait and talk about this later."

"Well, Lucius is still a good marriage match for her. I think we should talk to his parents," said Calitoria.

Vita's neck turned a blotchy red as she held her thoughts to herself. *I can't accept this. Justa marrying Quintus's son! Calitoria is acting like she is Justa's mother.*

Telesphorus and Gaius sat alone in the tablinum surrounded by wax tablets containing legal documents about the farm and loans.

"What do you think about Justa receiving training at the Temple of Isis?" asked Gaius.

"A young child can't choose what is best for them. Even though Calitoria says so, they lack knowledge. It is the responsibility of the parent to make a straight path for them. Justa will have free will when she is an adult to choose. I am a Jew and have accepted that the Messiah has come and follow the faith of The Way. My faith is important to me. I know Vitalia feels strongly about her faith and takes responsibility for Justa's growth and education. It is natural that Vitalia is strongly against the goddess Isis instruction. She will want to protect her child from wrong teaching."

"How can you approve of teaching her about your faith when it was only a few years ago that Emperor Nero blamed the Christians for starting the fire in Rome, feeding them to the beasts during gladiator games, even burning their bodies as torches of light during his festivals! How can you worship some criminal who was crucified? It is a very unpopular religion in the Empire. It requires too much."

"It's true. Much is required. The faith in The Way is different from the worship of gods and goddesses."

Why has this conflict entered my household. The Empire tolerates so many religions why can't my home do the same. "I will continue to take my sacrifices to the gods and be done. Isis is a religion with secret rites that women like. Calitoria can continue with that. Since Justa is in our home she will study all of them. We can't have the women fighting."

CALITORIA PURCHASED a new shift for Justa, cream white with knots tied at the shoulders, belted at the waist, dropping down to the floor.

"Thank you for the new shift, but why?" asked Justa.

"Let's fix your hair, too. Talistia, please, a crown of braids," said Calitoria.

"Where are we going?"

"It's time you made some local visits. We will visit the Isis Temple, then I want to show you where Telesphorus has his classes and meet the young men. I want you to meet Lasennia of the Balbus family, too. We should shop for some nice jewelry. It is time for you to look more grown up. It won't be hard."

Secret activities for Justa continued all week before Vita discovered the clandestine plan. Dismayed, ignored, and angry, she realized the time had come to leave. She furnished an apartment over the production facility, moved important personal items to the new home and entered the triclinium where Gaius, Telesphorus, and Calitoria reclined sampling a variety of meats and fruits.

"I have created lodging for myself and will be moving out of the apartment at the front of your villa. Gaius, you will have no trouble replacing my rent with a new tenant. The location across from the Forum and near the Basilica is perfect for any vendor. I appreciate your support all these years and am thankful for all that you have done. Calitoria, you were wonderful to Justa and we have worked together to raise her to be a lovely young lady but it is time for me to leave."

"Of course, you can leave and we will stay your friends and family here," said Gaius.

That was easy.

"We will all miss having you here," said Calitoria.

"I will help you with your things," said Gaius. He stood and walked to the atrium.

"I don't need your help. I just need Justa and will leave."

"Oh no, Justa will not leave," said Calitoria as if surprised.

"Yes, she will. You have undermined my authority with my daughter. You have been to the Isis Temple, you are grooming her for marriage with Lucius. You have taken her places to meet others as if she was yours. Those are not your jobs."

"She is...as our daughter." Gaius put his arm around his wife, worried about rekindling jealousy.

"But she is my daughter," said Vita.

"You have no husband," said Calitoria. "Here she has a real family. She is ours. You can leave now."

"Telesphorus! You must say something!" Vita pleaded. "I won't stand for this. You can't have my daughter!" Her eyes rested on each stone face. Tears began to blur her sight. "Telesphorus?" *I am alone. No one here will help me.*

BIRDS SANG AN ANNOYING TUNE, the workers could be heard downstairs arriving to prepare cosmetics, her new unfinished home felt cold and empty. Vita had paced the floor, the same movement back and forth all night, swearing in Etruscan. Pax rested his chin on his paws, his black eyes watching her.

How can this be happening? I have no plan. They are so powerful, this can't be stopped. Why is God letting this happen? Exhaustion clouded her thinking, unfamiliar anger consumed her heart, thoughts of ending her life to remove the hurt tempted her. *How can I watch these former friends raise my child, controlling Justa's life, molding her into a stranger I can't respect. I need to talk to someone.*

She cleansed her face with a splash of cool water and tied a leather strap to hold her hair back. She could not remove the puffy eyes from crying or the exhaustion from a sleepless night. *The only believers I know besides Telesphorus, who is now a betrayer, are Marci and Korinna but I don't know where they are staying. The Rabbi will know.*

The early morning streets were coming to life with pedestrians crowding her path hindering her mission. Hunched over, clutching her mantle under her chin, walking quickly, with Pax shadowing behind, she appeared the destitute beggar reflecting her state of mind.

The bronze knocker rang loudly jarring her nerves.

"I'm here to see Marci Helvii Erotis and his wife Korinna."

"My dear, they are not here, they move from place to place. I'm not sure where they are in the city. May I help you?"

"Perhaps." She needed this stranger's wisdom, the Rabbi, the one who studied the scriptures. She stepped in and removed her mantle. The story poured from her heart like rushing water. She even shared all her deepest secrets.

He listened, occasionally stroked his unkempt white whiskers, offered her water, repositioned his regard, sensed her torment.

"It seems that your friends and added family to your life, some you loved, have betrayed you. That is an old story, released from slavery. It echoes ancient stories of Joseph's betrayal by his brothers and the exodus from Egypt. Joseph also thought of his brothers as family and friends. Friends he could trust, loved without judgment. He shared his most precious joy of receiving the beautiful coat from his father." He paused to let Vita make the analogy of sharing the joy of her beautiful daughter.

"Then, they turned on him, wanted to kill him, wanted to get rid of him, lied to the father. In the end, Joseph did not die. He became a highly respected man of Egypt." He walked over to the pitcher of water, slowly lifted it and poured more into Vita's cup allowing Vita to remember her valued place in the community.

"Now, Joseph encounters his brothers again wanting grain in Egypt because they are starving. What did he do? Vengence? They deserved it."

Vita searched her soul. *Of course they deserved it. They were guilty.*

"He was betrayed by family he wanted as friends. What did he do?"

Vita's head swirled with answers not knowing the end of the story. *I just want to know what to do.* She watched the Rabbi stand up and rest his hands on the back of the chair, gazing at her. She dropped her head studying her hands.

Finally, he spoke. "He did the opposite of what was natural. He did what was right."

"But I don't know what is right," she said softly.

"Let's think about this. God gave you a Divine Spirit, His design. If you choose to hate, it will shape you, a deep wound, devastation to lose your daughter. I understand. They are not acting like friends and family. You become the victim, locking your true self away, fearful, hurt, angry, ugly in your spirit. You wonder, how could they do this to you? Always angry, that is not who God created you to be. Your Divine Identity is still in you." He paused again, nearly irritating her with silence.

"I want to fight for my daughter. I will go back to them and ask them to release her to me."

"If God is for you, who can be against you? It is important to prepare intelligently. Pray first to our Father."

"I will give them the chance to do what is right, to act like family. Maybe they will. If not, I will file a suit of theft at the Basilica. They are stealing my child."

The Rabbi shuffled over to a small table, opened a box, pulling out an amulet with engraving on it. "Here, a Sator Square. To others it is an interesting palindrome of five words, to us it is a secret Christus symbol of God's redemption for our sins and love for us. It will remind you of who you are.

SATOR
AREPO
TENET
OPERA
ROTAS

"The Empire does not condone stealing," he advised. "Our God can even use the Roman Empire for His will. Now that Emperor Nero is gone, Emperor Vespasian has legitimized the courts. You have an opportunity for justice."

Vita stood straight to leave, pausing to thank the Rabbi, when he added, "As for Telesphorus, I know this man. He is not a fool. Perhaps, he is choosing to be careful not for himself but for you and your daughter. He is still in the villa and can watch over her, you are not. Do not condemn his behavior until you see clearly. He will be here this evening to celebrate Shabbat. Would you like me to say something to him?"

"No, our conversation today is confidential. Please share nothing of my private situation with anyone. I have told you what no one else knows."

"Of course, there will be no violation with anyone."

Chapter 43

G aius watched Telesphorus tying up his parchments, preparing to leave.

"Where are you going?"

"It's Shabbat. I will spend it with the Rabbi as usual."

"You spend a lot of time there. I know that is your faith, but surely, you and the Rabbi are aware of Rome's intolerance with the Jews? Sometimes, I worry about you. Here there are a small number and you all are friends, but since the rebellion in Jerusalem, the harmony with the Jews is lost."

"Yes, I am aware that Christus Jews and any Jews are the most unpopular, so we meet quietly," Telesphorus acknowledged. "But these are my inherited traditions. All Jews learn the Torah, and I strive to study the scriptures and memorize them. I chose to settle on Christus of all the sects and schools."

Gaius's pride of being a Roman soldier in the greatest Empire of the world made him unable to understand why Telesphorus insisted on following a religion drawing so much hate from the Empire.

"Emperor Vespasian is building a most spectacular coliseum arena in Rome. He finances it with the spoils plundered from the destruction of the Jewish Temple in Jerusalem, all the gold has been melted down. They are talking about building an arch celebrating the defeat of the

Jews right there in Rome on the Via Sacra. With it, they honor his son, Titus, as a war hero for the victory. Doesn't that anger you?"

"I am aware. We have lost our beloved Temple, the dwelling place of our Lord. It is God's will that we are scattered."

"You confound me," Gaius said. "The Jews are seen as antisocial, not celebrating the many festivals to the gods, and disrespectful, not recognizing the deity of the Emperor. Your meetings are secret causing suspicion, and refusing to work on Shabbat is just lazy."

"We don't mean to be disrespectful, but the essence of our faith is that we have one God we worship, not multiple gods."

Gaius shook his head and turned his back to Telesphorus. The friendship was in jeopardy. Telesphorus placed a hand on Gaius's shoulder.

"I will always be loyal to you. You are more than a friend, you are family. We are like brothers supporting each other in all things. I am thankful to be here with you, I hope you feel the same."

Gaius breathed deeply.

"I could not do this by myself. Your acts of goodwill, assistance, loyalty, and affection are true friendship. I wish to reciprocate these acts to you."

WHEN THE RABBI opened his door, he welcomed Telesphorus with the customary kiss. They walked to the table prepared with wine goblets and the ceremonial candles.

"How are you?" the Rabbi asked, hoping for an honest answer. "And how are things at the Petronius villa?" *Will he tell me?* "Do you still love the young business woman Vitalia? And the little girl?"

"Of course, my feelings are the same."

"All peaceful? And the farm?"

"The same. I try to make the farm profitable, but it is more and more difficult. Emperor Nero devalued the currency printing more and more coins out of substandard metals. Now all costs are inflated. But Nero is gone. Banished and then committing suicide. The civil war is over and peace is restored. Opportunity for our Emperor Vespasian to create fiscal reforms and settle inflation is open, and his

laws and tax reforms are helping. Things are more stable at the Petronius villa."

"You have a good position with the Petronius family, comfortable."
He prefers to hide from what they are doing to Vitalia, thought the
Rabbi.

He continued, "I have been studying the Hebrew books, one is
worth the study, Judges. It is about Gideon. He is quite the interesting
character, popular military victor. However, at first he tries to avoid his
responsibilities with excuses but I sympathize, he feels inadequate,
timid. Doesn't think he can be who God wants him to be."

Rabbi pulled out his chair and sat.

"He hides from the Midianites that steal crops, take animals, and
destroy land. They were actually cousins of Gideon, family. Guess they
knew him. He was hiding in a sheltered wine press, threshing wheat,
protecting his harvest. Didn't want to lose what he had. No threat to the
Midianites. Gideon trembled with fear. Everyone knew he was a coward,
but an angel came and said, 'The Lord is with you, you mighty man.'"

Rabbi motioned for Telesphorus to sit in the best chair.

"People called him a coward, Lord calls him a mighty warrior, interesting, don't you think?"

Rabbi paused. Telesphorus shifted uncomfortably in his seat. He
knew the Rabbi delivered a lesson. Thoughts of leaving somehow and
not being rude possessed his mind.

"Sometimes we think we can't do what God wants us to do. Cost is
too high, might lose everything. But if God asks us to do something, He
will be there to help us. Hard to do the right thing." He loosened his
belt preparing to eat.

"A mighty warrior he turned out to be. Telesphorus, will you pour
the wine?"

VITA ENTERED the Basilica and took her place in line. She inched
toward the Magistrate's table patiently, finally able to ask, "How do I file
a suit?"

The Magistrate waved her over to a young man standing
behind him.

"First, you talk to me, then you must present the suit in public to the defendant. We will take statements from plaintiff and defendant and then go to the judge. What is your complaint?"

"Gaius Petronius Stephanus and his wife, Calitoria Themis, are holding my young daughter and keeping her from me. I am a freed-woman from the Petronius family."

He scribbled on parchment head down. "What is your name and your daughter's name? And the father's name?"

"My name is Petronia Vitalis, freedwoman *vindicta*, of Petronius, legally independent. She is illegitimate, *daughter of Spurius,* Petronia Justa."

"Married?"

"No."

"You know if you are married you can't file this suit. Your husband would have to file it and all your property including your daughter would belong to him."

"I said I am not married."

"You are a freed slave of Petronius. The law does not allow you to file suit against your patron."

Vita closed her eyes. *This stain of slavery follows me in every endeavor casting me into a class for life. Now, I am stopped again in the most destructive way, unable to regain custody of my child.*

Nearby, M. Nonius Balbus stood holding court with friends Q. Tamudius Optatus and M. Vinicius Proculus, mutual friends of Gaius. He recognized Vita as a respected business owner of Herculaneum and read the stress on her face. Balbus walked over to see why she confronted the Magistrate. Always respected and visible in the Basilica, he functioned as prominent politician and benevolent patron of the city.

"Vitalia, or Vitalis," he chuckled, knowing her business used her male nomen. "Successful business woman, I am surprised to see you here. Your lotion and cosmetic business is so prosperous in our city, much valued by my wife and the ladies of Herculaneum, Pompeii, and abroad. Can I help you? Is there a problem with your business?"

"No, not the business. It is fine. Gaius Petronius Stephanus and his wife, Calitoria Themis, are holding my daughter and keeping her from me. I am here to file suit."

"That is difficult to believe." Balbus stepped back and stood for a moment concerned about getting involved in a family squabble.

"Now, I am told I can't get her back because I am a former slave. I have no right to file a lawsuit against them," added Vita.

"But your child is *ingenua*. She can file a lawsuit to be returned to you. She was born after your manumission, a citizen by birth. You would have to file the lawsuit on her behalf, but I am sure that won't be necessary. Gaius always speaks so highly of you. I'm sure you can work this out," he remarked and returned to his friends to share the news. *I wonder if Lasennia knows about this.*

Vita returned her attention back to the clerk who recorded Balbus's comments on a scroll. "So, your daughter is *ingenua* and you are filing the lawsuit on her behalf. It sounds like your daughter has a case. We shall make an appointment for the delivery of the lawsuit to the defendants."

A PERFECT OPPORTUNITY TO publicly deliver the suit would be at The Festival of the Dead when the culmination of the celebration honored the deceased patron of Herculaneum, M. Nonius Balbus, ancestor of the current Balbus family. The last day of the four day celebration specifically honored the Balbus patron, including a parade to the palaestra where athletic games and competitions were played in his name. Vita knew the Petronius family would be attending.

On the scheduled day, Vita and the clerk from the Basilica entered the palaestra searching the open field for Gaius and Calitoria. The field held a large crowd enjoying picnics and track and field races. They walked east along the colonnade toward the larger swimming pool. Vita shaded her eyes searching. The clerk became frustrated hoping to deliver the suit and move on to other legal deliveries. Finally, Vita pointed and identified them standing in a group of friends including the Balbuses.

Gaius's gray hair and deeply lined face startled Vita as she hadn't realized how rapidly he was aging. Calitoria stood stiff and haughty, proud to stand with the elite residents. Vita motioned for the young clerk to follow her and enter the circle.

"I, legal clerk of Herculaneum, serve you notice of suit regarding the unlawful theft of freeborn daughter of Petronia Vitalia, named Petronia Justa. Statements are to be submitted swiftly to the Magistrate." He handed them the tablet, turned and left. Vita faced Gaius and Calitoria.

"This is so embarrassing!" hissed Calitoria. "This is not how the elite are treated. How could you be so cruel?"

Vita straightened. "You should know this is how the law requires delivery of a lawsuit."

"This is all a misunderstanding, Vitalia. You can see Justa any time you want," said Gaius.

"So, you are returning Justa to me?"

"We are treating her like a daughter. She is a part of our family. We have given her a home. We have even allowed her to be educated. She will remain in our family," said Gaius.

Calitoria supported Gaius. "I have a future in mind for her, meeting all the fine people, educating her in all the fine ways."

Friends slipped away, quietly, including Balbus, guilty of enabling the trouble with advice on how to file the lawsuit.

"If you return her to me, there will be no suit. Are you returning her to me?"

"No, that is not possible," said Gaius.

THAT EVENING GAIUS and Calitoria sat with Telesphorus in the tablinum to prepare their statement.

Calitoria fretted, "This is so wrong and humiliating. I have lost my friends. How can I explain? I can't go out. I can't see anyone. To have a lawsuit filed against us makes us criminals."

"Calitoria, we can fight this. It is only right that we have Justa because we have raised her here. I love that little girl. She is the light in this villa, especially bringing happiness to you and me after all the babies we have lost. She is our only one."

Telesphorus read through the suit and analyzed what both parties wanted. "You want to continue having Justa, Vita needs her daughter with her without influence from both of you."

"She will not have her!" Gaius asserted raising his voice. "We have supported Justa financially with clothing, food, and education. We could claim her as an orphan, that her mother has abandoned her, making Justa our slave."

Telesphorus recoiled. "But that is not true. Her mother has also lived here, and Justa was born after manumission."

"Don't forget Vitalia put a curse on our family," Calitoria said bitterly. "She could do it again."

"My mother was convinced Vitalia was the goddess Minerva," Gaius said, remembering his own mystical experiences with Vita.

"Let's find some agreement," counseled Telesphorus hoping to calm them both enough to see reason. "We all love Justa. Her mother loves her, too. We all want to keep seeing Justa as part of our lives. If we can find a way to share Justa, we can settle this lawsuit without going to trial where we could lose all contact with her."

Calitoria looked stricken and Gaius affirmed, "We want Justa as part of our lives."

"Can we think of a way to see Justa daily and have her live with her mother?" Telesphorus prompted. "Can we include Vitalia in our family again? If we do, we will ask Vitalia to hear our proposal and stop the lawsuit."

THE BASILICA CROWD seemed quiet for the number of people present. The massive building with detailed architecture, columns, and frescoes commanded respect but Vita hardly noticed. Even though the sun warmed her back, a shiver of fear chilled her body. If she could not win this lawsuit and have her daughter, life had no meaning. The Petroniuses and Telesphorus waited at the entrance between two magnificent sculptures, one portraying the Proconsul Balbus the Elder and his son Balbus the Younger on horseback.

"Vitalia," called Gaius. "We want to talk to you before we go in. Telesphorus is our Advocate."

"How nice, I don't have an Advocate." She glared at Telesphorus.

"We propose to share Justa." Telesphorus began formally. "You can take her to be with you. If we keep your apartment and store front exclusively for your use, we would like to see you and Justa during the day when you are working there. Justa loves to use your paints and easel and practice her drawing and painting. Those items are still there. It will be a perfect place for the two of you, and we could visit and continue to watch Justa grow up."

Vita waited. She looked at Gaius, suspecting they wanted more. "I would still pay rent?"

"Yes," Gaius said. "And we want to be reimbursed for the money we have spent raising Justa in our home since her birth. Telesphorus will negotiate an amount for you to pay."

Calitoria blurted, "And the lawsuit would be dropped, settled, no more talk of it."

Vita was suspicious. "I would have full custody and all decisions concerning my daughter if I pay your ransom?"

"It is not a ransom, it is money we are owed. Yes, that is our offer," said Gaius.

What choice do I have? Two powerful families against me, the Petroniuses and the Calitoriuses.

"I agree to this settlement," said Vita.

"We need to go in the Basilica and inform the Magistrate that the lawsuit is settled and there will be no trial," said Telesphorus.

Chapter 44

"Oh, Mama." Justa fell into her mother's arms. "What has happened? They wouldn't let me go anywhere or come see you for so long. No one would tell me why. Where have you been?"

Vita comforted her daughter, kissing her forehead, holding her close. "It is over now. We will not be separated again. I promise. Let's go pack your things."

Vita retraced the familiar steps to the top floor where she and Aquilina stayed so many years ago. She remembered all the insulting comments she and Aquilina had about the family, laughing until they held their sides in pain. She thought of that first night when she silently crept to the front door to escape. At last, her escape would be final. They packed Justa's possessions in a soft tote and headed back to the front door.

"Wait," said Vita. "I want to say goodbye to Lavinia and Talistia." Mother and daughter walked to the kitchen to find the one who mothered Vita when she first arrived. Lavinia and Talistia circled them with hugs.

"It is right that you are together. Will we see you again?" asked Lavinia.

"Yes. It took me awhile to collect the money to pay the Petroniuses for Justa but I have managed and our settlement includes renting the storefront. It is just a few steps away for you to come and visit."

"How did you convince them?" said Lavinia. "I'm afraid I was not hopeful,"

Talistia wiped a tear.

"Sometimes you have to be brought to your knees and pray to find justice in this world," said Vita.

With the last hug, Vita and Justa walked out of the kitchen and past the peristyle to the front door. This time Vita opened it and escaped, finding total freedom for them both. As she stepped out onto the street, she felt a weight lifted from her shoulders. She took her daughter's hand and walked to their home.

FOR TWO YEARS Vita and Justa lived and worked together in perfect harmony, running the cosmetic business, talking of expanding to purchase an inn and transform it into a spa facility with restaurants like the one in Pompeii. They were cordial with the Petroniuses, friendly with Telesphorus, and occasionally took their meals in the kitchen with Lavinia and the slaves of the villa.

Pax became elderly. The big white dog tried to keep up, following Vita, then following Justa as if he still had the job of protector. Soon, his life energy slowed until he slept on a pallet most of the day, either in the storefront watching Justa and Vita paint or at the production facility.

Mother and daughter had fun bonding together over their art, Vita transferring her knowledge to Justa. How to use a grid pattern, soft shadowing to show depth, shading for rounded columns, copying from nature, foliage, birds, flowers, people. She taught her daughter all she knew.

"Justa, you have such an eye for detail, and it seems to come so easily for you. I have to study and try and you just make the art happen," Vita said watching her daughter at the easel. "I like the way you have formed the eyes of your subjects. They seem to be a bit too large. Why do you do that?"

"The eyes are the entrance to the soul, the most meaningful part of the face." Justa replied tilting her head to study her work. "It is hard to emphasize and still capture the likeness of the individual."

New supplies brought new excitement, new paint colors to mix with charcoal for darks and lead white for lights. Justa used a procedure that her mother taught her for drawing the face, placing the eyes, nose and mouth accurately for each individual. The images were sometimes transferred on fine linen stretched on a wooden cross-hatched frame painted with tempera. Another technique used pigments mixed with wax heated over a burner and painted on flat, smooth wood. Sharp tools carved texture into the wax for hair and skin. Both linen and wood surfaces were popular with patrons wanting portraits to hang in their homes. Men wanted to look educated and intelligent, ladies wanted their jewels included, or if they were educated, they wanted some symbol such as a writing tablet or stylus included.

Frequently, the rumbling of earthquakes shook the paints, spilling them over the burners. To avoid a mess and cleanup, Justa learned to quickly pick up the tray of paint pots and hold them until the vibrations ceased.

"Mama, I have a boy I like," Justa announced one day while painting. Her mother was not surprised. "I think he likes me, too. But another boy likes me and I like him. I should choose."

"I think I know the two young men you talk about. Is one Lucius, Quintus's son? Is the other the son of Balbus?"

"Yes."

"Both young men recognize your virtues. Had you been born a slave, both would not be choices for you. You are a freeborn citizen, free, you must remember that. It is important. It is good that you are a citizen."

THE LAST OF the summer months came with torrential rain and rising temperatures. Day after day, rain caused eroding soil and flooding. Puddles and ponds appeared where none existed before. The deluge filled the swamps outside the city, causing an annoying stench that settled on the city of Herculaneum. Vita and Justa sold sage and lavender bundles for patrons to burn in incense pots. Telesphorus visited them in the storefront as he calculated the profits, informing Vita that the scents were one of the best sellers.

"This miasma is dangerous," warned Telesphorus. "This odorous air carries disease. Rome is having the same problem from the Pontine Swamps outside their city. The Magistrates are encouraging residents to stay inside as much as possible."

"What happens if you don't?" asked Justa.

"You might get the fever, Roman Fever. I fear that Gaius has it. He has been confined to bed. Calitoria says invisible flying creatures have invaded us. She is in the lararium making sacrifices to the gods," said Telesphorus.

"I don't think they are invisible," said Vita. "I have found them landing on my arms for days. The stench carries them here."

A few days later both Vita and Justa had the fever. Justa recovered quickly. Vita did not.

The fever took over her body and left her unable to leave her bed. Justa gave her honeysuckle in white wine, and chicken broth mixed with bits of chicken. She nursed her mother with cool cloths placed on her forehead, bathed her with sponge and water, and changed her linens often, but the disease progressed quickly. Vita struggled to breathe, her eyes yellowed and her legs became swollen. Chills were followed by fever and sweating.

Justa knelt by her mother and prayed, then watched her sleep, remembering her calm wisdom, her talents, the loving way she guided and taught, always accepting her as if she was a rose bud, not expecting more, waiting for the blossom to open gradually, not rushing, waiting for the rose to develop into full bloom. "We can't expect the seed to be the bud, we can't expect the bud to be the rose. We have to be patient, savoring each stage for the beauty it exhibits," she had said.

As the time neared for Vita to pass, Justa sat next to her day and night, caressing her head, holding her hand.

On the last day, Vita took the necklace holding the golden ring from Quintus and handed it to Justa. "I love you, Justa. This is yours now. Someone I loved gave it to me a long time ago. I hope it helps you find true love and happiness."

"I love you, too, mother." Their eyes met.

"When I am gone, you must beware of Calitoria," Vita whispered and closed her eyes.

The lullaby came to Justa's mind that Vita sang to her as a babe.

"Lay you down in peace, with Adonai, and raise you up to life renewed." Justa sang the simple, unvarying melody softly, over and over, then noticed her mother no longer took a breath or moved. She was gone.

Justa sat staring at the floor through tears. *My heart is broken. How can I go on?* Time stalled. *I need help. There is only one place to go where anyone will understand.* She left her home and went to see Lavinia. Pax followed her down the street and around the corner keeping pace with her at a labored trot. People on the street dodged left and right to open a path. *How can people carry on as if nothing has just happened? My mother died!* She wanted to shout. *How dare the sun shine! Where is the rain and storm that the earth should deliver when I don't have my mother anymore? Who do I live for now?* Inside the Petronius villa she found Lavinia.

"Is Vitalia gone?" Lavinia asked when she saw Justa's tear-streaked face.

"Yes, just now," she sobbed. "If I didn't love so much, it wouldn't hurt so much."

The elderly woman held her tightly, just as she comforted Vita years before as an orphan.

"Gaius has died also," she whispered.

SADNESS PERMEATED THE VILLA. Every step, every look, every project was affected by the memory of Gaius and Vita. Even Lavinia found herself conflicted in preparing meals. Gaius's favorite foods were no longer needed. When Talistia shopped at the market, the usual items were replaced with only desires of Calitoria. The miasma killed so many of the slaves and townspeople, it caused shortages of supplies and workers to deliver them. Telesphorus rummaged through the accounts for the farm, working the numbers to balance assets with expenses. New expenses caused by Gaius's death were daunting.

It had been more than a decade since Telesphorus created Gaius's will. He pulled it out to remind himself of his friend and former master's wishes. As he read the will, Telesphorus despaired, afraid the cost of administering it created an impossible life for Calitoria. Perhaps she would not be able to keep the villa and the remaining slaves. In fact, the most daunting obstacle was the issue of the slaves. Telesphorus would have to arrange a meeting with everyone.

As the slaves shuffled into the tablinum to hear the will, they were confused to be in the presence of Calitoria and Telesphorus in a somewhat equal status. Lavinia, Certa, Brit, and Talistia studied the individuals that were present and each one wondered why Telesphorus called them to the tablinum.

Telesphorus began his message knowing the turmoil that would follow. "Today, I will be reading the legal document that Gaius Petronius Stephanus declared as his Will."

Calitoria sat down in the chair usually inhabited by her husband, confident that the villa would remain her property and that Telesphorus would care for her. He had been appointed her Guardian by the Magistrate. Roman law required a widow to have a male Guardian upon the death of her husband, to administrate legal and financial matters. Telesphorus was the obvious choice.

"The Will begins with transference of the villa to Calitoria. The farm continues as before with myself as administrator. Gaius states that all the slaves that he owns will now be free. All have manumission upon his death as allowed by Roman law. In addition, I will share this with the farm slaves."

Each slave stood shocked not expecting this reversal in their social status. Calitoria sat upright searching her thoughts on this loss and its effect on her.

"Each slave will receive a percentage of the estate to support their life as freedmen and women. The five percent tax required by the Empire for each slave's freedom will be paid by the estate."

At this time Telesphorus paused, setting his jaw firm, shaking his head at the strain he anticipated to pay the tax and stipend for each slave and still sustain the farm and villa.

"In addition, he states that Petronia Vitalia will receive a percentage of the estate as gratitude for the happiness she brought to the family and, should she be deceased, the percentage shall be delivered to her daughter, Justa."

"What? He did what?" screamed Calitoria.

Lavinia's eyes widened. *Now I know. Gaius must have been the father.*

Telesphorus continued. "As the Advocate Lawyer for Gaius, I must fulfill his wishes. However, if all of you that received manumission would like to continue as part of this family and continue your duties in this villa, you are welcome here. We will support you. The Will has now been read and you may leave."

Calitoria stayed, paralyzed by anger and her sense of betrayal.

JUSTA SPENT her days avoiding the home that she and her mother had shared. Too many memories haunted the walls, reminding her of the void in her heart. Memories of happy times filled with love, memories of the safe comfortable existence they enjoyed, memories that turned into sharp weapons of loss. Lavinia's kitchen provided an escape. Since the news of Gaius's Will, Justa was able to take time to grieve before facing the sole ownership of a thriving business.

Rumors circulated that Justa was spending time in Lavinia's kitchen. It served as a location for friends to submit their appreciation of her beautiful and wise mother who created a business transforming lives with employment, allowing others to feed and care for their families with respectable jobs. Many came to share stories of her helpfulness in times of need and the joy she brought through friendship. Quintus and his son Lucius heard Justa spent time in Lavinia's kitchen and came also. It seemed Quintus struggled with his emotions more than Lucius and, to the reader, it is understandable knowing the love he shared with Vita when they were young.

Lavinia studied the group as they sat in her kitchen.

Quintus offered condolences and suggested, "I would be honored to be your Guardian in business and personal affairs if you do not have one."

"I understand I will need one as the law requires it for women. I know my mother used Telesphorus for that role. I will consider it."

Lucius and Justa have the same regular features and their expressions
are similar in a childish manner, perhaps because they are both young, but
the straight white smile and the dark hair cause a resemblance. Quintus
must be the father, thought Lavinia. *But most of Herculaneum residents*
have dark hair.

Lucius tried to lift Justa's spirits distracting her with light-hearted events in town. The race at the festival where his buddy tripped at the starting line, the way his horse flirted with his mare and the self-absorbed rich customers coming into the jewelry shop. It seemed the rich couldn't tell the different between the real gems and the glass beads. Even though they had riches to spend, they secretly chose the glass instead. Everyone in the kitchen laughed. Lucius kept his eyes on Justa. He touched her hand and sat as close as possible. Justa did not mind the attention.

Other visitors came but most notable was the visit from Lasennia when she brought her son Marcus Nonius Balbus IV. Impressed by Justa's accomplishments, Lasennia bragged to her son that Justa's beauty complimented her intelligence, talent, and business sense. Even though her pedigree lacked Roman family history, her inheritance compensated for her class. This young Balbus stallion knew Justa to be one of the most thoughtful girls in Herculaneum. Her countenance reflected a child brought up with love, spreading kindness to everyone. He was eager to court Justa. Again, Justa did not mind the attention.

Another visitor came to see Justa. It was Calitoria accompanied by the court official from the Basilica employed by the Magistrate, carrying a scroll.

"Petronia Justa is to appear before the Magistrate in Herculaneum in response to the lawsuit filed by Calitoria Themis regarding her status as a freed slave and the issue of the inheritance from her mother Petronia Vitalia."

Chapter 45

It started to rain, a soft constant rain mimicking the unending sorrows that Justa endured. The rain washed the sidewalks and filled the gutters, but for Justa trouble was not washed away. The lawsuit demanded urgency, pushing her out of her grief, forcing her mind to unravel the emergency of the present. Justa opened the door to leave Lavinia's kitchen, gathering her will to cross the threshold and soak in the shower.

"Even if you lose everything, I will love you," Lavinia remarked. "Remember there are many here who care about you, and we will take care of you. This is a dark moment but the future holds a plan for you."

"I know. Right now I must remember all that my mother taught me. I am strong enough to get through this. I am free. My mother fought hard for her freedom and now I must fight for mine. I will not let Calitoria claim me as her slave."

She stepped out in the weather returning to the home shared with her mother, a safe and loving home.

When she arrived, a notice had been nailed to the plain wooden door.

THIS PROPERTY - VITALIS COSMETICS - BELONGS TO
CALITORIA THEMIS OF HERCULANEUM

I guess she thinks by saying it is her property that it makes it hers even before we go to court.

The sign caused embarrassment to Justa but it had an unexpected effect. Everyone in Herculaneum became aware of the injustice plaguing a fellow business owner of unremarkable lineage, including the cloth maker, the baker, the owner of the granary, the fullers, the cafe cooks and waiters and so many others. Indignation toward Calitoria and her elite connections to the influential Calitorius family fueled support and a level of loyalty Justa was not expecting.

However, elite citizens said hateful things about Justa, that she was new money without breeding, that she didn't deserve the inheritance. *Just because they say it doesn't make it true,* Justa counseled herself.

Lavinia came to check on Justa with her favorite lentil cakes and dates.

"How are you doing?"

"I am trying to understand Calitoria. I know she wants my mother's money."

"Telesphorus is her Advocate, so he can't help you."

"I will ask Quintus to help me. He has offered."

EVEN IN THE small town of Herculaneum, the courts were overwhelmed with cases. While Calitoria awaited her time at trial, finances became difficult and more money needed to be found somewhere.

"If we transform the adjacent front room into an additional store-front, we can rent it out. I already have talked to a tinker who will rent the space. The upstairs can be converted into an additional apartment to rent. I think your friend and his wife would like to settle there," she said.

"You mean Marci Helvii Erotis?"

"Yes, he and his wife."

"I will talk to them." He happily agreed to having his friends nearby.

"Also, sell the horses for coins, no bartering. You can save the bridles and saddles, we might use them again when we get Justa's inheritance. Put them in the lararium for storage. I won't be using that room anymore. The gods have never given me favor. Why should I worship them? I will take care of myself. Now, we must prove Justa was born a slave, and her mother was a slave at her birth.

"I will claim that I gave Justa her freedom. The only way I could do that as a woman was if Gaius was already dead. It establishes a recent informal manumission, setting the timeline. That would make Justa born a slave of the Petronius family." She stood and paced the floor of the tablinum. "Junian Latin freed slaves cannot inherit an estate in the eyes of the law. The slave owner, me, would inherit Justa's possessions under Roman law."

"But that is not true," said Telesphorus. "You can't do that."

"There is no documentation to refute it! A beautiful plan!"

"But it will take all of her mother's business and inheritance away from her. I can't help you with this."

"You have been assigned by the Roman court as my Guardian and my Advocate Lawyer. You must protect my situation as I instruct."

"I can't. It is not true."

"Do you want to stay here? Keep your position of prestige? Keep your home? Keep your school? Or be one of the ex-slaves on the street begging?" Calitoria drew herself up to her full height, feeding on the power she now wielded. "I will destroy you. I will ruin your reputation so that no students will come to your school, you can never again be an Advocate for any of my elite friends. I will tell everyone what a horrible person you are. I will have my revenge and you will help me do it."

She ceased her rant murmuring to herself. "Vitalis is a goddess, Justa is so perfect," she mimicked. "Now my best friend Lasennia wants her son to marry Justa. Well, she won't if Justa is a Junian Latin freed slave, the lowest level of freed slaves. She can have no inheritance, no money, and no business. She can never have a legal marriage and any children will be illegitimate." Calitoria's need for revenge was exposed. "Vitalis's daughter will never marry Lasennia's son or anyone else!"

The two conspirators did not know that Lavinia hid behind the entrance, straining to hear every word. Her previous passive attitude of compliance had been replaced with eavesdropping and snooping. Lavinia retreated from her hiding place to the security of her kitchen. *I must tell Justa.* She wrapped her mantle around her shoulders and scurried to Justa's home.

When she entered, she found not only Justa but a room full of visiting friends, including Quintus and Lucius. Lavinia couldn't wait to warn Justa, revealing the whole hideous scheme to the outraged clique.

"Can she do that?" asked Justa. "Can she say I am a Junian Latin when I am not? How can I prove I was born free? Mother always said I was. Telesphorus knows! How can he do this?"

Quintus stood and captured Justa's shoulders. "Don't despair. I will find those who know. I will bring them with us to court."

THE WITNESSES for each side were registered, three for Calitoria and nine for Justa. The Calitorius family and other elite families seemed to be distancing themselves from the unpopular case, causing a fraction of the classes. Fearing repercussions, they were unwilling to take sides. The one witness Calitoria found from her side of the prestigious family was the slave Gaius purchased years ago from them, the slave they called Certa. She rewarded his testimony with coins. Telesphorus was registered as her Advocate. The day in court was finally scheduled.

A BOY SAT on the client bench outside the Petronius villa waiting his turn. Odd in the queue of older men, he sat patiently. His turn came and he was ushered into the tablinum.

"How can I help you?" smiled Telesphorus.

"I have a note for you from the Rabbi. I was told only to give it to you in private."

Telesphorus read the note and responded. "Tell the Rabbi I will be there at the appointed hour."

In the deep of night, Telesphorus extinguished his lamp and slipped out of the villa heading toward the Rabbi's home. The Rabbi opened the door to the darkened atrium, illuminated by one oil lamp, contrasting the usual cheerful welcome he always expected. Telesphorus followed his cleric to the familiar seating.

"I hear you are Calitoria Themis's Advocate and Guardian. I am aware that the trial is tomorrow."

"It is my job."

"You are organizing the case against Petronia Justa?"

"Yes."

After a long pause the Rabbi said, "What are you doing, Telesphorus?"

Disappointment carved a furrowed brow on the Rabbi's face. Telesphorus did not answer. The pointed question left a wound.

"Tell me, does the case pursued by Calitoria hold the truth?"

Telesphorus studied his hands, slouching in his chair. He felt the slings and arrows of a punishing parent and shook his head. "No."

"I called you here at night because a public meeting might jeopardize your position. It is well-known in Herculaneum that I feel this case is unjust. It is a manipulation of the facts due to the lack of documentation. Many lost their papers of manumission in the earthquake if they had any. Justa lacks her mother's documentation, but the truth is evident that Vitalia and Gaius proclaimed she was born free many years ago."

The Rabbi's voice filled the shadowed room with harsh reality. Then he softened his regard as Telesphorus sat, ashamed and unable to answer.

"Calitoria is using your reputation as a good and just man to prove her case. This truth will come out. You are flirting with Darkness. But I believe you are a follower of the Lord."

Telesphorus looked straight into the Rabbi's eyes. "She says she will destroy me if I don't help her."

"So, it is safer to remain in your position at the villa. Perhaps you have already lost what is most important to you."

"What do you mean?"

"The Lord sees you and knows you and loves you. Do you think He will abandon you? Are you abandoning Him?" The Rabbi walked to the door and held it open. Telesphorus followed and stopped at the threshold. "His love will not change whatever you choose to do."

"You are right. I am thinking of my own safety but losing my very soul. I can't live with myself if I go through with this."

"I'm proud of you for making that decision." The Rabbi took a deep breath considering his next statement.

"A few years ago, Vitalia came to me before she brought suit against the Petroniuses to force them to return Justa to her. Do you remember?"

The Rabbi's eyes glittered with a hidden challenge, holding Telesphorus spellbound. "Now that Vitalia is gone, I can tell you what she revealed to me in confidence. She came to me and told me everything." He paused. "You are Justa's father."

Telesphorus searched the Rabbi's face trying to understand what he heard.

"I thought Gaius was the father. I thought that all along."

"I believe everyone has a right to know the truth so they can behave properly. Now, it will help you decide what to do."

Chapter 46

The next day, the morning of the hearing, Justa prepared to appear at the Basilica. Justa wore her best tunic made of fine fabrics and a hand-tooled leather belt tied at the waist with a lavender palla wrapped over her shoulders. Her hair was pulled back in a simple style with a gold clasp. On the first finger of her right hand she wore the golden ring with ruby stone given to her by her mother. Wearing the ring, she felt her mother beside her.

She walked the street alone passing the usual clutter of humanity who carried out daily chores, people scurrying here and there, oblivious to her anxiety. A young girl with embroidered cap sat in a small niche against the wall playing a flute. A cup was placed in front for coins. *That might be me after this,* she thought. She dropped a coin in the cup.

She could see the majestic Basilica ahead with its bronze chariot and horse statue high above. Entering the main hall, a red and white sign confronted her stating the Balbus benefactors had repaired the building after the earthquake. Stately marble horse sculptures on each side of the foyer depicted the elder Marcus Nonius Balbus and his son the younger as riders, continuing the theme. Justa passed between them, daunted by the length of the hall facing her. A hum of subdued voices echoed in the respected court as she moved forward toward the sitting official. Today, she would give her statement with witnesses that graciously volunteered to testify.

The Basilica was meant to be intimidating. The long nave led to a raised apse far ahead where the powerful Praetor sat. Behind him on either side were frescoes of mythological stories done by the most talented craftsmen. In the center, a niche held another fresco portraying a naked Hercules, observing his son suckling a doe.

Justa gracefully walked the long hall barely feeling her body other than a slight dizziness. She glanced past the fluted side columns on either side to see the gallery packed with spectators. Searching left and right she noticed familiar faces, Balbus, his son and Lasennia, along with elite citizens of the Empire. She noticed the blacksmith, the bakers, mule drivers, wine makers, and some of her workers from the production facility offering a hidden wave of the hand or a respectful nod telling her they were there for her support. Tears almost filled her eyes but she drew them back summoning courage, standing straighter, imagining her mother walking with her, clearly an apparition, but very real to Justa.

By the time she reached the throne of the local Praetor, judge of Roman law, who was seated next to the recently placed statue of Emperor Vespasian, her mouth was dry, her hands trembled. Quintus stood waiting for her at the end of the long hall as Advocate, with Lucius next to him giving a supportive grin. She stood ready to defend herself. As Justa tucked a stray curl behind her ear, Quintus noticed the gold and ruby ring on her finger that he'd given her mother, Vita, so many years ago and he knew she'd never forgotten him and might even have forgiven him.

On the other side, Calitoria and Telesphorus stood waiting. Calitoria wore her finest stola with golden clasps at the shoulders. It dropped to the floor but still exposed the elegant open toe sandals and delicate embroidery around the hem. Her jeweled earrings and necklace matched the golden leafed headband holding blond curls around her face.

"The case of Calitoria Themis against defendant Petronia Justa is called for a hearing of the evidence," called the Praetor. "Calitoria Themis, what is your complaint?"

Justa turned toward Calitoria already in place beside her.

"I am Calitoria Themis of the Calitorius and Petronius families.

This girl, who calls herself Petronia Justa, daughter of Spurius (illegitimate), was freed by me this past year after my husband, Gaius Petronius Stephanus, died leaving me a widow with Guardian and Advocate Telesphorus to support my cause. Justa, the recently freed slave of mine, was born to my slave urbana years ago, a deceased woman named Petronia Vitalis. A slave we allowed to build a lucrative business in Herculaneum which is now mine following the laws of inheritance of worldly goods."

The crowd hummed their disapproval. Someone yelled, "Liar!" Justa felt the blood pool in her feet.

"What documentation do you produce?" asked the Praetor.

"I do not have documentation but I have witnesses."

Telesphorus stood to the side and motioned for the first of three witnesses.

Each stood before the Praetor giving their statement supporting Calitoria, handing their written document to the clerk. When the third witness approached, Justa recognized the slave they called Certa. *This man does not speak. How can he testify?* He mumbled and moaned a garbled testimony and was asked two times by the Praetor to repeat. "Do you have a written statement?" Certa motioned that he could not read or write. A third attempt was initiated and the clerk recorder wrote the statement down to the best of his ability.

Calitoria explained, "My witness's tongue was amputated when he was captured at war and sold as a slave. We must have sympathy for him." The elite in the gallery voiced support, "Yes, of course" and "A strong witness."

"All right, document that he is witness in support for Calitoria Themis on the matter under discussion," said the Praetor.

Next, Justa presented her statement.

"I am the daughter of Petronia Vitalis, formally manumitted freed slave of Gaius Petronius Stephanus. I was born after my mother gained her manumission. Therefore, I am a freeborn citizen, *ingenua*. Calitoria Themis is mistreating me by trying to take my inheritance. She claims my mother was still a slave when I was born which is not true."

"Do you realize that masquerading as a free slave or citizen has a stiff penalty? You would be branded and whipped."

"Yes."

"Where is your documentation?"

"I do not have documentation but I also have witnesses."

Quintus motioned for the first of nine witnesses to come forward. It was Q. Tamudius Optatus, a good friend of Gaius. He testified that years ago he heard Gaius say to Vitalis, 'Why do you begrudge us? We are treating Justa as if she was our daughter.' Therefore, I know she is the freeborn daughter of Petronia Vitalis, business woman of Herculaneum."

Another good friend of Gaius, M. Vinicius Proculus, was sworn to tell the truth and testified that he heard Gaius say, 'I am about to manumit a slave.' The following Ides she was formally manumitted when the Proconsul traveled to Herculaneum. The daughter did not exist at that time. The woman under discussion is the freeborn daughter of Petronia Vitalis."

The rest of the witnesses testified to her free status and all proceedings seemed concluded. Then, a tenth witness crossed over to stand beside Justa and spoke.

"I, Gaius Petronius Telesphorus, swear by Augustus and his children that I know about the girl Justa about whom this case is being discussed. She is the freeborn daughter of Petronia Vitalis, my fellow in manumission. I negotiated with Gaius Petronius Stephanus and Calitoria Themis for the release of Justa to her mother and to receive a maintenance allowance in return. From this, I know that the woman Petronia Justa, about whom this case is being discussed, is the freeborn daughter of Petronia Vitalis."

"Aren't you the Guardian and Advocate Lawyer for Calitoria Themis?"

"Yes, I am."

The crowd cheered. But someone called out, "He can't do that. He is Calitoria Themis's lawyer."

"You are testifying against your client? This is most unusual and changes validation in this case." The Praetor sensed the disapproval in the crowd. Fists were raised in defiance, plebs called out prejudice and injustice. Avoiding a disruption of the court, he spoke, "This court cannot rule on this matter due to the confusing testimony and lack of documentation. We will move this trial to Rome. You and all your witnesses are summoned to Rome on the third of December. Bail is one thousand sesterces as pledge for appearance of the plaintiff and the defendant."

Calitoria's face colored, "But I need more time to find a new lawyer!"

"When you hire one let me know."

All witnesses and spectators filed out of the Basilica spilling out to the street.

"This is in your favor, Justa," said one.

"We will be with you," said another.

The Rabbi gleamed with pride and wrapped his arm affectionately across Telesphorus's shoulder with the words, "Well done, you are the warrior God wanted you to be."

Quintus joined the circle of friends and thanked Telesphorus for his unexpected testimony. "Will you plead her case in Rome? You are the more qualified and I will loan you my son, your student, to assist you."

Telesphorus smiled in return. "Yes, Lucius, will you assist me?"

Of course, I would be honored." Justa watched the exchange feeling protected by those that cared about her and also loved her mother.

"We will take this to Rome. I will plead your case for you," said Telesphorus. Justa hugged him and Telesphorus held her tight knowing he had a daughter with the only woman he had ever loved, Vitalia, better known as Vitalis. On this day, his choice cost him everything except two important things, his daughter and his faith.

Epilogue

The case went to the Augustus Forum in Rome in front of the Temple of Mars at the third hour of the twelfth of March A.D. 76. All the witnesses, Advocates, Plaintiff, and Defendant were required to travel and appear. Calitoria rehired an Advocate named M. Calitorius Speudon to plead her case, obviously someone from that influential family. In the actual trial, plaintiffs and defendants could not speak, only their Advocate Lawyers could plead their case, trained by their education in public speaking and persuasion. However, the judges in Rome could not come to a decision and needed to confer with others. The case was continued to the next year's court session and another year and another year. Justa and Calitoria continued to wait.

When Mount Vesuvius erupted in the early fall of A.D. 79 a decision had not been made. We will never know how the case ended, but we know that Herculaneum and surrounding towns were buried for nearly two thousand years. Perhaps, we can hope that they escaped.

The story is based on real events found in the debris of Herculaneum. The villa and family existed. There was a slave or former slave named Vitalis that gave birth to a child named Justa. Vitalis became free but we do not know in what manner, whether she was given her freedom by Gaius Petronius Stephanus, whether she bought her own freedom or both. There were wax tablet records of two court cases found in the upper room of the villa, both dealing with Vitalis and Justa and their relationship to the Petronius family. Vitalis had become a very wealthy woman. It is only through my speculation of how she became wealthy.

Justa should inherit her entire fortune as her daughter, but if it was decided that Justa was born before Vitalis was freed, then the Petronius family would acquire the fortune. Telesphorus, the former family slave and tutor, behaved curiously during the two court appearances and created suspicious speculation. He did switch sides at the last moment.

The family eventually fell upon hard financial times as reflected in the changes in the elegant villa. During the excavation, it was found that the outer rooms had been converted into storefronts opening onto the street, probably to generate income. A room upstairs had been rented out to another family. It is in this room that the image of a cross exists on the wall. A signet ring was found in that room with the name Marci Helvii Erotis.

After I had determined a way for Vitalis to create her fortune, I found in my research that during excavation one of the storefronts contained pots of crushed pigments and wax that an artist left behind. Someone was an artist.

So here in this villa, now called the house of the Bicentenary, a young woman named Justa was the focus of lawsuits. The last one sent to Rome.

So now we know. Such was the life available to women in Herculaneum: Roman Empire, Law and Power, conflicting Religious Beliefs, Slavery, and Forces of Nature Within and Without...with Vitalis and Justa at the crossroads.

by the author

Timeline

ROMAN EMPIRE A.D.

A.D.

14-37 Emperor Tiberius

33 Traditional date of Jesus crucifixion

37-41 Emperor Caligula

41-54 Emperor Claudius

54-68 Emperor Nero

59 Vita is sold

59 Death of Nero's mother, Agrippina

59 Pompeii/Nuceria riot

60 St. Paul spent a week in Puteoli

60-61 Boudicca Rebellion

62 Nero's first wife killed, Octavia

62 Nero marries Poppaea

62 Campania Earthquake

62 Justa born

64 Great fire in Rome

65 Death of Poppaea

65 Traditional date of St, Paul's beheading

68 Nero's suicide

69 Four Emperors

69-79 Emperor Vespasian

70 Jerusalem Temple destroyed
72 Vitalis fights for Justa's return
73 Death of Vitalis and Gaius
74-75 Lawsuit
75-76 Lawsuit goes to Rome
79 Eruption of Mount Vesuvius

Glossary

HISTORICAL CHARACTERS

Acte - Slave mistress of Nero, also known as Livia Acte

Apicius - Author of an ancient cookbook

Agrippina - Nero's mother

Augustus - Ceasar, also called Octavian

Balbus Family- Influential family in Herculaneum

Boudicca - Queen of Iceni

Burrus - Nero's consult

Calitoria Themis - Former slave of Calitorius, wife of Gaius

Claudia Octavia - Nero's first wife and stepsister

Claudius - Emperor

Craestus Brethren - Followers of Jesus

Druids - Spiritual advisors in Britannia

Etruscans - Ancient settlers of Campania

Gaius Petronius Stephanus - Owner of villa

Iceni - Tribe in Britannia

Jucundus - Banker in Pompeii

Justa - Daughter of Vitalis, subject of lawsuits

Livineius Regulas - Exiled politician, sponsor of Gladiator Games

Lucius Venidius Ennychus - Neighbor wanting citizenship

Marci Helvii Erotis - Resident at time of eruption, signet ring found in lararium

Marcus Nonius Balbus - Politician, benefactor generations in Herculaneum with same name

Minerva - Ancient goddess

Mithras - God of war

Paulinus - Governor of Britannia

Philodemus - Ancient philosopher

Poppaea Sabina - Second wife of Nero

Romulus and Remus - Legend of twins, founders of Rome

Samnites - Settlers of Campania

Seneca - Nero tutor, philosopher and advisor

Silures - Tribe in Britannia

Telesphorus - Slave and Advocate in villa

Trinovantes - Britannia tribe

Veranius - Previous Governor of Britannia

Vitalis - Vitalia and Vita, slave of Petronius family, Vitalis real historical name

Volasennia - Balbus, widow, mother, mother-in-law

FICTIONAL CHARACTERS

Amedius - Slave at farm

Aqualina - Slave in villa

Certa - Slave in villa

Dracus - Fellow architect

Fradia - Female slave at farm
Korinna - Wife of M. Helvii Erotism
Lasennia - Current wife of current M. Nonius Balbus
Lavinia - Kitchen slave
Lucius - Son of Quints
Pax - Dog companion
Pontius - Fellow architect
Quintus - Lover of Vita
Regulas - Calitoria's baby
Reticulus - Foreman at the farm
Severus - Gladiator and bodyguard
Talistia - House slave
Thana - Mother of Gaius Petronius Stephanus

HISTORICAL TERMS

Ankh - Symbol of eternal life
Atrium - Large entrance room
Baiae - Town along coast
Baldric - Part of soldier uniform
Basilica - government building
Bireme - ship with double oar teams
Britannia - Ancient Great Britain
Cacare - Swear word
Camulodunum - Colchester England
Cella - chamber behind statue in temples
Cellarius - Wine steward
Cena - Dinner
Collegia - Group, usually tradesmen
Cubicula nocturna - Bedroom
Daughter of Spurious - Illegitimate person
Defrutum - Boiled down grape juice, must
Dolia - Hole holding food at food bar
Domus - Villa
Familia rustica - Farm slaves
Familia urbana - House slaves
Forum - Area for market and gatherings
Fullers - Clothes cleaners
Garum - Salty fish sauce
Gustum - Appetizers
Ientaculum - Breakfast
Impluvium - Collects rainwater in atrium
Ingenua - Born free
Isle of Mona - North Britannia holy area for Celts
Lake Lucerne - Holds oyster farm
Lanista - Owner and trainer of gladiators
Lararium - Shrine to guardian spirits in villas
Mantle - Women's head covering, shawl, palla

Mensa prima - Meat dishes
Miasma - Bad air, probably carrying Malaria
Mount Vesuvius - Volcano
Mulsum - Syrup wine
Murillo - Type of gladiator
Nuceria - Nearby town, part of riot
Palaestra - Swimming and exercise area in town
Palanquin - Travel seat carried by slaves
Palla - Like a shawl or mantle
Patricians - Inherited wealthy upper class providing leadership
Peristyle - Interior garden in villa
Pillei - Hat
Plebians - Average working class
Posca - Acidified wine with water
Pozzulana - Volcanic dust
Praetor - Judge
Prandium - Lunch
Proconsul - High level magistrate
Puteoli - Nearby port visited by Apostle Paul
Quadrireme - Ship with four oar levels
Retiarius - Type of gladiator
Sapa - Sweetened reduction of grape juice
Secutor - Type of gladiator
Sesterces - Money
Sica - Curved sword
Silphium - Plant used for birth control
Sistrum - Egyptian rattle
Slave urbana - City slave
Spectacula - Pompeii's coliseum 20,000 seats
Stola - Like a tunic or shift
Tablinum - Like an office or receiving room
Trireme - Ship with three levels of oars
Vesperna - Supper
Vindicta - Freed slave

Recipes

Gaius's Soft-Boiled Eggs in Pine-Nut Sauce

3-4 soft boiled eggs
3/4 cup pine nuts
1 teaspoon ground pepper
4 Tablespoons Garum

Soak the pine nuts in water 8 hours. Drain and grind them (Lavinia used mortar and pestle.) Add pepper, honey and garum. Heat the sauce. Peel the eggs and leave whole. Serve in a bowl with sauce poured over them.

*Asian Fish Sauce can be substituted for Garum.

Thana's Mulsum

1 part honey
4 parts Italian wine

Thana likes it heated. Do not drink in a lead cup. Thana liked the white sugary crust from boiling the wine in a lead pan. Don't do this either. Causes insanity and other maladies.

Honey Mushrooms

1 Tablespoon olive oil
1 Tablespoon Garum
1 Tablespoon Honey
2 teaspoons chopped Lovage
1/2 teaspoon ground Pepper
8 ounces large Mushrooms

Combine liquid ingredients and bring to a boil. Add lovage and pepper and thickly sliced mushrooms. Cook quickly to reduce liquid to a glaze.

*Celery leaves can be substituted for Lovage.
*Asian Fish Sauce for Garum

Parthian Chicken

4 pieces chicken, leg or breast (or use open whole chicken cut and spread flat)
ground pepper
3/4 cup red wine
2 Tablespoons Garum
1/2 teaspoon asafoetida powder
2 teaspoons chopped lovage
2 teaspoons caraway seeds

Combine wine, fish sauce and asafoetida, add crushed lovage and caraway seeds. Pour sauce over chicken. Bake 375 degrees for 1 hour. Covered. Remove lid halfway through.

*Celery leaves can be substituted for Lovage.
*Garlic powder or Onion powder can be substituted for asafoetida powder.

*Asian Fish Sauce for Garum

For more recipes from Apicius: <u>A Taste of Ancient Rome</u> by Ilaria Gozzini Giacosa or <u>The Classical Cookbook</u> by Andrew Dalby and Sally Graiinger

Acknowledgments

Thank you to all my loved ones who encouraged me to write this story. Thank you to my friend and fellow writer and artist, Sandy Orr. A special thank you to my editor, Marilyn Benedict.